T0129241

"*More Than A Savior* is an emotional and insightful book that weaves together biblical truths with practical help and applications to everyday life. It will reveal the heart of Jesus and draw you, as it has me, into closer communion with our Lord and Savior and Friend. Thank you, Robert—this is my kind of book."

Ron Mehl
Pastor, Author of *The Ten(der) Commandments*

"Jesus Christ is not only our Savior, our Redeemer, and our Messiah, but He is also our Friend. Robert Crosby tenderly encourages us to enjoy the width, depth, and breadth of that eternal companionship. Like that dear old hymn reminds us, 'What a friend we have in Jesus.'"

Janet Parshall
Nationally Syndicated Talk Show Host

"Bob Crosby is one of the best! Clear. Concise. I don't want to put down his writings."

Dr. Don Argue
Past president, National Association of Evangelicals

"Bob Crosby has a heart to see Christians become all they were meant to be in Christ. He communicates with a keen sense of human need, both helping people identify the issues they face as well as giving superb guidance in finding practical solutions. Perhaps more than anything, Bob is a conveyor of hope."

Steve Fry
Author, Recording Artist

"In a world where the approach to spirituality too often is 'do your own thing,' Robert Crosby shows what true intimacy with Jesus is like through the example of the apostle John, through what it has meant to Christians over the ages, and through its impact on our lives today."

Leslie H. Stobbe
Evangelical Association of New England

Other Books by
Robert C. Crosby

Creative Conversation Starters for Couples
Fun-tastic Conversation Starters for Parents & Kids
Living Life from the Soul

More Than a Savior

WHEN JESUS CALLS YOU FRIEND

ROBERT CROSBY

Multnomah Publishers® *Sisters, Oregon*

MORE THAN A SAVIOR
published by Multnomah Publishers, Inc.
© 1999 by Robert C. Crosby
International Standard Book Number: 9781590528334

Cover photo of hands by Mike Houska
Cover design by David Uttley

Unless otherwise identified, all Scripture quotations are from *The Holy Bible,* New International
Version (NIV) © 1973, 1984 by International Bible Society, used by permission of
Zondervan Publishing House

Also quoted:
Holy Bible, New Living Translation (NLT) © 1996. Used by permission of Tyndale House
Publishers, Inc. All rights reserved.

The Holy Bible, King James Version (KJV)

The Living Bible (TLB) © 1971. Used by permission of Tyndale House Publishers, Inc.
All rights reserved.

The Holy Bible, New King James Version (NKJV) © 1984 by Thomas Nelson, Inc.

The Message © 1993 by Eugene H. Peterson

Revised Standard Version Bible (RSV) © 1946, 1952 by the Division of Christian Education of
the National Council of the Churches of Christ in
the United States of America

Contemporary English Version (CEV) © 1995 by American Bible Society

Multnomah is a trademark of Multnomah Publishers, Inc., and is registered in
the U.S. Patent and Trademark Office.
The colophon is a trademark of Multnomah Publishers, Inc.

ALL RIGHTS RESERVED
No part of this publication may be reproduced, stored in a retrieval system, or transmitted,
in any form or by any means—electronic, mechanical, photocopying, recording, or
otherwise—without prior written permission.

For information:
MULTNOMAH PUBLISHERS, INC.•POST OFFICE BOX 1720•SISTERS, OREGON 97759

Library of Congress Cataloging-in-Publication Data
Crosby, Robert.   More than a savior: when Jesus calls you "friend"/by Robert C. Crosby.
p.cm. Includes bibliographical references. ISBN 9781590528334
1. Christian life. 2. Jesus Christ—Person and offices. 3. Friendship—Religious
aspects—Christianity. I. Title. BV4509.5.C77 1999 99-21883 248.4–dc21 CIP

146651086

To
my fantastic four

Kristin Anne
Kara Joy
Robert Christian ("Robbi")
Kandace Grace

I'm so glad
I get to be your dad.

May you know in Him a Savior
And always find in Him a Friend.

Contents

Part Four

Jesus, My Consuming Desire

Acknowledgments

$\mathcal{S}$omeone has wisely said that writing a book is akin to giving birth. You carry the dream around inside for quite some time. You know that it has potential, but, at first, you cannot quite see what it will look like. In the end, you are eager to see it born.

This volume has gone through quite a metamorphosis. It began more than ten years ago in an embryonic form. Never did I know then what it would one day become. I have carried it, prayed over it, worked at it, and waited. It has changed along the way because I have changed. I hope it will inspire fresh life and grace within your soul. May you know him better as a result.

To my wonderful wife, Pamela: You are Encourager #1 in my life. Thank you for loving me, praying for me, challenging me and walking with me every day. Thanks for believing in the writer in me. It's time for another Passionate Getaway.

To the Christian Center congregation and staff: It is exciting to watch Jesus being formed within you. Thank you for being more than a fellowship. You're family.

To Les Stobbe: for seeing more in a manuscript than I could see.

To everyone at Multnomah: for the serious and thorough commitment you show in all you do.

To Bill Badke, my editor: for challenging the socks off of me and giving me hope all the while.

To my parents, Bob and Beverly Crosby: for giving me a most marvelous gift—the fear of God.

To my faithful cadre of intercessors: You know who you are and so does heaven. One day, so will everyone else.

To Jesus: Thank you for the anchor of knowing you are my Savior and for the adventure of discovering you are my Friend.

"Look! Here I stand at the door and knock.
If you hear me calling and open the door,
I will come in, and we will share a meal as friends.
I will invite everyone who is victorious to sit with me on my throne,
just as I was victorious and sat with my Father on his throne."

Jesus Christ
REVELATION 3:20–21 (NLT)

PART ONE

JESUS, MY FRIEND

Chapter One

THE ASTOUNDING
INVITATION

I no longer call you servants…
JESUS
JOHN 15:15

[God] can't be used as a road.
If you're approaching Him not as the goal but as a road,
not as the end but as a means,
you're not really approaching Him at all.
C. S. LEWIS

What would it be like if you could come as close to Christ as did his disciples? What if you could literally walk with him and talk with him as they did? And how transforming an experience would it be if you had the chance to actually lean your back against Jesus' over dinner as did John the Beloved? Or to have him weep with you over your brother's unexpected death as did Mary of Bethany? How marvelous might it be if you could sit privately with him and ask the deepest questions of your soul as did Nicodemus, up close and personally? Or what if you could actually discuss with him the dark side of your life in the bright light of day as did the woman at the well? And how would you feel if he looked you in the face and called you *friend*?

The Bible shows Jesus to be more than a messenger of doctrine. Instead, the Gospels give us a broad tapestry of people's experiences *with* him and their encounters *of* him. Resounding within each of the four accounts of his life and ministry, from Matthew to John, is an appeal which reverberates with the message: Get to know *HIM*.

The invitation of the Gospels is something far more than an opportunity to learn more *about* Jesus Christ, it is a bold call to personal experiential knowledge. We are beckoned not just to look and consider, but to taste and see. We are invited to do much more than explore the events surrounding his life. We are called to encounter his presence within ours practically and powerfully. The message of the Gospels is not just a record of *inform*ation about his life, it is an opportunity to experience a *transform*ation in yours. The story of his life and ministry is not some piece of doctrinal propaganda being passed throughout the land, it is a message of an incredible opportunity for a life-changing relationship extended to you and to me.

But just how close can a person come to Christ today? And what does it take to cultivate the kind of closeness that quenches the God-thirst felt within your soul and mine? What were the secret insights and experiences shared by the people who were the closest to Jesus during his earthly life and ministry? What can we absorb from other followers throughout history and today who have experienced true intimacy with Jesus? How have they engaged the presence of God and discovered an abiding closeness with him?

I never would have guessed it could have all started in a library.

My intentions were to simply get a bit of homework done. When I sat down at the large library table with a few of my friends, and one of theirs I had never before met, I was just hoping to avoid studying alone. My focus was interrupted, however, when the young lady I had never met proceeded to tell everyone at the table that she was stuck in her reading assignment. It seems there was a particular word of which she did not know the meaning. As she polled the group, none of us knew it either. Being the college newspaper editor, I was a bit embarrassed. So I did the gentlemanly thing. I quietly left the table. Unbeknownst to my friends, I went over to the large collegiate dictionary, looked up the word, wrote the definition down, walked back to the table and placed the small piece of paper in front of this young lady.

I guess you could say it all began with a word.

In my mind, searching out the definition was merely the right thing to do. Also, I figured that until she got the definition, I was not going to be able to get on with my studies that night. The young lady saw it differently, as I later discovered. She thought it was somehow romantic and thoughtful. I guess it all has to do with the lens you view it through.

We struck up a friendship, and then it happened. A few days later, walking down the sidewalk which led to my dormitory, this particular young lady and I were enjoying a light-hearted chat and a few laughs when suddenly her voice tensed. I wondered why.

"Robert, I want to ask you a question," she ventured.

"Oh yeah, what's that?" I casually returned.

"You know there is this Sadie Hawkins party coming up next week? You remember—that's the one where the girls are supposed to ask out the guys?"

"Uh huh."

"Well," she reluctantly continued, "I was wondering if you would like to be my date for it?"

This was not an invitation I expected. What you don't know is that at this particular point in my life I had just begun dating *another* young lady in whom I had been interested for a year or so. No, it wasn't a steady relationship, but it *was* showing promise. Now, here I was, for the first time in my life, dating one person and being asked out by another. Such a glorious quandary!

My response was most immediate and surprising to me: "Sure, I'd love to."

Even though I had begun to date someone else, even though my affections had been aimed toward another, I found Pam's invitation that day absolutely irresistible. You see, underneath the surface of my intentions, the makings of a friendship were brewing. I had only known Pam for a few days, but I was starting to like her. I mean *really* like her. Not only did I enjoy being around her, talking with her, and discovering more about her, I even liked *who I was* when I was with her.

The next few weeks I fell out of mere *like* and into *love,* deeply in love with Pamela. Oh sure, I had known *about* her for a few years. I had passed her on the way to class or heard her name come up in conversations. Now something totally different was happening. The days that followed were something far more. Now I was getting to know her. Instead of light chit-chat in a public cafeteria, we were sharing deep conversation in more private settings. The days were graced with long walks and deep talks. There were interests to compare, dreams to share, hopes to discover, and challenges to face. The more we met, the more our hearts began to merge. The fit was right. The closeness irresistible. Intimacy was doing what it does best— knitting two souls together.

And I thought she had only invited me to a party. Little did I know where it would all lead.

In like manner, there is an ocean of difference between learning more *about* God and truly experiencing his presence and his power in your life. Jesus clearly was far more interested in sharing his life with the souls of the men and women who followed him than simply capturing their intrigue with his new ideas and teachings. The Gospels are accounts of people who not only knew *about* Jesus; they knew *him,* personally and intimately. God wants the same for you and me today.

EYE IN THE SKY

John Newton was probably the last person you would have expected God to use. But powerfully use him, he did. From age eleven on he worked on slave ships. When he wasn't sailing he was "collecting" slaves on the islands and mainland of the West African coast for sale to visiting traders. Eventually Newton became the captain of his own slave ship. His was a cruel and harsh experience. His skin had been roughened by the harsh seawinds and his heart hardened by the life that went with it.

Somewhere, somehow, something changed within John Newton. In addition to reading *The Imitation of Christ* by Thomas à Kempis in the fray of a particular life-threatening storm, perhaps another earlier experience had helped shape the soul of the man who would one day pen the words to "Amazing Grace."

I'm told that as a boy growing up in eighteenth-century England, John lived next door to a little old lady who was a bit of an adopted grandmother to him. He would, on occasion, stop by and visit her. On one of her walls hung a picture he always found quite curious. It was a depiction of the Old Testament character Hagar and her son, Ishmael, when they were abandoned to the desert by Sarah and Abraham. Over their wearied images was a mysterious eye peering down at them from the sky. The words underneath were Hagar's own, taken from the Bible: "Thou God seest me" (Genesis 16:13 KJV).

One day while studying the picture, John asked the elderly woman, "What is this picture about? What does it mean?"

The lady responded, "Well, John, some people would like you to think that this means God is a great big spy in the sky who is just waiting to catch you doing something wrong, so that he can punish you. As a matter of fact there will probably always be people who want you to believe just that. However, it is not so. Such a notion of him is incorrect. What this picture truly means, you see, is that God loves you so much, he just cannot take his eyes off of you!"

If your heart does not stop right here in amazement, go back and carefully, thoughtfully, read that last paragraph again.

Did you catch it? Was your perspective purged as mine was when I first read it?

First of all, I am not surprised to find that God expects me to *worship* him. I would expect that of any deity, wouldn't you? After all, it only makes sense that the God whose hands placed the planets into order deserves the worship of one whose hands often struggle just to get the checkbook balanced.

Second, I am not amazed that God sets a high standard for living in front of me that he calls *holiness*. Clearly, it only stands to reason that the one who created man from the dust of the earth knows what is our maximum functioning potential. It seems only fair that the one who most deserves the right to expect something from us is the one whose hands formed us. If he, in fact, put us together, certainly he knows how to put us to our greatest use.

Additionally, it does not catch me off guard to discover God has left a document that describes his purposes and plans for mankind. Why, every intricate appliance I have ever purchased comes with an owner's manual, which tells me how to most effectively put that resource to work.

However, one thing does amaze me. It was something I never expected, something I never even considered. You see, what astounds me about Jesus Christ the most is not his deity or his piety, and not even his sovereignty. What I find truly incredible about the Jesus of the Bible is his utter familiarity.

ONE UNSOLITARY LIFE

One of the greatest shows on earth has to be the annual Christmas Spectacular at Radio City Music Hall in New York City. The traditional closing is a Nativity scene back-dropped with the popular and moving piece of prose entitled "One Solitary Life." This literary description of Christ has been published in greeting cards and plaques in many languages over the years. Although it has been broadly read and embraced, there is one word within it that I have never been comfortable with. That particular piece just does not seem to connect with the Jesus I see in the Bible.

And all the armies that ever marched;
And all the navies that ever sailed,
And all the parliaments that ever sat;
And all the kings that ever reigned, put together
have not affected the life of Man upon this earth
as has that One Solitary life.

And the word I have a problem with? *Solitary.*

If by *solitary,* one means what the dictionary defines as "being alone or without a companion," I disagree. If it denotes "tending to avoid the society of others," it doesn't sound like Jesus. Or what about these definitions: "characterized by the absence of companions," "being the only one," or "a person who lives alone."

Did Jesus embrace and enjoy solitary moments or seasons in his life? Certainly. Did he live a solitary life? I hardly think so.

Remember, he chose twelve individuals for a special reason: "That they might be *with* him" (Mark 3:14, emphasis mine).

Do these sound like the words of a loner? What about these words:

> "Come to me, all you who are weary and burdened, and I
> will give you rest." (Matthew 11:28)
>
> "Let the little children come to me, and do not hinder
> them, for the kingdom of heaven belongs to such as these."
> (Matthew 19:14)
>
> "Here I am! I stand at the door and knock. If anyone
> hears my voice and opens the door, I will come in and eat
> with him, and he with me." (Revelation 3:20)

No, Jesus was usually surrounded by people. In and around his life and earthly ministry we see him with:

The multitudes.
The five thousand.
The four thousand.
The seventy.
The twelve.
And...The three.
Even...The one.

ONE UNFORGETTABLE MOMENT

Jesus frequently made it clear by word and deed just how important people were to him, but never more profoundly than at one point in his ministry, which was both reported and savored by his youngest disciple, John the Beloved. In the midst of perhaps Christ's most intimate conversation with his disciples, the Savior said something so incredible and intriguing that at least one disciple would never forget it.

That revealing conversation Jesus had with his disciples (recorded in John 13–17) began with his sharing the Passover celebration meal and modeling the priority of servant-leadership by washing their feet. Jesus delivered an intimate discourse in that room, speaking to them of many vital issues and desires he had. He bared his soul. Shared his heart. Extended his vision.

Jesus spoke of many things precious and personal during these climactic moments.

He predicted his betrayal.

He prophesied Peter's denial to his face.

He comforted his disciples ("Do not let your hearts be troubled").

He described himself as "the way" to know God.

He emphasized his deity ("I am in the Father and the Father is in me").

He promised to send the Holy Spirit.

He referred to himself as "the vine" and his followers as "the branches."

And then...

He came to a point in his conversation with his disciples that was perhaps his most personal and familiar moment with them. What he said is nothing short of astounding. What he promised is absolutely amazing.

These were the last few moments Jesus had to speak into his disciples' lives. The next day he would be crucified. These were the last few moments in which he could say what he wanted to say. This was, if you will, the closest thing we have to his death bed experience. His words were not parabolic or vague. They were strong and direct. And, remember, this would be the last close up and personal chance Jesus would have to

- prepare his followers.
- affirm his devotees.
- ready his soldiers.

THE NEW COMMAND

Suddenly, Jesus became like a general issuing a new command: "My command is this: Love each other as I have loved you" (John 15:12).

Jesus' command would at one and the same moment become John's compelling passion and focus, his priority and compulsion, his preoccupation. Loving God and loving each other. That would become the goal of it all. John would spend the rest of his long life pondering its depth and significance, experiencing its potential, and mining its wealth. For in those words and moments, John caught more than a message, more than a concept, more than a teaching... he caught something of a new kingdom.

THE SUPREME EXAMPLE

Ever the practical one, Jesus, on the immediate heels of the command, followed with an illustration that put flesh on the bones and breathed life into the paramount principle of love.

"Greater love has no one than this, that he lay down his life for his friends" (John 15:13).

This is the manner in which Jesus chose to describe his own crucifixion, his own suffering. This is the context in which he chose to paint his most vivid image of love.

Interestingly, he did not choose to portray this greater love in the image of a war hero, a political prisoner, a religious martyr, not even a dying family member. No, he chose to paint his suffering and crucifixion in the context of *a man* who "lays down his life for his *friends*" (emphasis mine).

Jesus was not laying down his life for his *followers*. He was not laying down his life for his *students*. He was not laying down his life for his *witnesses*. He was not laying down his life for his *disciples*. He was not even primarily laying down his life for his *brothers*. No, first and foremost, the crucifixion was Jesus laying "down his life for his friends."

The context was relationship. Better said, it was *friendship*. The crucifixion would not be just some theological event to satisfy part of God's nature. It would be a personal expression from Jesus to every one of us that he wants friendship with you and with me. It is in this sense that Jesus wanted his followers to look upon his suffering and death.

Let's zoom in on those words for a moment.

"Lays down his life"—Jesus, the Friend, did not have his life *taken*. On the contrary, it was *given*—given for you. He laid it down. In every aspect he presented his sacrifice as a gift, not a loss; as something surrendered, not stolen. Jesus laid it down willingly, decisively, with a deeply motivating purpose in mind.

"For his friends"—Jesus, the Friend, had at the forefront of his mind not merely a mission, a movement, or an objective. He did not lay down his life for some*thing* but for some*one*…you and me. It seems he wanted that to be quite clear.

Jesus, the Friend, just hours prior to Gethsemane, was counting the cost. Sitting in this room, amidst the privacy of the Passover, I envision Jesus studying the faces of his followers. Faces. Hearts. Lives. The very ones he was about to die for. It is as if he was not just preparing *them*; he was preparing *himself*. Somehow, incredibly, as he faced the most harrowing and torturous experience of an impending crucifixion, as he looked upon his beloved followers, I believe his mind recited something like this: "It is worth the cost. *They* are worth the cost."

Somehow, the crucifixion of Christ would bring about a change in his relationship with his followers. In his death Jesus had something to prove, not simply to God or to the world, but to those who would follow him. The drastic depth of his sacrifice spoke of a certain depth of relationship he desired with them. The cross was not some gesture on Jesus' part to preserve the relationship he had with his disciples. It was the passageway to an intimacy more lasting than they could imagine.

FAMILY AND FRIENDS

The Bible uses more than one word and meaning for *friends* or *friendship.*

Friendship as *obligation* is the essence of the Old Testament word (*Rea*) for friendship. It is perhaps best illustrated by the responsible assistance offered by loving "your neighbor as yourself" (Leviticus 19:18b). This concept is later echoed in the New Testament story of the Good Samaritan (Luke 10:25–37). This word defines a friend as someone who shows his love to others by helping them, assisting them in their needs, supporting them in their difficulty, rescuing them in their despair.

Friendship as *sharing of experiences,* (Greek: *Philos*), however exemplifies the way in which Jesus related to the lost people around him. Instead of being shocked by their behavior and removing himself from their fallen culture, he chose to engage them and their misconceptions about love and life. As a result, his friendly disposition was misunderstood by some who sought to hurriedly label him instead of seeking to understand, as they said: "Here is a glutton and a drunkard, a friend of tax collectors and 'sinners'" (Luke 7:34). This label of a friend was meant as a slam. Somehow I believe Jesus wore it as a badge of honor.

Finally, **friendship as *the loving fellowship of family*** (ie: *Agape*) is the path to which Jesus called his followers. Real community. Genuine intimacy. Larry Richards writes, "While friendship among humans may be expressed in table fellowship and neighbor-liness (John 12:18), friendship with God is expressed in commitment to Jesus and in a life lived by His Words."[1]

Abraham is described in the Bible as "God's friend" (James 2:23, NIV). This was perhaps the most intriguing title ever given to a created being.

The nineteenth-century biblical biographer Alexander Whyte describes the significance:

> You may take sarza to open the liver, steel to open the spleen, flower of sulphur for the lungs, castoreum for the brain; but no [substance] opens the heart but a true friend—a true friend to whom you may impart griefs, joys, fears, hopes, suspicions, counsels, and whatsoever lies upon the heart to oppress it....
>
> The great office of a friend is to try our thoughts by the measure of his judgments; to task the wholesomeness of our designs and purposes by the feelings of his heart; to protect us from the solitary and selfish part of our nature; to speak to and to call out those finer and better parts of our nature which the customs of this world stifle; and to open up to us a career worthy of our powers."[2]

Deep within my heart and yours, we crave for that kind of a friendship, don't we? We long for a relationship with someone who will love us enough to understand us and yet challenge us enough to help us rise to our potential in life. Someone to encourage our dreams. Someone to confront our oversights. Someone to shield us in our insecure moments. Someone to guide us in our bolder ones. Someone who will be interested in what interests us. Someone who will hold us and never let us go.

THE ASTOUNDING INVITATION

In this atmosphere of devotion, modeled by Christ's foreshadowed description of the kind of death he would die, the Lord extended to his rough-edged band of followers the most incredible invitation the world would ever receive. Minus the gilded type and the fancy stationery, it went something like this:

> *"I no longer call you servants,*
> *because a servant does not know*
> *his master's business.*
> *Instead, I HAVE CALLED YOU*
> *FRIENDS,*
> *for everything that I learned*
> *from my Father I have*
> *made known to you.*
> *You are my friends*
> *if you do what I command."*
> JOHN 15:15, 14 (EMPHASIS MINE)

No invitation has ever been more inviting than this one—a personal relationship with the Son of God himself.

If I had to guess what Jesus would want to call me, it would have been something different. Perhaps *follower,* or *disciple,* or *servant,* or *student*…but *friend?* That I never would have expected. No invitation could have surprised me more.

The significance of such an open door is overwhelming.

It is opportunity unparalleled.

Such privilege unimaginable.

The implications are staggering.

SOMEONE MORE

John the Beloved knew Jesus as his Savior, yes, but as far more. You see, a savior is someone you need. A king is someone you admire and respect. A general is someone you follow and obey. But a friend is someone you know and love.

The Lord does not just call us to be a bunch of workers or laborers who go out and try to do something for God to win his favor. Instead, he calls us to be his friends. He's called us into a friendship, so living the Christian life has much to do with cultivating your friendship with Jesus. Walking with the Lord is not just trying to live up to the Ten Commandments. No, the beauty of the gospel is that Jesus says in essence "I want to fill your life and empower you so that you can live those commandments not out of constraint, but out of desire. I want you to know me so well that you want to do the will of God, that you delight in doing the will of God." Succeeding at the Christian life, then, is not as much about working harder as it is about *coming closer*.

There is a big difference between approaching God primarily as a servant or primarily as a friend. *Serving* is task-oriented; *befriending* is relationship-oriented. *Serving* always begins with *doing* something; *befriending* always begins with *knowing* someone. *Servants* don't dare pry into their master's business; *friends* are regularly given the "inside track." *Servants* serve in order to gain their master's approval; *friends* serve because they already possess it. *Servants* have a field to tend; *friends*, a garden to share.

When Pam invited me to attend a Sadie Hawkins party that day, I was taken aback. Little did I realize that my "yes" that warm Florida afternoon would lead to experiences and commitments I did not know I had the capacity for. Love, marriage, four children, living in three different states (so far), the joys and challenges of taking on life together, and an absolute redirection of the course I thought I was on. To think that it all began with just one little word.

When Jesus invites you and me to walk with him in friendship, we are astounded, aren't we? When we say "yes", he takes us by the hand and leads us into a journey that will turn our lives inside out. On the way, there are joys we never thought attainable, mountains we never thought scaleable. There are spiritual intimacies to fill our souls and spiritual trials to stretch them beyond what we ever imagined. Entering this relationship is one thing, navigating through it is quite another. And it all begins with one word—*Friend*. Of all the relationships in life, when we say "yes" to this one we enter into an unparalleled open door and find ourselves on the adventure of a lifetime.

MEDITATION

Take some time in prayer today to consider the incredible lengths Jesus Christ has gone to in order to forge a friendship with you. Carefully consider the one verse of Scripture the church reformer Martin Luther called "the heart of the Bible, the Gospel in miniature": *"For God so loved the world that he gave his one and only Son, that whoever believes in him shall not perish but have eternal life"* (John 3:16).

Told differently:

"God" . . . . .The greatest Lover
"so loved" . . . . .The greatest Degree
"the world" . . . . .The greatest Company
"that he gave" . . . . .The greatest Act
"his one and only Son" . . . . .The greatest Gift
"that whoever" .The greatest Invitation
"believes" . . . . .The greatest Simplicity

"in him" . . . . .The greatest Person

"shall not perish" . . . . .The greatest Promise

"but" . . . . .The greatest Difference

"have" . . . . .The greatest Certainty

"eternal life" . . . . .The greatest Possession

That's *great* news! Take time today to consider it.

Chapter Two

EDEN AGAIN

THE GARDEN OF INTIMACIES

Thou hast been in Eden the garden of God.
EZEKIEL 28:13, KJV

Eden, where Adam and Eve lived in the pleasure of a connected
relationship to the fullness of God.
They were fully satisfied and sustained. They were safe.
They were never alone. They had all they needed and more in God,
each other, and the created order around them.
JOSEPH STOWELL

Computer chips are formed out of the dust of the earth, or should I say the sand. Interestingly enough, these tiny microprocessor devices that have revolutionized the way we live have two primary enemies: dust and viruses. Computer companies spend millions of dollars to create environments that make micro-processor construction free of both. Elaborate filters are utilized to purge the air and to create what are called clean rooms.

When God created the earth, you might say that he designed his own clean room upon it and called it Eden. The Garden of Eden was heaven on earth. It started out that way, at least. What was shared and enjoyed there by a man and a woman was astounding and incomparable, the likes of which have never been seen since, not on *terra firma* at least.

Man's friendship with God began and, for a time, flourished in the Garden. Regardless of what particular geographical area the Garden of Eden occupied, it represents the place in which our kind originated, the place to which God wants to bring you and me...and in the depths of our souls, the place we most long to be.

Birds have migratory flights that bring them back to familiar territory and, ultimately, to the spot where they originated. Certain fish have their arduous return to their spawning sites, and they will go to incredible lengths to get there. Salmon are known to spend hours leaping repeatedly up waterfalls sometimes ten and twelve feet high against the tide to make their way back to the place of their origins. With a craving for Eden, there is a desperation within us, in a real sense, to do the same.

Just imagine what the Garden must have been like: a man and his God in intimate friendship; a man and a woman in deep love and harmony; a completely pure environment, untainted, uncontaminated. No unwanted dust particles to be found anywhere.

In the Garden prior to the fall of man, Adam feasted upon intimacies of all kinds. There was a fullness, a wholeness, and a balance to his life in the Garden that stands out like a bright star against the dark backdrop of the lives that have followed all the way to yours and mine. In a real sense, Eden remains our model for relationship with God.

What sabotaged the heavenly design was sin itself. Man chose to follow the dictates of what was *around* him instead of staying faithful to the call that was *above* him, and, tragically, he fell from grace. This produced much loneliness, emptiness, and confusion *within* him. After the fall of man, sin contaminated the clean room environment and played havoc with the lives of its inhabitants. The ripples of that rebellion have followed all the way into your home and mine to this very day. For us to appreciate, however, the devastation that event brought upon us, we need to go back and consider just how wonderful Eden and its intimacies must have been. To more fully understand what *we* have lost, you and I must recognize just how much *they* possessed.

A DAY IN THE LIFE OF ADAM

As the sun crested over the horizon of Eden, its warm rays tapped Adam on the shoulder and he awakened. Stretching the sleep out of his muscles, the man stood and once again beheld the beauty of that place. He often found himself doing just that—gazing at every kind of beauty imaginable. How often his days were filled with moments when his soul marveled at the creative handiwork of the Father.

The Garden was *safe*. Within it, the Father had surrounded Adam with creative reminders of his faithful love and constant care. The portraits of the Painter filled his environment. The gallery of God's handiwork, of this particular wing at least, was his home address. Each tree, each river and brook, each majestic sunrise and sunset reminded him of yet another facet of his Father's character. The sun rose every day just as faithfully as his Father's afternoon visits came when it set. The rivers that joined at his doorstep kept a flowing sound in life's background and reminded him of the wonderful way the Father wove together the pieces of his every day. He had never felt fear. Even the lion rested peacefully beside the lamb.

The Garden was *uncluttered*. Time was of no concern within its gates. Adam's walks with the Creator could last as long as they wanted them to. There was never any rush. The present moment was what always mattered most. Yesterday didn't matter and tomorrow was never considered.

The Garden was *abundant*. Through it Adam had been supplied with every kind of fruit and vegetable imaginable. It felt as if the entire garden was a gift from the Creator to him. He had not yet begun to explore all of the varieties of delectable foods that always grew around him. Somehow, wonderfully and mystically, these fruits represented the very characteristics of the Creator. The sweetness and sustenance they brought to his body served constantly to remind him of the Father's words and ways and of the nourishment they brought to his soul. He feasted not on apricots, but on the *awesomeness* of God; not on pomegranates, but on *providence;* not on june berries but on *joy* unspeakable.

The Garden was *productive.* Adam had been given Eden not only as a place to live, but as a garden to tend. He possessed a purposeful call—to cultivate and to create. Working the soil was a daily part of his life. He continually felt as if he was a co-laborer with the Father in his Garden. Adam's efforts at cultivating were exactly what it took to enhance and increase the harvest. He broke open the soil and God blessed it. As the man took obedient steps to work the ground, the Father worked behind the scenes bringing fruitfulness and abundance, always an abundance. It was quite a partnership.

The Garden was meant to be *shared.* To the Father, the picture was not complete with a man walking through it alone. God had not intended nor imagined such an image. It was as if he allowed Adam to live alone just long enough to recognize how *not good* such a state was. Then the Father sent the man a perfect complement in the form of a woman, a partner, a soulmate. Despite the fact that Adam and the Father shared regular times of encouragement every day, the Father wanted something more for the man. Eve arrived, not as some second-class add-on to the master plan, but as a divine intention from the beginning (*see* Genesis 1:27). She was like no other creation in Eden; she too was filled with the very breath of God (*see* Genesis 2:7–8).

The Garden was *inhabited*. Animal life of all kinds filled the majestic tapestry of Eden. There were birds in the sky. Creatures on the ground. Fish in the waters. All in all, Adam was anointed to be the king of this Garden jungle, and Eve the queen. God gave him the creative assignment of maintaining order by naming each and every animal. His role was to rule and to govern. Just as God had given him a name, so Adam would give each of them one.

The Garden was *verdant*. Lush and lovely and alive, it was a place of sheer beauty. Each of Adam's senses was daily enlivened by the sights he was privileged to behold, the sounds of peace, and the fragrances of joy. Everything about it was enchanting. There was not a dull corner to be found anywhere. Everything reminded Adam and Eve of the Father. His fingerprints were all over it. Each creation, animate and inanimate, presented itself as a letter of love addressed to him and signed by the Father's hand. The Word of God was not black ink in a book; it was what filled the atmosphere, what brightened every color and enlivened every creature. Everything around him reminded him of his Father and Friend. How could it not have done so, since God was the artist who originated every piece? How could a painting be truly admired apart from its painter? How could a sculpture be absorbed without consideration of the sculptor? Eden was God's gallery and every creature a masterpiece.

The Garden was *sacred*. The highlight of Adam's every day was not the spectacular sunrises or sunsets, not the incomparably delicious fruits, as marvelous as they were. The main course of his day was a walk filled with intimate conversation with the Father in the cool of the afternoon. There was nothing like it. Peace, joy, and love within Adam's soul were always rekindled as he took these walks through creation with the Creator himself. Somehow life in those moments was brought back into perspective. Adam felt most at home during those walks. They anchored his soul and provided a fresh burst of purpose. Empty places within his soul were regularly filled by the companionship of his Father.

After all, what must it be like to view a breathtaking sunset while in the company of the one who first imagined it, the one whose very hand had painted it? How marvelous it must have been to behold the stunning grandeur of a mountain range while rubbing shoulders with the one who used them to rest his feet upon. What joy surely erupted within the soul to observe the able wingspan of an eagle mounting a windy turbulence and to hear the Father say to the accompanying man, "As you wait upon me and my will, you too will surmount every turbulence of life."

THE WAY WE WERE

When God took out his canvas of clay called *Earth* and began his paramount work of art, the angels must have been on the edge of their seats. *What was God making this time? Would it look like any of his other creations? Why did he seem so much more excited about this project than the others?*

The palette of the Creator was dotted with a rainbow of colors, absolutely brilliant colors, radiant with his character. As the Creator selected a brush and soaked the bristles with the color of his choice, he made his first stroke of the brush. It went on as the light of the sun. The Painter of Light made his second stroke, which went on as the blue of sky. His third stroke of the brush went on the canvas as browns, greens, and more blues of land, plants, trees, and oceans. The fourth turned the light of the sun and the moon on the canvas. The fifth stroke painted animals and birds of every kind. But the most important impression on the canvas was yet to come.

All of the previous work of the Artist was in preparation for this stroke of the brush. Each brilliant color had been placed upon the canvas of time and space to provide a setting for what he would now create and place. The sixth stroke went on as the man and the woman. Though perfectly set against the backdrop of his majesty, the picture, however, was not complete.

Now that the Garden had color and life, God would fill it with the one missing ingredient: sound. And not just any sound. The sound of his voice. The first words that poured from his lips were promises and blessings, at least eight that I count:

- **A promise of reflection**—*"they will be like us"* (Genesis 1:26, CEV). The man and the woman were designed originally to be mirrors of God on this planet. By virtue of their composition and design they had the innate potential of reflecting the image and the glory of God to the earth's inhabitants below and to the angelic hosts above. As you and I now look above and view the stars against the dark canopy of space, so God would look below and enjoy the brightness of his ever growing company of saints. As they would stay close to their heavenly Father, they would eventually become an important expression of his character and heart.

- **A promise of rulership**—*"let them rule [the animals]"* (1:26), *"Rule"* (1:28). Adam and Eve were called to rule over the Garden. They were the caretakers of this corner of creation. God selected them to be the overseers of this portion of his world. Their task was to lead God's world God's way.

- **A promise of blessing**—*"God gave them his blessing"* (1:28, CEV). The Father extended his full support to man—his favor, and his inward strength and grace. He not only promised to guide, but also to provide for all of his needs.

- **A promise of replenishment**—*"Fill the earth [with people]"* (1:28). God called Adam and Eve to be fertile, "fruitful," and fulfilled. God was so pleased with them that he wanted to fill the earth with more and more people just like them. He had placed within their makeup the godlike potential to procreate, to initiate the extension of the creative work of his hand.

- **A promise of influence**—*"bring it under your control"* (1:28, CEV). Even before the Fall, before sin entered the Garden, there was work to do. The work was to bring order and leadership to the opportunities and challenges Project Eden presented. Just as God had initiated Eden's creation, man was commissioned to daily initiate its upkeep and development.

- **A promise of God's pleasure**—*"God looked at what he had done. All of it was very good!"* (1:31, CEV). When an artist finishes his best-done painting, he sits back, observes and enjoys the moment. When a writer or sculptor finishes a project, he enjoys a glowing moment of accomplishment. Apparently this experience is tied to our God-breathed design. Most affirming of all is the recognition that God looks at his creation of man, as well as the rest of creation, and says, "It [is] very good."

> *"Thou hast created all things, and*
> *for thy pleasure they are and were created."*
> (Revelation 4:11, KJV)

- **A promise of responsibility**—*"God put the man in the Garden of Eden to take care of it and look after it"* (Genesis 2:15, CEV). Eden was glorious, but it was no vacation resort. It included full employment, with all the accompanying benefits. Work was a part of God's plan for man before his fall. The curse that came as a result of man's sin simply added hardship to the duty. The ground, which had once been fertile, became stubborn and uncooperative. What began as *destiny* turned toward *drudgery*.

- **A promise of refreshment**—*"You may eat fruit from any tree in the garden; except the one"* (2:16–17a, CEV). This passage is the first in the Bible to establish any boundaries for God's creation. What stands out is that the provisions of the boundaries were *wide* (i.e.: "from any tree in the garden") and the limitations were *narrow* (i.e.: "except the one").

MAN—A REFLECTION OF GOD'S IMAGE

God is personable; so are we.

God is creative; so are we.

God is relational; so are we.

God is a communicator; so are we.

God is intelligent, purposeful, emotional, and intentional; so are we.

God is Spirit; and we have a spirit as well.

The intricacies and varieties of human personalities form a reflection of some of the very characteristics of God. We are made in his image, after his likeness. We have within us his very breath. As a result, we can only be fruitful and fulfilled, strong and satisfied, in his company. Whether or not we claim to be Christians, our souls long for what he alone can provide. We need desperately to be in relationship with him and to find our lives through him. We are drawn intrinsically back to a place called Eden.

DUST IN THE WIND

When Adam and Eve chose to do what God had commanded them to avoid, the clean room of Eden was contaminated. Theirs was an entire Garden to explore, cultivate, engage, and enjoy, and yet they chose their own way over God's. The results were nothing short of

cataclysmic. In an instant they became alienated from God, suscep-
tible to sin and sin-sickness. Something entered the Garden that
had never been there before—selfishness. Man became more
focused on the creation than the Creator. Adam's faith was shattered, his peace shaken, his purity tarnished, and his friendship
with God violated. Intimacy with God was interrupted. Read the
record in Genesis 3.

From then on, the saga of God's rescue mission for the souls of
men and women would be unfolded. The process of recovering a
friendship with man, which is the central theme of God's Word,
would come at a high cost.

CONNECTIONS

The Bible is a book of connections—connection with God and connection with our neighbor. It began with a man in deep and meaningful connection with God—personal, close, intimate, and
consistent. Within just a few chapters of the Bible's beginning, however, man forfeited this significant place of relationship when he
allowed sin to enter the Garden.

Most of Scripture after the Fall describes a roller coaster of
men's weak attempts at getting to know the God of the universe.
Throughout their stories and experiences, one thing stands clear.
There is a God calling man back into meaningful relationship with
himself, and there are men and women often struggling to find that
simple place we so desire of being "one with the Father" (John
17:22, CEV). The nature of the connection God wants us to have
with him is presented throughout Scripture in various metaphors.
Among the more prominent are:

- **The Vine and the branches**—In this relationship model, the
  key responsibility of man is *abiding*. This was one of the apostle

John's favorite concepts. Abiding in Christ to him meant more than just staying in his presence; it involved depending, trusting, believing, leaning on, relying heavily upon, and holding firmly to him in life. In this scenario God is our absolute source of life, nourishment, and attachment. And, like the original setting of Eden, this model takes place in a garden (John 15).

- **The Shepherd and his sheep**—Another of John the Beloved's favorite models, this one involves pleasing God by *following* (John 10). Sheep are known to be among the dumbest of all animals. They possess virtually no sense of direction and often will unknowingly eat themselves into a state of lostness. In this metaphor, God is seen as our soul tender, the Psalm 23-like overseer who daily watches over not only our state of submission, but over the deepest needs of our soul. The setting of this model is a pasture, or the place of feeding. He makes me "lie down in green pastures."

- **The King and his subjects**—We are called to be faithful in *submitting* to God. Jesus made it clear that he was doing more than putting together a movement—he was establishing a kingdom, the kingdom of God. The kingdom was his constant message and preoccupation on this earth. It is the most otherworldly concept that he spoke of and yet the one illustrated by the most down-to-earth stories. This model presents God as our ruler. He has come to do more than simply provide us with a relationship with himself. He is determined to impart to us a kingdom (Luke 22:29).

- **The Captain and his soldiers**—Jesus is described in the book of Hebrews as the captain of our salvation (2:10, KJV). In this capacity our priority is *obeying*. It is the one way we can convey our loyalty and our love, our consecration, and our commitment. Serving as soldiers, we see God as our leader. He understands the objective we hold, he recognizes the enemies we face, and he alone gives us our daily marching orders. In this model, we are on a mission and life is a constant battlefield.

- **The Bridegroom and his bride**—Perhaps the most mysterious model is the one described by the apostle Paul when he taught that Christ is the Bridegroom and his church (i.e.: all those who follow Jesus) is his bride. Paul said of it, "This is a profound mystery" (Ephesians 5:32). His words virtually invite us to ponder the significance of this place of privilege. The implication is that we are to *embrace God* by way of a deep and intimate relationship. This model presents God not primarily as our Lord or our leader, but as our lover.

These various models of our connection with God, of the nature of our relationship to him, should not cause us confusion. They represent not a variety of choices for how to approach him, but rather an assortment of views, or camera angles, that describe just five of the premier privileges afforded to the person that Christ draws close to himself. To the Christian, Jesus is at once a nurturing Vine, a watchful Shepherd, an admirable King, an assertive Captain, and an admiring Groom. He is that and so much more. He is all in all. John knew that better than any of the rest. To know Jesus is to know life and to find yourself once again at home in Eden.

NONE
WALKED CLOSER

"THE DISCIPLE WHOM JESUS LOVED"

I want to know Christ.
PHILIPPIANS 3:10

God is not satisfied until there exists between Him and His people
a relaxed informality that requires no artificial stimulation.
The true friend of God may sit in His presence
for long periods of silence.
Complete trust needs no words of assurance.
A. W. TOZER

*I*f Adam seemed closer to God than any other Old Testament figure, certainly John was that man in the New. From the beginning of his relationship with Christ, John the beloved—Jesus' trusted disciple and confidant—always seemed to be more aware of Christ's words and actions than the others, more determined to stick by Jesus' side, and more ready to respond to his desires and commands.

John grew up in Galilee initially as a disciple of John the Baptist. No doubt having caught some of the Baptist's prophetic zeal, he and his brother were dubbed by Jesus the "Sons of Thunder" (Mark 3:17). John, the younger of the two sons, is considered by many to have been the youngest of Jesus' disciples. Interestingly, this successful fisherman, whose name means "one whom Jehovah loves," became one of the select triumvirate, Jesus' inner cabinet of confidants.

Of all the disciples, John was arguably the closest to Christ. He sat next to the Lord at the Last Supper. Among the disciples, he alone stood by Christ all the way to the Cross. And on that eventful Resurrection morning, his passion caused him to outrun even Peter to the empty tomb.

Whatever it is that causes one man to be closer to Christ than another, John possessed it. Of all the characteristics he exhibited in his relationship with Christ, this one stood out: he was *close*. John possessed that vital quality that turns a mere man into a man of God. A. W. Tozer refers to it as "spiritual receptivity":

> Why do some persons "find" God in a way others do not? Why does God manifest His Presence to some and let multitudes of others struggle along in the halflight of imperfect Christian experience? Of course the will of God is the same for all. He has no favorites within His household. All He has ever done for any of His children He will do for all of His children. The difference lies not with God but with us.
>
> [What set great saints apart was] *spiritual receptivity*. Something in them was open to heaven, something which urged them Godward. They had spiritual awareness and they went on to cultivate it until it became the biggest thing in their lives. They differed from the average person in that when they felt the inward longing they *did something about it*. They acquired the lifelong habit of spiritual response. As David put it neatly, "When thou saidst, Seek ye my face; my heart said unto thee, Thy face, Lord, will I seek."[1]

Responsiveness to God. John had it in great measure. *Faith* prompted him to ask more of Christ than others were willing to ask.

Hope motivated him to run more diligently toward Christ than others. *Love* stirred him to open his eyes and take full notice of the man who came to show God to us.

Jesus was no stranger to questions. On one occasion, he was confronted by a notorious Pharisee ("expert in the law") who sought to test and confound him with what the Pharisee seemed to think was a trick question:

> "Of all the commandments, which is the most important?"
>
> "The most important one," answered Jesus, "is this:...'Love the Lord your God with all your heart and with all your soul and with all your mind and with all your strength.' The second is this: 'Love your neighbor as yourself.' There is no commandment greater than these" (Mark 12:28b–31).

Men such as this ill-intentioned Pharisee had taken the law and complicated it. Jesus, conversely, took the law and simplified it. He broke it down to the irreducible minimum.

God desired for his people to apply themselves spiritually ("heart"), mentally ("mind"), emotionally ("soul"), and physically ("strength") to cultivating their love relationship with him. That, as Jesus expressed it, is Vital Commandment #1.

Second, Jesus taught that we are to put at least as much into caring for others as we put into caring for ourselves. Unselfishness captures the spirit of Vital Commandment #2. It seems that the questioning Pharisee thought he might stump Jesus, but with savvy insight Christ offered an immediate answer that makes complete sense. Consider how appropriately the Ten Commandments fit under these two categories Jesus presented:

LOVE FOR GOD	LOVE FOR NEIGHBOR
(Exodus 20)	
1. "YOU SHALL HAVE NO OTHER GODS BEFORE ME"	5. "HONOR YOUR FATHER AND YOUR MOTHER"
2. "YOU SHALL NOT MAKE FOR YOURSELF AN IDOL"	6. "YOU SHALL NOT MURDER"
3. "YOU SHALL NOT MISUSE THE NAME OF THE LORD"	7. "YOU SHALL NOT COMMIT ADULTERY"
4. "REMEMBER THE SABBATH DAY BY KEEPING IT HOLY"	8. "YOU SHALL NOT STEAL"
	9. "YOU SHALL NOT GIVE FALSE TESTIMONY AGAINST YOUR NEIGHBOR"
	10. "YOU SHALL NOT COVET…"

Jesus accused the Pharisees of "strain[ing] out a gnat" but "swallow[ing] a camel" (Matthew 23:24). In other words, they were caught up in the minutiae when it came to their faith and they overlooked what really matters—love for God and for people. Jesus said, "You have neglected the more important matters of the law—justice, mercy and faithfulness" (Matthew 23:23c).

Instead of cultivating a sensitive awareness of God's heart, a true spiritual intimacy, the Pharisees put their two cents worth into the law, making it complicated, bulky, and debilitating. And yet, in like manner, some fallen thing within all of us wants to try to work our way to God, to earn a place before him—whether it is chanting a mantra or obeying human laws. God, however, calls us not only to outward obedience to his Word, but inward intimacy with the Holy Spirit.

Jesus painted love for God and love for his fellow man as the central theme of all of life. His supreme purposes for us in this life are served when we obey those commandments from the heart, and, as we do, we obey the whole law. The stone-etched mandate becomes a heart-inscribed desire. Such love is evidence of a close walk with Jesus. Such love is evidence of genuine intimacy.

"THE DISCIPLE WHOM JESUS LOVED"

The Gospels picture different levels of closeness to Jesus by those who knew and lived around him. When Jesus cultivated friendships in Galilee with twelve disciples, he chose them to "be with him" (Mark 3:14). He invested his heart, life, and teaching into this chosen team of men.

Within the Twelve, however, was an inner circle of three who, according to the scriptural account, were closer to Jesus than the rest. They saw more, heard more, and experienced more. This triumvirate consisted of Simon Peter, and James and John, the two sons of Zebedee. Jesus seemed to confide in these three more than the rest, allowing them to share in his pain (Garden of Gethsemane) and glory (Mount of Transfiguration) on a unique level.

One of the three (Peter) was the first of the twelve to acknowledge that Jesus was the Christ or the Messiah (Matthew 16:16). Interestingly, the other two, James and John, had a mother who made a bold request of Jesus one day:

> She said, "Grant that one of these two sons of mine may sit at your right and the other at your left in your kingdom." (Matthew 20:21)

Much like the remaining disciples, many a Christian has viewed this mother's request as selfish and a bit audacious. However, how many mothers after this one have not asked in prayer that their offspring might be as close to Christ as possible? Perhaps her request was not an expression of power-coveting, but rather a tender plea of intercession on behalf of her sons' souls. Regardless, her sons were both a part of Jesus' close cabinet of three, and one of them, John, appears to have been the closest disciple of all—the "disciple whom Jesus loved" (John 13:23), or at least that's how he described himself.

At the Last Supper, it was this young disciple who, upon hearing the prophecy that one in their midst was a betrayer, leaned back against the Master and asked, "Who is it?" Secretly identifying Judas as the culprit, Jesus answered the concerned inquiry of this devoted man, reassuring him at the same time.

John was present at the Transfiguration and ultimately was the only disciple present at the cross. In that fateful broken moment, Jesus called on the trusted disciple to fill his earthly role of "son" to his mother Mary in his absence (John 19:25–27). Clearly, Christ had a deep confidence in this young follower who had remained faithful to identifying with him even to the cross.

Throughout the biblical record of his life, there is something special and intriguingly unique about the disciple whom Jesus loved. *What was it about John that drew Jesus to him so? How did this follower gain such a trusted place in the Lord's heart? What did he do to cultivate his own friendship with Jesus? What did his eyes see that other's missed? What did his ears hear and his soul store? And, even more importantly today, what can I learn from John's life and character to fuel the flame of my own personal pursuit to know Christ? How did John come to love him so?*

Imagine thinking of yourself as "the disciple whom Jesus loved." John, as he wrote his gospel account, was not into self promotion; he wanted to promote his Savior. His gospel was unique and the most personal of the four. His gospel began with these Genesis-like words: "In the beginning was the Word... The Word became flesh and made his dwelling among us" (1:1, 14). And he ended that gospel by saying,

"Jesus did many other things as well. If every one of them were written down, I suppose that even the whole world would not have room for the books that would be written" (21:25).

Thank God for the synoptic gospels, for Matthew, Mark, and Luke and their accounts of Jesus. They focused much on connecting the events in Christ's life to the Old Testament prophecies that forecasted them. They presented the story of Jesus to specific and varied people groups.

But in their accounts there is not near the color that we find in John's Gospel. That gospel is so simple that it is the first book we often recommend to new believers to read. And yet it is so profound that many scholars and literary experts say there is no more beautiful piece of literature in the world. John's soul was full of all the things Jesus had done. He not only saw those things, he recorded them for us.

Learning how to love God and to let God love you is what Christianity is all about. Every other aspect of it flows from that dynamic experience. Loving God with all of our heart carries a call to have a real *passion for God*. Loving him with all of our mind challenges us to absorb *the wisdom of God*. Loving the Lord with all of our soul invites us to experience wonderful *devotion to God*. And loving him with all of our strength calls us to offer our diligent *service to God*.

Surely arguments could be made that other apostles figured more significantly into the early events of the church. One might consider the zealous preaching of Peter a preeminent trait. Another may cite the theological and church government insights and missionary journeys of Paul as being paramount in their influence. Yet, by virtue of the places he shows up and the passages he penned and remembered, John held a privileged place in proximity to the Master.

Many waxed *bolder*.
A few even seemed to stand *taller*.
However, surely none walked *closer*.

Chapter Four

A FAITH
WITH A VIEW

*I pray also that the eyes of your heart may be enlightened
in order that you may know the hope to which he has called you,
the riches of his glorious inheritance…*

EPHESIANS 1:18

Faith is the gaze of the soul upon a saving God.

A. W. TOZER

My eyes could pan the entire city of Toronto at a glance from the vivid perch high atop the CN Tower, the world's tallest self-supporting structure. The first time I stood beneath this behemoth spire I was overtaken with awe as my eyes surveyed this man-made structure soaring some three-hundred times my own height (1,815 feet, 5 inches to be exact). Just an hour earlier, as my car approached the outskirts of the megalopolis, the same structure that now engulfed me was merely an intriguing blip on the horizon. It was reduced by distance. From afar, this same tower had actually fit between my two fingers; up close, my senses were absolutely overwhelmed by the view. It stretched above the cityscape to create a suncanopied futuristic skyline that stamped a modern and unmistakable image on the memory. The closer I got the more impressive it seemed.

My mind for a moment was stunned when I considered just what the tower represented: the merging of minds and the mountain of calculations, the pooling of ideas and cascades of cooperation, the teaming of manhours and the energies expended. A sight to behold. For a lingering moment, the convergence of considerations was more than my own set of senses could fully absorb.

Paul the Apostle apparently had a similar experience with an engulfing presence of a different kind. In a familiar passage, he cites a doorway of great insight and responsibility in the path of every believer. In Romans 12:1, Paul draws our attention as Christians to his incomparable view: "Therefore, I urge you, brothers, in *view* of God's mercy, to offer your bodies as living sacrifices, holy and pleasing to God—this is your spiritual act of worship."

Interestingly enough, while pounding out a strong sense of the duty given to every person who would honor God, Paul attaches this essential doorway of commitment to a hinge in the form of a phrase: "in view of God's mercy." In essence, the principle of offering one's body as a living sacrifice is, first of all, connected with a perspective. The motivation to do God's will is somehow connected to the grace of being able to see more of who he is and more of what he has already done for us. To the writer of Romans, the best way to strengthen our commitment is to improve our view.

As long as I continue to journey on the outskirts, the view is too manageable to ever be marvelous, too scaled-down to ever be truly significant. From a distance...no wonder is ever too wonder*ful*, no power too power*ful*, no master ever too master*ful*.

Many choose to view God in such a manner. Distant. Observable. Manageable. Close enough to consider. Distant enough to never impose nor interfere. Gail MacDonald has said, "Today we have large thoughts about man and small thoughts about God."

THE DEEP END OF THE POOL

Just prior to this paramount verse in Romans, Paul draws our attention to his own vivid view of the mercy of God. Since the verse just cited begins with the word *therefore,* it, of course, implies that the writer is collecting the essence of the material that he has just presented, which serves to build the case he is now stating. Looking back at the verses just preceding actually reveals much of Paul's own vivid view of God and of God's vast provisions. His view is expansive, to say the least. It includes a strong sense of the fathomless riches of God's wisdom and knowledge, his unsearchable judgments, his unmappable pathways, his inexhaustible mind, his invariable rightness, and his unlimited resources. Paul reveals himself as a man obviously caught up in the depth of God's character and person. Read it for yourself:

> Oh, the depth of the riches of the wisdom and knowledge
> of God!
> How unsearchable his judgments,
> and his paths beyond tracing out!
> "Who has known the mind of the Lord?
> Or who has been his counselor?"
> "Who has ever given to God, that God should repay him?"
> For from him and through him and to him are all things.
> To him be the glory forever! Amen.
>
> ROMANS 11:33-36

Clearly, Paul's view of God and his mercy was no distant image. Rather, there was a depth to his own awareness and experience in God. Take a closer look at what he said: "For *from* him and *through* him and *to* him are all things" (Romans 11:36, emphasis mine). In other words, God is the *origin* ("from him"), the *propulsion* ("through him"), and the *destination* ("to him") of life itself. These verses at the close of Romans 11 were clearly meant not just to be read and pondered, but experienced and searched out. They come on the heels of Paul's legal masterpiece, the first ten chapters of this letter, in which he describes the fallen state of man, the resultant wrath of God, the faith of Abraham, the sacrificial work of Christ on the cross, and the overcoming of sin by living in the power of God's Spirit. Coming out of these heavily doctrinal issues, Paul proceeds to invite us into the deep end of the pool. He beckons us from the water-temperature-testing exercises of weighing insights and calls us to ponder no longer, but to plunge—to experience God, to surrender our lives—and in the real responsibilities of life, to devote our very bodies to his service.

AN URGENT CALL

Taking time to consider and record his own sense of the greatness, vastness, and graciousness of God, Paul's eyes unrelentingly turn from the glories above to the reflections below. "Therefore, I *urge* you, brothers..." With passion, he musters a trumpeting call, a piercing mandate, a determined challenge to every believer within striking distance. By now, he is so overwhelmed with God's grace toward mankind that his words swell with passion in his effort to relay his sense of duty—his eager responsibility—to believers at large. As he considers the phenomenal richness of God's gifts to man, the apostle recognizes that commitment and obedience on man's part is neither an astounding response, nor above and beyond the call of duty. It is reasonable, right, and, in every sense, appropriate. From Paul's perspective, any other response would be criminal.

Jerry White paints it this way: "Over my twenty years as a Christian and thirteen years in full-time Christian ministry, I have watched hundreds of men and women living out their lives. Some flourishing; others languishing. Some who made an impact; others who made no mark whatsoever. Some grew in the Lord; others dried up spiritually and withered. Some walked in a certain joy and offered encouragement; others complained and griped. Some deepened and softened; others became more shallow, hardened and, even, callused. Some grew with grace and godly influence, others just grew old."[1]

What fork in the road led them to one or the other? What choice? What decision? What attitude? What posture? What disposition?

The answer is one thing: A purposeful commitment!

"Ordinary people who make simple, spiritual commitments under the lordship of Jesus Christ make an extraordinary impact on their world. Education, gifts, and abilities do not make the difference. Commitment does."[2]

A SOCIETY OF "OPTION TENDERS"

Too often today we are more determined to keep our options open than we are to lay down solid commitments. Much of our culture praises the free spirit who, despite his relative satisfaction or dissatisfaction with his job, always has a resume out. Society applauds the person who, while tiring of her marriage, her kids, and her job, leaves it all to "find herself". All the while, the age-old Psalm remains unchanged, honoring the person "who keeps his oath even when it hurts" (Psalm 15:4b).

Ellen Goodman, the widely-read syndicated Boston Globe columnist, writes, "The fear of commitment is epidemic in the Western world. Students wait longer and longer to make a choice of major. Couples enter marriage tentatively with an easy escape clause. Men and women take jobs with a wary reserve that keeps them looking for something better. Company workers too rarely demonstrate loyalty and commitment. Couples postpone having children to retain their personal freedom and options. Children find themselves in the backwash of mothers and fathers pursuing their personal freedom. What is the root? Selfishness."

Goodman cites the problem as selfishness. Perhaps the apostle Paul would diagnose it this way: You just don't have a good enough view! In order to experience the deep blessings of relationship, we must have a close-up view of Jesus.

BETWEEN MY TWO FINGERS

Enjoying lunch while sitting atop the 143,300 tons of reinforced concrete that makes up the CN Tower, my wife and I took our time while celebrating our honeymoon at the revolving Sky Pod Restaurant. We were determined to savor every morsel of an incredible lunch and to give our senses ample time to absorb the vivid panorama of this beautiful city. As we ate lunch and, later, toured the structure, my mind reeled with wonderment over all that must have gone into creating this place. The dreaming. The imagining. The planning. The drawings. The countless calculations. The construction. It was such an undertaking. Such an impressive accomplishment. The more of it I pondered, the bigger it seemed and the smaller I felt. The more I considered its precision and its very presence, the more content I was to just stand still, to behold, and, for those moments, to simply be engulfed by it all.

As overwhelming as the tower was to me in those moments, there still existed in the back of my mind a thought of absolute contrast. It occurred to me that this same structure, which now elicited my wonderment and seized my imagination, had just hours earlier (twenty-five miles away to be exact) fit between my two fingers and done little more than spark a bit of intrigue. In much the same manner, we often want a god like that…one who fits between our two fingers. You see, if you have a god who fits between your two fingers, you can place him wherever you want. You can move him out of your way whenever you want. A god who fits between your two fingers is accessible enough to be periodically admired, and yet small enough to be quickly placed out of sight when you just don't want to be bothered. Rather than having to fit ourselves into *his* world, *his* kingdom, *his* directives and values, this kind of god, instead, conveniently fits into ours.

THE VIEW FROM HERE

The apostle-general Paul not only delivers marching orders in the first verse of Roman's twelfth chapter; he appeals to our reason and calls us to our senses, as well. Paul makes it urgently clear that our commitment to serve God faithfully is fueled by our vision of what he has already done for us. In sizing up the root problem of our hesitations and resistance to commit, perhaps Paul would say it this way:

"If you are neglecting prayer...the problem is...*You don't have a good enough view*...of God and who he is!"

"If God is only a Sunday-morning focus in your life...*You don't have a good enough view!*"

"If you are not engaging in honoring the Lord with your resources, your finances, and your offerings...*You don't have a good enough view!*"

"If you're not entering into worshiping God with all your heart, mind, soul, and strength...*You don't have a good enough view!*"

"If you are not actively sharing your faith with others...*You don't have a good enough view!*"

"If you are not taking time to pray with your Christian spouse or family...*You don't have a good enough view!*"

John transcribed Jesus' indictment of the self-sufficient Laodicean church in a stinging postcard rebuke: "These are the words of the Amen, the faithful and true witness, the ruler of God's creation. I know your deeds, that you are neither cold nor hot. I wish you were either one or the other! So, because you are luke-warm—neither hot nor cold—I am about to spit you out of my mouth. You say, 'I am rich; I have acquired wealth and do not need a thing.' But you do not realize that you are wretched, pitiful, poor, *blind* and naked. [YOU DO NOT HAVE A GOOD ENOUGH VIEW!] I counsel you to buy from me gold refined in the fire, so you can become rich; and white clothes to wear, so you can cover your shameful nakedness; and *salve to put on your eyes, so you can see*" (Revelation 3:14–18, emphasis mine).

UNSEEN REALITIES

A few years ago while viewing a documentary on *LIFE* magazine, "40 Years of Life," I watched with great interest a series of former editors being interviewed. One of the early editors, who served the publication during the Civil Rights movement in America, was asked to give his own opinion of Martin Luther King, Jr. In his response, I believe I heard one of the clearest definitions I have ever come across of what faith is. The editor's assessment was: "Martin Luther King was a hero…and heroes are a rare breed. They have the uncanny ability of being able to rise above their fears and do what they really believe in. To a hero, what he cannot see is infinitely more real to him than what he can see."

Rising above our fears. Doing what we believe. What motivates such an effective and purposeful lifestyle? Consider the second part of the quote again: "To a hero, what he cannot see is infinitely more real to him than what he can see." People of faith not only live from the soul, they see from it. The writer of Hebrews said it this way: "Now faith is

being sure of what we hope for and certain of what we do not see.…
And without faith it is impossible to please God" (Hebrews 11:1, 6a).
Unseen realities. In a sense, faith is perceiving the imperceptible, believing the unbelievable, and somehow, by God's grace, knowing the unknowable.

Paul obviously prayed that the Ephesian Christians would similarly gain a better view. Before he ever entered into the oft-taught disciplines of this famed epistle (i.e.: building unity; living as children of light; marriage and parenting relationships; and wearing the armor of God), he offered a prayer that their eyes would be opened, that they would see and know God more fully: "I keep asking that the God of our Lord Jesus Christ, the glorious Father, may give you the Spirit of wisdom and revelation, so that you may know him better. I pray also that *the eyes of your heart may be enlightened* in order that you may know the hope to which he has called you, the riches of his glorious inheritance in the saints, and his incomparably great power for us who believe" (Ephesians 1:17–19a, emphasis mine).

The Greek word used in the passage to speak of enlightenment is powerful. It is the word *photizmo* and is associated with our word "photography" today. Jack Hayford suggests that if Paul were to use the words of contemporary technology he would have said: "I pray that God would cause there to come by the ministry of His Spirit of wisdom and revelation a burst of the strobe light of heaven's glory into the negative of your soul and it would burn an image in technicolor of the glory of His purpose for each one of you."

THE GAZE OF THE SOUL

From a distance, perception is deceiving. An 1,800-foot-tall tower can turn into a toothpick I can twiddle between my fingers. Up close, however, the truth is made known. In fact, I am the "toothpick" by comparison when I see things as they really are. Distance distorts reality. Closeness has a way of confirming the truth.

A.W. Tozer defined faith as "the gaze of a soul upon a saving God."[3] He further explained that by "its very nature [faith is] scarcely conscious of its own existence. Like the eye which sees everything in front of it and never sees itself, faith is occupied with the Object upon which it rests and pays no attention to itself at all. While we are looking at God we do not see ourselves—blessed riddance. The man who has struggled to purify himself and has had nothing but repeated failures will experience real relief when he stops tinkering with his soul and looks away to the perfect One. While he looks at Christ the very things he has so long been trying to do will be getting done within him. It will be God working in him to will and to do."[4]

Intimacy with Jesus begins and ends with the view that we find through our faith in him. The Lord not only wants to help us walk uprightly, he desires to help us see fully and brightly.

The invitation is clear. Faith is not some moral adrenaline that we force into action by gritting our teeth and trying hard to look holier. It is a fountain of God-confidence that flows from our souls as we become less concerned about ourselves and more aware of the greatness of the God we serve. A god who fits between our two fingers will never inspire genuine faith within us. However, as soon as our eyes are opened and we begin to see with our souls the God who is "great" and only "greatly to be praised," faith will flow, and the view will be like nothing we've ever seen.

Chapter Five

WILL THE
REAL JESUS
PLEASE STAND UP?

I keep asking that the God of our Lord Jesus Christ, the glorious Father,
may give you the Spirit of wisdom and revelation,
so that you may know him better.

PAUL THE APOSTLE

EPHESIANS 1:17

He delights in us when we enjoy not just the gifts he gives,
which are many, but the person he is.

JERRY SITTSER

*I*t is amazing to see how powerfully our lives can be shaped by the lives of others. Throughout history, leaders have come to the forefront at strategic times. Often, their words and their examples have changed society. See if you can guess who said the following after a life-changing encounter with a leader:

At that moment I was reborn! Now I knew which road to take...Like a rising star you appeared before our wondering eyes, you performed miracles to clear our minds and, in a world of skepticism and desperation, gave us faith. You towered above the masses, full of faith and certain of the future, and possessed by the will to free those masses with your unlimited love for all those who believe…For the first time we saw with shining eyes a man who tore off the mask from the faces distorted by greed…

You grew before us to…greatness…What you said are the greatest words…You expressed more than your own pain…You named the need of a whole generation, searching in confused longing for men and task. What you said is the catechism of the new…belief, born out of the despair of a collapsing, Godless world…We thank you.

Who do you think wrote those words? And at what time in history were they penned? And, more importantly, who were they written about?

These words speak of "miracles," so was it about some *miracle* worker? Additionally, the writer focuses on the subject of "faith," so surely it must have been a religious leader. We read of freeing the suffering "masses" and of an "unlimited love for…those who believe." If the person this writer was speaking of was not the Messiah, then surely he was a prophet.

Well, the scribe of these sentences was not focusing on Christ, Mohammed, or Ghandi. And he was not speaking of the faith of a convert to Christianity, Judaism, or Islam. Still his devotion was fueled with a religious dynamic.

His name? Paul. No, not Paul the Apostle, but *Paul Joseph Goebbels*. And his influencing leader? *Der Fuhrer.* Adolf Hitler.

Goebbels's words, although riveted on a man who ultimately became full of the devil himself, were nonetheless passionate, powerful, and compelling. His deep-rooted convictions would light a flame of faithful devotion in the hearts of countless thousands of others. His misdirected dedication would lead him to become Hitler's most loyal follower and the Overseer of Berlin. Even though

Hitler stood for something most of us now abhor, his life brought change to his hearers and his followers, a fact that cannot be denied.

Earlier in Hitler's political career, Goebbels knew *about* this man. He reached a point in his life, however, where he came to know him in a greater sense. At that point, the flame was lit and Goebbels was sold on him.

There is a vast difference between knowing *about* Jesus Christ and *knowing him* personally. Christianity is not a mandate to simply espouse a new creed or doctrine; it is a call from heaven to every soul to experience God, to encounter the person of Jesus Christ in our very hearts and lives.

Not only do we need a close-up view of Jesus, we must be viewing the right one, not one of the counterfeits.

Interesting, isn't it? Those times when you think you know someone and really don't can be confusing and downright disheartening.

Jesus, on at least one occasion, told his new-found followers something absolutely central to the Christian faith. It was as if he was saying, "If you miss everything...do not miss this!" His paramount principle? That there is a major difference between doing religious things and really knowing Christ. Listen to his words:

> Not everyone who says to me, "Lord, Lord," will enter the kingdom of heaven, but only he who does the will of my Father who is in heaven. Many will say to me on that day, "Lord, Lord, did we not prophesy in your name, and in your name drive out demons and perform many miracles?" Then I will tell them plainly, "I never knew you. Away from me, you evildoers!" (Matthew 7:21–23)

The principle contained in this passage is at the same time remarkable and terrible to consider. *Remarkable* in that Jesus is reasserting the purpose for which he came into the world—to bring men and women into intimate spiritual relationship (i.e.: friend-ship) with himself. *Terrible* because his words make it clear that there will be many individuals who will do things that on the surface appear to be very spiritual, but in reality are not. This revelation makes it powerfully clear that being a Christian is not simply about *doing* a lot of Christian things; being a Christian is all about *knowing* Jesus Christ intimately, personally, and meaningfully.

Imagine the desperation that will unfold one day when people line up anticipating their place in heaven, only to discover that their seemingly Christian works did not earn them one cubic inch of heaven's territory. Most of us know how difficult it is when temporal hopes are put off or shattered. Imagine the immensity of the moment when a soul discovers that its *eternal* hope is shattered and lost.

When Jesus said there would come a time when he would declare "I never knew you," he was underlining and highlighting the important call of his life to every individual, to you and to me. He came to give us eternal life and the eternal, abundant life that he offers consists of knowing him, of sharing in an interactive, personal, and growing relationship with Jesus Christ.

In the long run it will prove true that the place in which we begin to please God is not simply in the works we do, but in the knowledge we share, the knowledge of God through Jesus Christ. As a matter of fact, the Scripture makes it clear that all of our efforts at doing godly things in our own strength "are like filthy rags" (Isaiah 64:6). The works of service that truly please God are the ones that flow out of our love relationship with him, out of our friendship with Jesus. Oswald Chambers said that "the lasting value of our public service for God is measured by the depth of the intimacy of our private times of fellowship and oneness with Him."[1]

Christianity is not a faith built on our terms, but on Christ's.

And clearly the love that allowed him to endure this sin-riddled earth and the agony of the cross was a love riveted on winning not our blind oblation, but our loving obedience.

THE LENS WE SEE THROUGH

How we *view* Jesus has much to do with how we serve him. It is vital that we see him clearly, that we grow in our understanding of the Jesus of the Bible. Most of us have grown up with a culturally conditioned view of who Jesus is. I have often thought that the most fortunate new converts to Christianity are the ones who knew nothing of Jesus until shortly before they made their commitment to him. Such people have minds that are free of the misconceptions of Christ that cover the planet. They are free to allow the Holy Spirit to reveal Christ to them.

In recent years there has come a fresh consideration of the man Jesus, of who he truly was and is, of what he stood for, of what his message was and was not.

For many of us, however, growing to know the Jesus of the Bible involves shedding much misinformation about him. The New Testament teaches us that God's will is that you and I be conformed into the image of Christ (Romans 8:29). I am suspicious, however, that in our culture and too often in the church today we are quick to make Jesus *after our own image*. For years we have done so ethnically. All you have to do is examine various Christmas cards with nativity scenes from around the world and the truth emerges. We see the pasty white Jesus, the black Jesus, the Asian Jesus, and on and on. Somehow it is important to us that Jesus is in our camp.

We mistakenly view him in several major ways, the more popular including:

- **The white, Anglo-Saxon Protestant Jesus**—Much of America today has been taught to worship a Jesus who looks like the majority of American citizens. We are often quick to forget that Jesus entered this world long before Martin Luther did. Although Christianity funneled out through the post-resurrection centuries in a number of various streams, we must look back to where it began—with a sun-tanned Hebrew sojourning the countryside among his rough-edged cadre of misfit men, his disciples. Out of this initially unimpressive group of men, Jesus proposed to turn the world upside down (or should I say, right-side up).

- **The Republican-conservative Jesus**—Jesus never ran for public office and neither did any of his disciples. Although we must not use this as a premise to avoid political involvement (after all, we are called to be "salt" and "light" in the culture), it is important that we not brand Jesus as the spiritual mascot of any political party. Was he opinionated about the social issues of his day? *Definitely.* Was he determined to confront injustices in the culture? *Absolutely.* Was he focused on effecting social change through political methods? *Never.*

  The kingdom Jesus came to build was not a political one, but a spiritual one. And he did not come to lead a political revolution, although many hoped he would; he came to lead a spiritual revolution. His conquest was not one precinct at a time, but one heart, one soul, at a time. While the Zealots sought to carry out a revolution from outside the ranks of the ruling majority inward, Jesus came to carry out one from the inside out. He first sought to establish his kingdom not in the halls of justice, but in the hearts of men. Most of the people in his day did not know what to do with that approach— several would soon learn.

  Certainly we are free to make our political decisions and to be involved in government. I hope and pray that more and more Christians will do so. However, it is essential that we remember that the greatest hope for any country is not a new king or a new president, but a radiant, loving, devoted, and confident people of God. When God saw a planet that needed a gift of hope and direction, he raised up not a new political party, not a military regime, but the church.

- **The social activist Jesus**—Many view Jesus as someone who was primarily riveted on social reform. After all, didn't he feed the hungry, care for the sick, and watch out for the children? And was his work not most often among common people, amidst the neighborhoods and among the poor?

It must be noted, however, that Jesus invested the bulk of his time not just dispensing help, but communicating hope. Not only did his loaves of bread and cures for diseases come into people's lives, they came with words—words of hope. Of course the Scripture does teach us to "not love with words or tongue but with actions and in truth" (1 John 3:18), but Jesus brought words of hope along with provisions of help. To him, apparently, they were interconnected. As a matter of fact, on one occasion he put it this way:

"Man shall not live by bread alone, but by every word that proceeds from the mouth of God." (Matthew 4:4, CEV)

One urban pastor, Buster Soaries, has put it this way: "Jesus came to bring more than just *help*; he came to bring *hope*. In the world today, if you just give someone in desperate need *help,* they might still commit suicide. If you bring them *hope,* however, they will probably learn how to get their own *help.* Then both needs will be met."

Jesus never separated his social activism from his spiritual ministry.

- **The passive Jesus**—Many of us were raised in churches with stained glass windows. For hours and hours of worship services over the years we gazed at pictures of the Good Shepherd. My mind is still filled with images of a mild-mannered, milquetoast-of-a-man sort of Jesus, with nicely-combed hair and soft skin. He is the Jesus carefully holding a fragile little lamb. The image conjured many thoughts in my mind about him. The assumptions I came away with included:

  He could never hurt a flea.
  He is the most easy-going person who ever lived.
  He never got worked up or angry in any way.
  His life consisted of just being nice to everyone he met.
  His emotions always stayed at the same temperature.

Philip Yancey challenges our misconceptions of an emotionless Jesus:

The personality that emerges from the Gospels differs radically from the image of Jesus I grew up with, an image I now recognize in some of the older Hollywood films about Jesus. In those films, Jesus recites his lines evenly and without emotion. He strides through life as the one calm character among a cast of fluttered extras. Nothing rattles him. He dispenses wisdom in flat, measured tones. He is, in short, the Prozac Jesus.

In contrast, the Gospels present a man who has such

charisma that people will sit three days straight, without food, just to hear his riveting words. He seems excitable, impulsively "moved with compassion" or "filled with pity." The Gospels reveal a range of Jesus' emotional responses: sudden sympathy for a person with leprosy, exuberance over his disciples' successes, a blast of anger at coldhearted legalists, grief over an unreceptive city, and then those awful cries of anguish in Gethsemane and on the cross. He had nearly inexhaustible patience with individuals but no patience at all with institutions and injustice.[2]

If anyone ever lived life from the soul, it was Jesus. There was nothing bland about him whatsoever. The more one reads the gospel accounts, the more clear it becomes that he held his audiences spellbound, he captured the fascination of children, he confounded the contemplations of the wisest, and he certainly never conjured a yawn from anyone.

- **The icon Jesus**—Some people treasure their icons of Jesus: whether in the form of a crucifix or a rosary or a favorite old Bible or a WWJD bracelet or whatever reminds us of him. Not long ago Bobby Vinton was interviewed on the *700 Club* and when asked about some of his early hit records he said he felt they were blessed because of his prayers and because he kissed a statue built to honor a particular patron saint.

It is one thing to have memorials and mementos that remind us of Jesus. These may convey much the same significance of love letters kept, treasured, and reread by a lover. However, it is altogether another thing if we treat them like a good-luck charm, a rabbit's foot or an idol themselves. After all, the second commandment was "to make no graven images," or no idols.

Jesus never sat for a portrait to be painted of himself. He lived before the Renaissance. And he came at a time when no picture could be taken of him. Perhaps there is a reason for this. As a matter of fact, we have no substantial record of a physical description of him prior to his resurrection. It is as if there was so much to absorb and record about Jesus' spirit, about his heart, about his authority, and about his actions that none of the four extensive Gospel records gave so much as a hint of a physical description. Even John, who referred to himself as an eyewitness of Jesus, was much more caught up in his perceived glory than any distinguishing physical characteristics. The only biblical physical description we have of him is the one John saw at the Revelation.

- **The good teacher Jesus**—Perhaps the most often used description given of Jesus by people who do not embrace the Christian faith is that of the good teacher. An imagined conversation might go something like this:

  Christian: So, who do you believe Jesus was?

  Nonbeliever: Oh, I believe he was a good teacher. He had a lot of good, moral, and philosophical things to say.

  Christian: Does that mean that you would place him right alongside Socrates and Aristotle?

  Nonbeliever: Sure, and Mohammed and Thoreau and the Dalai Lama. They all had a measure of light.

  Christian: But, do you know that Jesus professed to be the Son of God? Was that a good teaching? Do you believe it to be true?

  Nonbeliever: Well, that was his reality. To him, that was the truth. I guess in a sense all of mankind are the sons and daughters of God.

In a day and age when it is unpopular to judge one religion as being more right than another, an honest reading of Jesus' words in the New Testament reveals much. One of the most blatant revelations shows a Christ who was far too dogmatic about truth to fit within today's pluralistic and tolerant environment. After all, he didn't say that "I am one of the ways" to God, but I am "THE way…THE truth…and THE life" (John 14:6, CEV, emphasis mine). Additionally, he made it clear that he was God in the flesh when he said, "If you have seen me, you have seen the Father" (John 14:9, CEV). And, he expressed a clear religious intolerance when he said, "I am the door…All who ever came before me are thieves and robbers, but the sheep did not hear them" (John 10:7–8, CEV).

JESUS AND THE PERSONALITY TEST

One interesting tool in team-building within any organization, including the family, is a personality assessment. My favorite is probably one of the simpler ones—the Smalley-Trent test. In it, people taking the test are scored on a range of four key personality types based on various animal-types, including the following:

The "Lion"—This represents the person with a strong personality who is prone to take the lead in any given situation. What matters to them is who is in charge.

The "Golden Retriever"—This represents the individual who is empathetic, caring, and concerned about the people around him. What matters is people's needs.

The "Beaver"—This is the industrious personality who is concerned about the details of life and work. What matters is covering all the bases.

The "Otter"—This is the personality best described as a party waiting to happen. What matters is having fun, no matter what he's doing.

Over the years I have enjoyed using this personality assessment to counsel couples, teach classes, and evaluate employees. Recognizing personality styles can assist much in team-building. The thought occurred to me one day, *How would Jesus do on such a personality test?* It may seem a bit sacrilegious at first to even think that, and yet it became an inspiration as I thought it through. After all:

Was Jesus a *lion?* Was he a leader? Oh, yes. The "Lion of Judah" as a matter of fact. He boldly led his disciples and masses of people across the countryside of Palestine.

Was Jesus a *golden retriever?* Was he empathetic? Consistently. He was "filled with compassion" (Mark 1:41). On one occasion, he looked at the masses and saw them as "harassed and helpless, like sheep without a shepherd" (Matthew 9:36).

Was Jesus a *beaver?* Was he industrious and precise? Certainly. He came "in the fullness of time"—not a minute too soon, not a moment too late. He made sure there was plenty of food for the five thousand and even pulled a gold coin out of a fish's mouth to pay his taxes.

But, was Jesus an *otter?* Was he fun to be with and around? I believe he was magnetic. Many of the more conservative eyes of his day saw him as a partier, in fact. Since he spent time with the sinners of his day and the rabble-rousers, he was referred to by them as "a winebibber" (Luke 7:34, KJV).

> If our greatest need had been information,
> God would have sent us an educator.

If our greatest need had been technology,
God would have sent us a scientist.
If our greatest need had been money,
God would have sent us an economist.
If our greatest need had been pleasure,
God would have sent us an entertainer.
But our greatest need was forgiveness,
so God sent us a Savior![3]

The bottom line is this: *Jesus defies our persistent attempts to label him.* Perhaps what is most intriguing when one undertakes a prayerful and open-hearted study of the Gospels is not just the depth of the man, but his breadth as well.

Only Jesus is at the same time full of grace and full of truth.

Only he could show such outright compassion to societal outcasts and, yet, such utter defiance to the self-righteous ruling classes.

Only he could be so forceful and yet so kind.

Only he could confront political powers and somehow never seem at all political.

Only he could wash the feet of fishermen and, with the same hands, turn over the tables of errant religious officials.

Only he could be so authoritative and yet so approachable.

The Scripture confirms that intimacy with God comes by "looking unto Jesus..." (Hebrews 12:2, KJV). Paul Goebbels thought he had found a savior. As it turns out, a savior was, in fact, what he was looking for, but not what he saw. The sincere seeker of God will regularly dust off the lenses of his own prejudices, notions, and expectations and search for the genuine article. His soul is desperate to see not some icon or apparition, not a notion or a myth, but Jesus himself.

There is a wonder about Jesus. A wonder that the Holy Spirit himself wants to reveal within your heart and mine. There is a glory about him that is missed when we approach him on a merely human level. All the while that we are placing labels around his neck, he desires to pull chains off of our hearts. We are wise to invite the Holy Spirit to inspire our reading of the Gospels, to direct our prayerful interaction with Jesus, and to help us to see him clearly. Once our cultural conditionings are confronted, our eyes truly open, and our ears quite clear to hear, we will no longer see the Jesus we were looking for, but the one who was, who is, and who forever will be.

Chapter Six

FRIENDSHIP
WITH JESUS

You will seek me and find me when you seek me with all your heart.
JEREMIAH 29:13

*Full knowledge of one personality by another cannot be achieved
in one encounter. It is only after long and loving mental intercourse
that the full possibilities of both can be explored.*

A. W. TOZER

Given a close view of Jesus and a proper Jesus to view,
what kind of relationship can a follower expect? What
characterizes the type of relationship the Lord extends
to us as followers and companions?

My daughter was excited. Driving home from work with me
several years ago, my four-year-old was eager to tell me of her joy.

"I'm so excited, Dad. Know why?"

"No, Sweetheart. Why?"

"'Cuz Papa and Granma are coming to see me tomorrow and
they're going to bring me a surprise. I can't wait to get my surprise!"
Kristi asserted.

Seizing upon an opportunity, I decided to teach my daughter a
little lesson.

"Well, Kristi," I said. "I am really glad you are excited to see your grandparents. Even so, I just want to make sure that you are excited about seeing *them* and not just some prize they might bring. You see, it is really important that we not *love* things. It is alright to *like* things, but we are not supposed to *love* things according to the Bible. We are supposed to *love* God and people, and it is okay to *like* things. So, what you should be most excited about is that you get to see your grandparents, not the gifts they might bring. Got it?"

Kristi nodded her head, but I was not so sure.

A little later, when we got home, I told my wife all about our lesson. She quickly retorted, "Robert, don't you think that is a bit of a heavy lesson for a four-year-old to learn? It's probably more than she can grasp at this stage. Maybe you are expecting too much out of her."

On more careful consideration, I decided my wife might be right.

The next day, Saturday morning, we sat down to eat some waffles I had just cooked. As Pam dug into hers, she said, "Robert, I just love these waffles."

"Mom," Kristi interrupted. "You don't *love* those waffles really, do you? We're not supposed to *love* things. We're only supposed to *love* God and people. But, Mom, it's okay if you *like* them."

I exulted over the lesson learned. A good one for children—as well as adults—to remember. After all, we live in a culture in which the price tags are switched. What should be of great value (ie: our relationships) is too often devalued; and what should mean little to us (ie: positions, possessions, and power) is too often idolized and clamored after. Jesus made it clear that love for God and love for people are the most priceless possessions of the kingdom.

THE DREAM

One day a woman had a dream.

It was a dream so vivid that she felt as if she were right there. In this dream, she had died and suddenly found herself not in heaven, but at the glorious gates of heaven. A powerful looking angel greeted her and said, "You have a choice to make. One of these gates represents the way into heaven and the other three do not. They all look quite sacred, so be careful. There is only one which is the true way into God's presence. The others lead to a terrible place. Now, look at the gates very carefully and make a wise choice."

As the woman inspected the respective gates, she discovered that each of them had a sign emblazoned overhead with a word on it which represented a manner of approach to God.

One had the words—DEBT REPAYMENT.
Another had the word—PERFORMANCE.
Still another sign read—RELIGIOUS AFFILIATION.
The last door simply said—FRIENDSHIP.

Immediately, the woman knew what each of these doors meant. Or, at least, she thought she did.

The Debt Repayment Gate was designed for people who focused on paying God back for all the mistakes they had made, hoping that enough good deeds would one day outweigh all the bad deeds they had committed.

The Performance Gate was there for the individuals who were determined to live the kind of life that would meet with God's approval and get his attention. For these people, *looking* spiritual was what it was all about.

The Religious Affiliation Gate was set up for the person who was convinced that belonging to the correct religious group was the key. Being a member of the right group was the focus.

Lastly, the Friendship Gate was designed for the individual who simply wanted to have a relationship with God. This was the person who was aware of how much she needed God in her life and was convinced that every good gift comes from knowing Him.

The decision was a tough one.

In a way, the Debt Repayment Gate seemed to be the correct one. She was certain that she owed God an overwhelming debt, for she had sinned many times.

On the other hand, the Performance Gate also drew her. She felt that if she could just be *good* enough, it might get God's attention and he might allow her into heaven.

Still, the Religious Affiliation Gate was compelling. Bearing the right spiritual label seemed to be of value. After all, isn't true spirituality about being in the right group?

Of all the gates, Friendship seemed to be the least likely one. After all, who could presume to have a friendship with Almighty God? That seemed a far-fetched and unrealistic notion.

Which gate do you think she chose?
Which gate would your parents have chosen?
Which gate would you choose today?
Which gate would you have chosen five years ago?

The truth is...Jesus Christ settled the issue of debt repayment when he paid the debt of my sin and yours on the cross.

Christ also settled the issue of performance when he finished the work that God had sent him to do and marked the moment of completion on the cross once and for all with the words: "It is finished" (John 19:30).

He has settled the issue of religious affiliation. He said, "I am the way, the truth, and the life! No one can come to the Father except through me" (John 14:6, NLT).

The truth is that Jesus Christ calls us into the relationship best described as friendship with God.

THE APPROACH	THE GOAL	THE MEANS	SAYS
Debt Repayment	Paying God Back	(Works)	"Pay Up"
Performance	Impressing God	(Looks, Image)	"Act Out"
Religious Affiliation	Attaining God	(Labels)	"Sign Up"
Friendship	Knowing God	(Love)	"Draw Near"

FRIENDSHIP —
WHY IS IT SO IMPORTANT?

We all have a basic deep need for relationships. God has designed us so that we do not function well without meaningful relationships with other people. At the level of our souls we crave intimacy. Rod Cooper, a counselor, has aptly and succinctly defined intimacy as "into-me-see." Bottom line, we have a need to know others and to be known; to understand and to be understood; to share our hopes, dreams, hurts, and struggles with another human being. Friendship is truly not an option. It is a basic human need.

Additionally, when we avoid friendships and the cultivation of them in life, we find ourselves incomplete and unfulfilled. Friendships have a way of motivating us to live fuller lives. Friends have a way of challenging us and provoking us toward risk, honesty, and adventure.

The alternatives to meaningful friendship are undesirable. Our world is full of vices, bad habits, addictions, and traumas, many of which are compounded by the choices people make to avoid the effort it takes to build satisfying friendships. Alienation, isolation, and self-preoccupation are just a few of the miserable symptoms that can wrap their claws around the soul of a friendless man or woman. And those symptoms can come regardless of a person's age or socioeconomic condition. We live in an age of the Up-and-Outers as well as the Down-and-Outers.

Quality friendships magnify the depth and influence of our lives. But just how are we to fill the friendship vacuum that leaves a hole in our soul? What are the characteristics of a true friendship? How would we know one if we saw one? And, how can we be a true friend to someone else? After all, the Scripture says, "In order to have friends, a man must show himself friendly" (Proverbs 18:24, CEV). What does that involve?

SEVEN CHARACTERISTICS OF A TRUE FRIEND

As I search the Scripture, I find seven primary characteristics of a "true friend."

1. *A friend always loves you.* Proverbs 17:17 says that, "A friend loves at all times." Perhaps that is what is most refreshing about true friends. Their devotion to you does not change with the weather or the current circumstances. They can be counted on. Their love has been proven. Their commitment is unconditional.

2. *A friend always sticks by you.* "A man of many companions may come to ruin, but there is a friend who sticks closer than a brother" (Proverbs 18:24). Dave Roever is a Vietnam War veteran who had much of his face blown off when a hand grenade he held was hit by a sniper's fire. As he lay in a burn clinic, bandaged and in agony just days after the explosion, he painfully watched one wife after another come into the ward, take one look at their husbands, and throw their wedding bands on the beds and leave. They couldn't handle what they saw.

When Dave's wife finally arrived, his stomach tightened. After all, he had seen his face in a mirror and he looked like a monster. When his young wife sauntered up to his bedside, she leaned over, kissed him on his charred cheek, and said, "I love you, Davey." Roever responded, "How could you love me? I look like a monster." His wife wisely responded, "Oh, Davey, you were never good looking anyway!" His heart melted.

3. *A friend will tell you the truth.* Real friends are more than peace-keepers; they are the people who are willing to be truth-tellers. They will tell us the truth about ourselves when we need to hear it, because they care about us. They are even willing to risk our friendship if it means they might be of help to us.

Lee Iacocca tells of a friend who taught him most of what he knew in the automobile business. In his popular autobiography, Lee recounts a banquet where he stood up and honored this leader in his life: "Charlie (Beacham) could be a tough boss when he thought the situation called for it. At a dinner celebrating my election to the presidency of Ford in 1970, I finally got up the nerve to tell Charlie publicly what I thought of him. 'There will never be another Charlie Beacham,' I said. 'He has a special niche in my heart—and sometimes I think he was carving it out by hand. He was not only my mentor, he was more than that. He was my tormentor, but I love him!'"[1]

"Wounds from a friend are better than many kisses from an enemy" (Proverbs 27:6, NLT)

4. *A friend holds a crown over your head...and encourages you to fill it.* "As iron sharpens iron, a friend sharpens a friend" (Proverbs 27, NLT). In the popular animated children's movie *The Lion King* there is one scene where the father lion, King Mufasa, appears and says to his struggling young heir cub these memorable words: "Simba, you are more than what you have become..." When I first heard those words, they struck a chord in my soul. A friend knows how to play a note of encouragement in our lives and to stay on it.

5. *A friend is interested in what interests you.* "A man that hath friends must show himself friendly: and there is a friend that sticketh closer than a brother" (Proverbs 18:24, KJV). Dale Carnegie once

said, "You will gain more friends in three minutes getting interested in others than you will in three months of trying to get people interested in you." Real friends show real interest...and often.

6. *A friend operates on your schedule of need.* One of the best things about friends is that they are there when you need them. I will never forget the morning after my first venture as an amateur plumber. I simply had to install a new lavatory in my upstairs bathroom, but when I woke up I discovered a steady drip that had gone on all night. My upstairs and downstairs were flowing with water. The pastor of the church I served in came over in a flash when I called, and he stayed until the problem was fixed hours later. I will never forget the thoughtful response he gave to a friend in need.

7. *A friend is part of your life, not just your conversations.* Friends care about much more than how good the waffles are, don't they? Pythagorus put it this way: "Friendship, one soul in two bodies."

Alexander Whyte summed up the role of a friend well in these words:

> The great office of a friend is to try our thoughts by the measure of his judgments; to task the wholesomeness of our designs and purposes by the feelings of his heart; to protect us from the solitary and selfish part of our nature; to speak to and to call out those finer and better parts of our nature which the customs of this world stifle; and to open up to us a career worthy of our powers.[2]

JESUS, THE FRIEND

After examining these seven characteristics of a true friend, the question remains: Does Jesus Christ pass the test of true friendship? Before delving more deeply into your friendship with Jesus, what first steps has he taken toward striking up a friendship with you and how do you know he wants it to be even stronger than it is today? When our eyes fully open to view the Jesus of the Bible, what characteristics emerge? And what do they tell us about him?

1. *Jesus is...a friend who will always love you.* "Greater love has no one than this, that he lay down his life for his *friends*" (John 15:13, NIV, emphasis mine). In the face of rejection and blasphemous assaults, Jesus refused to treat a world of sinners with anything but a heart of compassion. Judas betrayed him; Jesus washed his feet. The executioners nailed him; he asked God to forgive them. No matter what you have done, he is determined to show you his love, even if it costs him a cross.

2. *Jesus is...a friend who will always stick by you.* "I will never leave thee, nor forsake thee" (Hebrews 13:5, KJV). In the face of a flock of followers with rough edges, Jesus stood by every one of them. His focus seemed to be more on their faithful following than on their imperfect condition. Their confusions, their immature blunderings and foibles did not break his commitment to them; they seemed, on the contrary, only to reassert it. Neither John's impulsiveness, nor Peter's impetuousness, nor Thomas's reluctance could deter him in his mission. He had gold to mine through the rocks and the rubble of their humanness.

3. *Jesus is...a friend who will tell you the truth.* "Apart from me you can do nothing" (John 15:5). Jesus was a consummate truthteller. When it came to calling things and people as they were, he never pulled a punch. His words could be stinging, but never without purpose and always laced with hope. When Peter rebuked him, he responded, "Get thee behind me, Satan." When John overreacted, he said, "You don't know what spirit you are of." And when the Pharisees pontificated, he told them they were "a brood of vipers." Jesus was far more concerned about conveying truth than about being thought of as nice. Straightforward honesty was the tool he

used to bring positive change to those he cared about.

4. *Jesus is...a friend who holds a crown over your head...and encourages you to fill it.* "You are the salt of the earth...the light of the world" (Matthew 5:13–14). It seems that the disciples not only liked the company of Christ, they liked who they were when they were with him. He brought out the true colors of their souls, the deep purposes of their hearts, the sincere motives of their thoughts. But most of all, when they were with him they felt the power of what had first drawn them to leave their pursuits and to walk with him: a call to follow. Somehow they, all twelve, felt sufficiently compelled when he first said the words "follow me" to leave all and do so. Imagine the implications of such a step in the life of any businessperson today. They found in him a hope of becoming something more that overshadowed all they were or had ever aspired to be.

5. *Jesus is...a friend interested in what interests you.* He was "moved with compassion" (Luke 10:33, CEV). He had a marvelous way of concerning himself with what concerned the people around him. Whether discussing a woman's ponderings about wells and the water drawn from them or his opponents' questioning about taxes and their overall appropriateness, Jesus was interested. On one occasion he looked at people and was "moved with compassion" because he saw them not so much as criminals and offenders as he did as victims, "harassed and helpless, like sheep without a shepherd" (Matthew 9:36, CEV).

6. *Jesus is...a friend who has operated on your schedule of need, more than on his schedule of convenience.* "While we were yet sinners [i.e.: When we needed him the most], Christ died for us" (Romans 5:8, KJV). One of the marvels of the Incarnation was that God was making himself available to man. Available to serve, to help, and to heal.

7. *Jesus is…a friend who is part of more than your conversations, but a part of your life.* "I have come that they may have life, and have it to the full" (John 10:10b).

Only two men are described in the Bible as having a friendship with God. First of all, there was Abraham, who through the ages has been considered the "friend of God" (2 Chronicles 20:7, Isaiah 41:8, James 2:23). And, second, Moses: Inside the Tent of Meeting, "the LORD would speak to Moses face to face, as a man speaks to his friend" (Exodus 33:11).

Jesus, however, often presented himself as a friend. Not only did he call his disciples friends, but he was viewed by the religious elite of his day as "a friend of the worst sort of sinners" (Luke 7:34, NLT). Even when Judas led the angry mob who, "armed with swords and clubs," arrested Jesus, the Master greeted him with the words: "My friend, go ahead and do what you have come for" (Matthew 26:47–51, NLT).

If Jesus is such a friend, then how can we respond except by seeking a friendship with him? If Jesus, in fact, offers you and me this astounding invitation of walking with him and cultivating that friendship into one of depth and strength, what keeps us from it?

GETTING CLOSER TO GOD

Earlier, we considered ways someone might consider finding a relationship with God. Ask yourself, "What am I doing to try to get closer to God? Which approach am I taking?"

If you are trying to repay a debt you owe, give it up. The bill is far too big and you just do not have what it takes. You don't now and you never will.

If you are banking on a good performance to get the attention and approval of God, it never will. Someone else has already performed the drama that has the heart of God riveted for eternity. It began in a manger and ended on a cross.

If your religious affiliation is the insurance policy you are hoping will get you through, you are in for a disappointment. Jesus shunned labels, but he pursued relationships.

If friendship with Jesus is your focus and desire, you are finding what matters the most. Remember, he never said that he came to lay down his life for debtors, for performers, or for church members; he laid down his life for his *friends*. Are you his friend?

Chapter Seven

"I WILL SHOW
MYSELF TO HIM"

Whoever has my commands and obeys them,
he is the one who loves me.
He who loves me will be loved by my Father, and
I too will love him and show myself to him.

JESUS

JOHN 14:21

Abandonment is practiced by continually losing your own will
in the will of God; by plunging your will into the depths of His will,
there to be lost forever!

JEANNE GUNYON

When you love someone, really love them, sometimes finding an appropriate means of expression can be difficult. Certainly, real friendship can never be forced, it must be cultivated. However, sometimes love has been known to drive us to extremes. Counselors and relationship "experts" tell us that being too pushy with people will usually backfire on us. Despite the warning, the *Los Angeles Times* carried a story about a man who never listened to such counsel:

> A lovesick man holed up in a $200-a-day Washington hotel
> has spent, at latest estimate, close to $20,000 demonstrating

to his beloved that he won't take "no" for an answer to his marriage proposal.

Keith Ruff, a 35-year-old former stockbroker from Beverly Hills, had proposed to 20-year-old Karine Bolstein, a waitress in a Washington restaurant. They had met in a shoe store the previous summer and had gone out a few times over several weeks before the proposal. Karen's response to the proposal was "No."

From then on a determined Ruff remained in Washington demonstrating his wish that she reconsider by purchasing and sending "everything but a partridge in a pear tree." When the article was written, he had almost spent all of his money. The gifts were numerous: a Lear Jet placed on standby at the airport; almost 5,000 flowers; a gold ring; $200 worth of champagne; catered lobster dinners; serenading musicians; a man dressed as Prince Charming bearing a glass slipper. Cookies, candy, and perfume; even sandwich-sign wearers bearing personalized greetings and walking in front of her home and place of employment with the message, "Mr. Dennis Keith Ruff LOVES Ms. Karine Bolstein."

Ruff has tried to gain Ms. Bolstein's father's support by sending him a basket of nuts and $300 worth of cigars. He has worked on her more-resistant mother by sending her flowers and a ladder with a note inviting her to "look at their relationship from a different angle."

When asked about his career plans, Ruff responded: "I don't care how many job offers I get. I'm not interested in any of them. I'd rather think about her than sit at a job." He said that he would "spend his last dime and beg for money if he has to, that he will keep on trying for 10 years, 20 years. I'll ask her to marry me 50,000 times…I wouldn't stop if she became a nun. I've never felt this way before!" He said that he spends a lot of time in his hotel room planning what to do next and occasionally crying.

Ruff reported that Ms. Bolstein called him once, "But I hung up on her. I didn't like what she said. Reality to me, is disturbing. I'd rather close my eyes and see her face. Fantasy is where I'm living. I'm living with hope, and some very big bills."[1]

Ah, the things you'll do for love.

My college roomate had a different experience: Frank and Sherry were a match made in heaven. Well, at least in Frank's mind.

I still remember when my college roommate set out to win the affections of a young lady on campus who seemed to have absolutely no interest in him. For weeks, Frank would talk to me about his irresistible interest in Sherry. Although unrequited, he talked about her and his determination to take her on a date. The fact that she had made it clear, via campus intelligence informers, that she did not want a date was only incidental in Frank's mind.

Night after night and day after day, Sherry was all I heard Frank speak about. If he had focused as much on his studies as on her, he would have graduated top of his class. Over the weeks that followed, I watched with amazement as he set out to win her affections.

Frank investigated Sherry in every way imaginable. He studied her to find out what her hobbies and interests were and he set out to win her, not on his terms but on hers. He was so love stricken that he became totally preoccupied with learning how to speak her love language. And learn it he did. In a matter of a few months, he had graduated from a first date to a strategically engineered moment when he asked her to marry him. To everyone's surprise, even somewhat to Sherry's, I believe, she said yes.

I sat in amazement. In my mind, these things were not supposed to work. Not only had Frank played his cards right, more importantly, he learned something prior to marriage that many people never learn even decades after it. It may sound romantic, but he found the way to read and to speak her love language.

Dr. Gary Chapman has popularized the concept of learning how to speak your spouse's or your child's love language. According to Chapman, there are five primary love languages. They represent the various approaches of expressing love which uniquely mean the most to us. The five *love languages* he cites are:

Gift-Giving.
Quality Time.
Words of Affirmation.
Physical Touch.
Acts of Service.

The underlying principles are that (1) we tend to like to have love expressed to us primarily in one of five key ways, and (2) we tend to express love to our spouse in the way in which we most want it expressed to us. Bottom line, if my primary love language is acts of service, I may try to express love to my wife today by washing the dishes. When I am done, I may expect her to take notice of my gesture. Chances are, however, if her primary love language is quality time, then my added chore will not do much for her need to feel loved by me. She won't be as impressed as I might have hoped. In my view, acts of service mean a lot; they are a primary love language in my life. In her mind, however, washing the dishes is not above and beyond the call of duty, nor especially romantic. In light of her primary love language, taking her out for a long and conversational dinner would go much further.

I wonder...*what is Christ's primary love language? In all the ways I might choose to express my love for him or to him, which of them really capture his attention the most? Which of them means the most to him? Which of my efforts at loving the Lord is he the most drawn to and blessed by?*

CHRIST'S LOVE LANGUAGE

The apostle John discovered what others missed. While many in his day were *looking for a way out* of Roman oppression, out of this life and into the next, out of an illness or dilemma and into health, John *was looking for a way in*—into the heart of Jesus, into his will and into his ways. Consider the following passage, exclusively pondered and penned by John the Beloved. Can you find God's preferred love language within it? Can you spot the treasure offered to the person who faithfully speaks that language?

> "Whoever has my commands and obeys them, he is the one who loves me. He who loves me will be loved by my Father, and I too will love him and show myself to him." (John 14:21)

There is no promise of Christ's more exciting or intriguing than this one. I have pondered it and pored over it for several years and it still leaves me absolutely fascinated with its sheer challenge and invitation.

I am convinced it is no accident that, of all the Gospel writers, only John recorded these words of Christ. You won't find them in Matthew, Mark, or Luke. Was it because they had never heard these words? Could it be that no other living witness had relayed such an amazing promise to them? Or did the other Gospel writers group these words with the many others of Christ which they just wouldn't have room for in their limited accounts? Were these verses left out for the sake of brevity?

Not only did John catch the principle contained in this passage, but he experienced in a most powerful manner the realization of its promise. Somehow along John's journey with Jesus, in some profound way, he discovered the fact that obedience *to* God inspired by love *for* God is what God wants the most from our lives. John found that when a man or woman begins to walk in *loving responsiveness* to the will and the voice of God, a powerful friendship is forged. As a result, such people's lives become more God-enriched than they ever dreamed possible; their prayers receive strong answers, their desires dramatically change, their influence in heaven increases, and their lives are powerfully transformed.

All through Scripture we see obedience and faith as the magnets within man that draw God near. After all, among all the people on the planet God could have chosen to initially bless and whose seed would become God's favored nation, why did he choose Abraham? The Scripture tells us. It was his great faith in God. We could say it was his responsiveness to the Word and to God in and around his life. Bottom line, Abraham's faith got God's attention and great blessings in his life and lineage resulted. And, remember, Abraham was called "the friend of God."

ABANDONMENT — GOD FINDS IT IRRESISTIBLE

I have often pondered the question: What does God find irresistible? In other words, what attitudes and dispositions in man is he the most drawn to? Yes, I recognize that man is basically sinful and alienated from God. Still, the fact remains that God had to start somewhere as he began his plan of redeeming mankind. What characterized the key people he chose? One cannot consider such a question without taking note of two people who evidently captured God's attention—one man and one woman.

Abraham, of course, is the man who uniquely captured God's attention in the Old Testament. In a sense you might say that it all began with Abraham, especially with regard to Israel's history. This man exhibited such a faith in God that it was "credited to him as righteousness" (Romans 4:9). The entire book of Romans, as well as the Protestant Reformation, led centuries later by Martin Luther, was predicated on the premise of his life: "The just shall live by faith" (Romans 1:17, KJV).

Abraham lived by faith, and God noticed. When the Lord commanded Abraham to move to a land he did not know, Abe packed up and followed without a map, without any specifics, simply on the basis of a word…but not just any word, the Word of God.

When the Lord spoke and told Abraham he and his wife would have a son, Abraham trusted. But when that miracle son came, God called Abraham to take Isaac to a mountain and there to sacrifice him, to give him back to God. Just before the knife pierced the promised child's flesh, however, the angel of the Lord stayed his hand. What Abraham was about to do would not seem logical, prudent, or beneficial by human standards. He did not obey because it made sense but because God had spoken. I believe God finds such faith irresistible, such response to his Word and his will magnetic.

As a result of Abraham's faith, God promised to make him the "father of nations" and to make his seed like the stars of the sky and the sands of the beach (Genesis 15:5).

Abraham's counterpart in the New Testament would certainly have been Mary, the mother of Jesus. Just consider: What was it about Mary that caused the Lord to choose her womb to bear his only begotten Son? Why was she among all women so highly honored?

Mary had an Abraham-like faith in the sense that when God spoke, she obeyed. Obedience is the key to the heart of God. Consider the conversation the Lord had with Mary when he brought news to her that she, a virgin, would bear the Christ child (Luke 1:26–38). Her reluctance was one of logic and natural confusion. She wondered how she could bear a child since she had never been with a man.

When the Lord made it clear that the Holy Spirit would cause her to be with child, Mary accepted the Word of the Lord and celebrated the fact with her famed Magnificat. Her words of response are full of faith: "I am the Lord's servant!...May it be to me as you have said" (Luke 1:38, CEV). Her response to God's command was quick and simple.

Surely Abraham and Mary were clay in the strong hands of the Lord. To understand that, you have to be aware of a few things:

- **You have to know what they had.** Abraham and Mary had this in common: What they both valued most was a son. Both of these sons had been promised by God and were much anticipated at their arrival. Mary was quite young when Jesus was born, probably a teenager. Abraham, on the other hand, had waited twenty-five years for the fulfillment of God's promise.

- **You have to know what they heard.**
  Some time later God tested Abraham. He said to him, "Abraham!"

  "Here I am," he replied.

  Then God said, "Take your son, your only son, Isaac, whom you love, and go to the region of Moriah. Sacrifice him there as a burnt offering on one of the mountains I will tell you about." (Genesis 22:1–2)

In Mary's case, on the eventful day of her son's dedication in the temple the exultant priest, Simeon, took pause as he cautioned her:

"And a sword will pierce your own soul too." (Luke 2:35b).

The compelling factor behind Abraham's and Mary's faith was a voice, the Voice of God. He had called them to surrender the person who meant the most to them. They chose to obey rather than to wrestle with God and his will.

- **You have to know what they handed over.** Abraham watched his young son climb up on an altar. Mary watched hers laid across the beams of a cross. In obedience, Abraham raised a knife to slay his son. Mary felt a sword pierce her soul that day at Calvary. Both were surrendering the one who had meant the most to them, their beloved sons.

These dark events echoed the surprising emotions of another Parent handing over his son:

> Surely he took up our infirmities and carried our sorrows, yet we considered him stricken by God, smitten by him, and afflicted. But he was pierced for our transgressions, he was crushed for our iniquities; the punishment that brought us peace was upon him, and by his wounds we are healed. We all, like sheep, have gone astray, each of us has turned to his own way; and the LORD has laid on him the iniquity of us all…Yet it was the LORD's will to crush him and cause him to suffer, and though the LORD makes his life a guilt offering, he will see his offspring and prolong his days, and the will of the LORD will prosper in his hand. (Isaiah 53:4–6, 10)

Our faith is exhibited by our yieldedness to God. Ask yourself…What do your actions tell you about your faith in God or lack thereof? Does your faith show up in your words? Does it show in your use of the resources God has given you? What has your faith led you to surrender? What is it that God is calling you to surrender to him in this season of your life? Your wife? Your husband? Your children? Your hobby? Your career? Your dreams? Your treasure?

Jeanne Guyon referred to the life of faith as one of abandonment:

> Become abandoned by simply resigning yourself to what the Lord wants, in all things, no matter what they are, where they come from, or how they affect your life.
>
> What is abandonment? It is forgetting your past; it is leaving the future in His hands; it is devoting the present fully and completely to your Lord. Abandonment is being satisfied with the present moment, no matter what that moment contains. You are satisfied because you know that whatever that moment has, it contains—in that instant—God's eternal plan for you.[2]

A REVEALING RELATIONSHIP

Marriage is a revelation or, better said, a series of revelations. And a Christ-follower, whether married or single, is greatly helped when he or she discovers how much our spiritual union with Christ is like a good marriage. As a matter of fact, Paul the Apostle encouraged his readers to make the connection and to ponder it when he said that the object lesson of marriage is "a profound mystery" (Ephesians 5:32a). Let's consider the mystery a bit.

When love captures two hearts they both find out soon that there is much to discover.

Usually the relationship begins with the first date or two. The revelations begin immediately; the intensities and time-tables of disclosure vary depending upon the couple.

There is a revelation of common ground.

A revelation of irresistible interests.

Then, things start to get thicker.

A revelation of two paths that could become one.

A revelation of shared hopes and aspirations.

Then, after the wedding, comes the wedding night.

A revelation of intimacy, physical and emotional.

A bed to share; a soul to embrace.

Then, forging a new life together.

A revelation of each other's strengths, weaknesses, and struggles.

All in all, a good marriage occurs when a man and a woman learn how to bare their souls to one another. The union is strengthened when they are able to become melded together into a commitment of ideals shared amidst a challenging world of realities. When that happens, intimacy occurs. In like manner, a relationship with God is built upon this process of revelation.

From the time of Abraham on, God has been revealing more and more of himself to those who love him enough to call upon his name and to seek his face. When Moses first inquired of the Lord's nature at the burning bush, he discovered God as the "I am." In a sense, that said it all. In another sense, the sentence was incomplete. The self-existent and self-sufficient nature of God disclosed to one of his followers that day was just the start to a sentence which God has been completing in the lives of true seekers ever since.

When Jesus promised to show himself to the person who walked in true obedience to him, the word used for "show" was *emphanizo.* This strong word meant he would "exhibit himself in person," "disclose his heart through his words," "plainly declare his purpose," and "openly appear" to his obedient follower.

When Jesus made this promise during his most intimate of

discourses it was at the same time shocking and profound. To the person who embraced his commands and actually chose to aim his or her life toward obeying the same, Jesus promised to *reveal* himself. The word used in the King James Version is *manifest* himself. Note that the promise was not simply to reveal his truth, or to reveal his will, not even to reveal more *about* himself, but to reveal *himself*. His promise was not universal, but personal; not inclusive, but exclusive. As A. T. Robertson wrote: "The Unseen and Risen Christ will be a real and spiritual Presence to the obedient and loving believer."[3]

To the listener who considers these words only in the light of Jesus as a man, the promise may seem quite ordinary indeed. To the person who receives them in the light of Jesus as God incarnate in a human dwelling, the promise is astounding. "I will show myself to him." It is an exhibition of Christ himself—an unfolding, a disclosure, a declaration, and an appearance.

The significance of John the Beloved being the lone pen who recorded these words of Christ in John 14:21 is found in the fact that of all the potential candidates, God chose him to be the one who would be shown the entire book of Revelation in vision and experiential form. John saw the revelation of Jesus Christ. How significant that fact is when you again consider these words of Christ, spoken years before to the writer of Revelation:

> Whoever has my commands and obeys them, he is the one who loves me. He who loves me will be loved by my Father, and *I too will love him and show myself to him*. (John 14:21, emphasis mine)

The book of Revelation is first and foremost presented as a revealing of Jesus Christ, not merely a prophetic forecast of end-time events. It begins with John actually seeing the Resurrected Christ:

I turned around to see the voice that was speaking to me. And when I turned I saw...someone "like a son of man," dressed in a robe reaching down to his feet and with a golden sash around his chest. His head and hair were white like wool, as white as snow, and his eyes were like blazing fire. His feet were like bronze glowing in a furnace, and his voice was like the sound of rushing waters. In his right hand he held seven stars, and out of his mouth came a sharp double-edged sword. His face was like the sun shining in all its brilliance. (Revelation 1:12–16)

Surely in that moment, in John's experience at least, the promise came true. John had, in fact, received the commands of Christ and shown his love for Christ by obeying them. He had felt what it meant to be loved by Jesus and by his Father, too. And now, Jesus was keeping his part of the promise by "showing" himself, "manifesting" himself, and "revealing" himself to John...powerfully and personally.

Whether you call them *rules, commands,* or *laws,* such mandates that the Lord calls us to obey tend to test the attitudes of our hearts. The black-and-white absolutes in our ever-graying culture are the tools whereby God measures and tests not only our obedience, but just how much we trust him and his character. These Old Testament verses paint a clear picture:

See, I am setting before you today a blessing and a curse—the blessing if you obey the commands of the LORD your God that I am giving you today; the curse if you disobey the commands of the LORD your God and turn from the way that I command you today by following other gods. (Deuteronomy 11:26–28)

How we respond to God's commands is fully dependent upon

the condition of our hearts. As a matter of fact, the commandments themselves *test* the condition of our hearts. Do we believe these commandments exist just to make our lives more difficult? Or are we convinced that God has his high purposes and our ultimate good in mind? Do we trust God and the heart of God?

Listen to the trust in God's heart expressed in the psalmist's attitude toward God's commands:

> Do good to your servant according to your word, O LORD. Teach me knowledge and good judgment, for I believe in your commands. Before I was afflicted I went astray, but now I obey your word. You are good, and what you do is good; teach me your decrees....The law from your mouth is more precious to me than thousands of pieces of silver and gold. (Psalm 119:65–68, 72)

Jesus taught that obedience *to* God is born out of relationship *with* God. The desire and ability to obey God flows out of a personal relationship with him and is motivated by love for him. In a real sense, the litmus test of the authenticity of one's relationship with God is shown by our obedience to him. *"Faith without works is dead"* (James 2:17, CEV).

Years ago, a young pastor had an opportunity to talk with Dr. David Cho, the pastor of the Yoido Full Gospel Church in Seoul, South Korea, the largest church in the world (approximately 700,000 members). Brimming with curiosity, the eager pastor asked the obvious question: "What have you done to see this kind of growth? To what do you attribute it?"

Calmly and serenely, Dr. Cho looked the pastor directly in the eyes and with a smile asserted: "I *pray* and I *obey!*"

Sounds almost too simple, doesn't it? Perhaps so simple that we trip over the principle and miss it. It is clear that John practiced this principle throughout his life. Again and again in his writings, John asserted that the best evidence of a person's close walk with Christ is a life of obedience. He put it this way: "We know that we have come to know him if we obey his commands" (1 John 2:3).

Obedience actually strengthened John's prayer life: "We have confidence before God and receive from him anything we ask, because we obey his commands and do what pleases him.…Those who obey his commands live in him, and he in them" (1 John 3:21b–22, 24a).

The power to obey clearly flows from a passion to embrace Jesus in our lives. John did so in such a manner that it was as if Jesus wore his life like a hand wears a glove—"live in him, and he in them."

Somehow John captured a manner of living that made obedience a joy and not a drudgery. Doing the will of God was not viewed as a chore, but a privilege and joy: "This is love for God: to obey his commands. And his commands are not burdensome" (1 John 5:3).

OBEDIENCE AND INTIMACY

In a religiously pluralistic society such as ours, it is easy to become confused over the way in which we should or should not approach God. Should we crawl to him on our knees with fear and trembling? Or should we pull up a chair, a nice devotional book, and a warm cup of coffee? Does God desire blind oblations *from* us or a heartfelt conversation *with* us? Is it fear he wants or love? Are we to hide our faces in his presence or spill our guts? Is it reverence or a relationship he is after? Awe or affection?

Clearly, the picture of our approach to God in the Old Testament is quite different from the New. Even the words for worship carry a quantum difference. The Old Testament word *shachah* means "to bow down and worship with awe and reverence; to fall prostrate in the presence of the Lord." The sense is one of great awe and rever-ence. However, the New Testament word, *proskuneo,* is much more intimate. It literally means "to kiss toward." The people of God in the Old Testament saw themselves as the servants of God. As we have observed, one of the changes Jesus brought about was the actual identity of his followers, choosing to refer to them no longer as servants but as friends.

Without surrendering the importance of the awesomeness of God and our need to reverence him, Jesus calls us closer. The Old Testament concept served as the line drawing; the New Testament teachings of Jesus added color, description, and depth. Jesus calls us out of the formality of mere servanthood and into the intimacy of friendship with him. And yet, how does a man or woman propose to be a friend of Jesus Christ? How is such a friendship strengthened and maintained? Again we must return to the image of marriage and the process by which intimacy is built in that sacred bond.

First of all, intimacy is maintained in a marriage by one thing—*responsiveness.* In a good marriage, when we recognize needs in our spouse's life or soul, we respond. When we detect concerns or struggles, we engage them. And even when we recognize dreams and desires brewing within our spouse's soul, we respond to them. This response forms the caring *give and take* within a marriage that somehow powerfully translates into intimacy, into a sense of close-ness and connectedness. Relationships are built upon responsive-ness to one another.

When a marriage partner ceases to respond to the apparent needs and desires of his or her spouse, the marriage begins to shut down. On paper, the covenant still exists; but in experience, it has atrophied. Responsiveness is what makes or breaks the relationship.

So it is in our relationship with Jesus. If we love him, we rec-ognize his desires and we respond in obedience. We recognize his commands, and we respond. We recognize his words and respond.

The Lord, in turn, recognizes our requests in prayer, and he responds. He recognizes our struggles and our desires, and by his grace he responds...sometimes so specifically. Somehow the Lord's engagement of our lives via his grace, and our engagement of his life via our obedience, cultivate a living relationship between our hearts and the heart of Christ.

He speaks. I obey.

I pray. He answers.

That's the way it works. It is a cycle of response, actions, and reactions that cause heaven and earth to touch.

The most important questions may be: Do I count on him? And can he count on me? As Jesus feels the response of our drawing closer to him, he moves in our direction. As we feel the response of his answers to our prayers and his words of direction and comfort, we move in his direction. A spiritual bond is built. Intimacy is created. A covenant is confirmed. The relationship becomes far more than a doctrinal belief; it becomes a living experience, and a transforming one at that.

It becomes a match made in heaven.

A love language is learned.

A revelation is experienced.

A friendship is formed.

Chapter Eight

FRIENDSHIP HAS
ITS PRIVILEGES

Friendship with God is reserved for those who reverence him.
With them alone he shares the secrets of his promises.
PSALM 25:14, TLB

This friendship means being so intimately in touch with God
that you never even need to ask Him to show you His will...
When you have a right-standing relationship with God,
you have a life of freedom, liberty, and delight; you are God's will.
OSWALD CHAMBERS

Opportunity is in the eye of the beholder. Just ask Ray.
The year was 1961, and when the order came for ten MultiMixer milkshake machines from one burger joint, Ray knew that
this customer warranted a closer look. After all, nobody ordered
more than one MultiMixer, the multiple milkshake machine that
made five milkshakes at once. Being one of the company's best
salesmen, he knew the capacity of his milkshake machine.

When Ray got that closer look at this local burger joint in San
Bernardino, California, he found something the public was ready
for—a restaurant that could serve a hamburger, french fries, and a
milkshake in fifteen seconds or less. Fast food history was being
made right before his very eyes. The McDonald brothers had struck

gold and Ray Kroc knew it. His response was, "I've got to become involved in this."

In the face of their success, Richard and Maurice (better known as Dick and Mac) McDonald had a shared dream. They both wanted to be millionaires. Not multimillionaires, mind you. They just wanted to have a million dollars in their accounts, then to get out of the business.

In the face of their success, Ray Kroc had his own dream. It was more far-reaching. He envisioned not a regional restaurant, but an international one; not just making millions, but multiplied millions; and not simply making his mark on the burger business, but becoming synonymous with it. Ultimately Kroc struck a deal with the brothers as their representative. He bought them out for, you guessed it, one million dollars each.

As John Love relates:

Since the [McDonald] brothers sold their rights...in 1961, McDonald's restaurants have rung up a total of $77 billion in sales. The royalty payments that would have been due the McDonald brothers had they not sold out come to a total of $388 million. Today, the McDonalds would be earning more than $55 million a year in royalties on their fast-food system.[1]

One business opportunity; two completely different perspectives.

The McDonald brothers saw an intriguing opportunity just waiting to be cashed in for a quick, cool million. Ray Kroc saw an astounding privilege just waiting to be taken on for a lifetime of possibilities.

John the Beloved saw what others missed. He viewed the same Jesus the other disciples saw, but on a level deeper and much fuller.

What they saw as a line drawing, he viewed in technicolor. What they simply noticed, he deeply pondered. When they challenged the words of Christ, he considered them. While they were testing the Lord's will, he was conforming to Christ's way.

You might say that while John the Baptist came to remind us of the fear *of* God, John the Beloved came to invite us into a friendship *with* God.

If John the Baptist came to "prepare the way of the Lord," then surely John the Beloved came to show us how to walk in that way. John the Baptist was a herald of the promise; John the Beloved was a harbinger of it. John the Baptist sounded an alarm to remind us that sin was keeping us from our highest privilege—knowing God; John the Beloved set an example of what it means to delve into his presence with a depth and passion. If John the Baptist led us to the pool's edge, surely John the Beloved was the first to plunge in, heart first.

What keeps us in the shallow end of the pool? Why do we settle to know him as Savior, when he desires that we know him as friend? And why do we focus so much on God as some sort of fire insurance policy when he has clearly called us to be his sons and daughters with all the privileges of inheritance?

When a man or woman sets their hearts on knowing God better, they are on the path of wisdom. And if wisdom is walking in the will and the way of God, then the "fear of the Lord" is where the first steps of that journey begin, because: "The fear of the LORD is the beginning of wisdom" (Proverbs 9:10).

Long before I ever befriended my earthly father as a son, I feared him. I feared him not in the sense of a stomach-wrenching worry that he would harm me. I feared him in other ways. He was bigger than me and stronger, as well. He was smarter and much more secure. He was my disciplinarian when my behavior or attitude called for it. And it did. He paid my bills, all of them! He had a voice that marshaled my attention as did no one else's. Perhaps most of all, I felt a deep and abiding respect for my dad. When I was a child my father was big to me, bigger than life.

Little did I understand that fearing the Lord was the path to calling him friend. Before expressions of love could be cultivated in my soul toward Jesus, impressions of the awe of his character and greatness would be made in a variety of ways.

BALANCING FEAR AND FRIENDSHIP

To John, friendship meant more than an annual Christmas card in the mail. It was far more than some social club to frequent. Friendship to him was not about small talk over a dinner table, but a close walk down a long garden path. It was a journey back to Eden. It meant intimacy, openness, and honesty between John and his maker—face to face, heart to heart, spirit to Spirit.

Just as the law creates an agenda for grace, the fear of the Lord is a means to friendship. The Old Testament image of God is predominantly one of God *over* us; the New Testament image is predominantly of God *in* us and God *with* us. The Old Testament describes God as the Gardener who prunes; The New Testament says that Jesus is the Vine and we are the branches. Something totally new is conveyed: that we are connected with him. The Old Testament tells us that the earth is God's footstool, while the New Testament promises that those Christians who overcome will be granted to sit *with* Jesus *on* his throne (Revelation 3:21).

The fear of the Lord is where God awakens us; friendship with Jesus is where he embraces us. It must *begin,* however, with the fear of the Lord. "The fear of the LORD is the beginning of wisdom" (Proverbs 9:10). The verse does not say that the fear of the Lord is where wisdom culminates or even continues, but where it begins. Fearing God means that we are in awe of his greatness. Without that sense of awe and reverence, we will never come to marvel over the fact that a great and awesome God calls us into friendship.

A friend of God. It sounds presumptuous, doesn't it? After all, who would presume to have a relationship with the one who placed the planets, the galaxies, into place? The fact is that Jesus made his friendship with you and me a focal point of even his crucifixion. Yes, he did come to save us, to rescue us from sin, Satan, and sadness. But he came for more; he came to draw us into a real relationship with God the Father. All too often, we find ourselves wading in the shallow end of God's divine purpose when we should be diving in deep. Consider these ways in which the fear of the Lord makes way for a friendship like no other:

Privilege No. 1—With the *fear of God* we pray in order to see our souls freed from sin and its contaminating influence. Through a *friendship with Jesus* our purged souls can be filled with the Spirit and his purifying presence.

"And Moses said to the people, 'Do not fear; for God has come to prove you, and that the fear of him may be before your eyes, that you may not sin'" (Exodus 20:20, CEV). The greatness of God and the perfection of his character are compelling and convicting when deeply weighed and considered. When the Spirit reveals more of God's awesomeness and holiness to our hearts, we become more aware of how small we are, and how sinful. This experience is better known biblically as conviction, and it is an emptying process. The good news of the emptying is that it makes more room in our souls and spirits for God himself to dwell.

Prayer is the tool God has given whereby we empty ourselves via confession and repentance. Through prayer our Friend leads us to become filled and refilled with the Holy Spirit. You will find soul fulfillment only in his presence.

Joy Dawson said it well:

So, for us, the fear of the Lord should do two things. First, produce in us the same attitude toward sin that God has, which is to hate it. Second, to give us a deep respect for and understanding of the holiness of God, the power of God, and the total self-sufficiency of God to meet man's need.[2]

Privilege No. 2—With the *fear of God* we see his every Word as a *command* demanding our *obedience*. Through a *friendship with Jesus* we see a *promise* behind every call to obedience, along with an *invitation* to know him more fully, to walk with him more closely.

Of all the Gospel writers, John hung most on Jesus' words. While other Gospels chose to give ample space to the parables and life-principle stories of Christ, John overlooked those in his account and elected, rather, to prioritize what he felt was most potent and needed of the words of Christ.

Not only is John's conception of Christian truth the loftiest, his experience of it is the deepest. His is perhaps the most Christ-like life that comes before us on the pages of the N. T. Scriptures...John's profound thinking grew out of his deep spiritual living. None of the twelve had a mind like John's. He has been called the Christian Plato. "John, fisherman's son and all," says Dr. Alexander Whyte, "was born with one of the finest minds that has ever been bestowed by God's goodness upon any of the sons of man."...But those things which engaged John's mind grew out of long and intimate companionship with his Lord. He had a receptive nature, perhaps the most receptive and teachable of all the apostolic band.[3]

Even the commandments themselves are given to point us to intimacy with God. For example, the second of the Ten Commandments is: "Do not make idols" (Exodus 20:4, NLT). At first glance, you might view this rule as binding, limiting, imposing, or difficult. However, behind this command is an acknowledgment of a positive privilege. In other words, look beyond the negative directive, which mandates that we make no idols for ourselves, and consider the positive outcome of such a rule. The pure purpose of such a command is that portions of our soul, our devotion, and attention that might have been captured by idol activity are instead free to be devoted to loving and following Jesus Christ. Being emptied of our idols qualifies us to be filled with his Spirit.

Privilege No. 3—With the *fear of God* we find motivation to avoid sin and sinful behavior so that our *reputation*, and his, are not berated. Through a *friendship with Jesus* we find motivation to avoid sin and sinful behavior because of our *relationship* with the Lord and an inner desire to please him and see nothing interrupt that relationship.

On at least a couple of occasions (Matthew 26:35; Mark 14:29) Peter boasted of his faithfulness toward God. Once he even asserted that if all the other disciples and followers deserted Jesus, he would surely remain faithful. Peter seemed to want Jesus to believe that absolutely nothing was going to get between him and his devotion to the Lord.

Sin eroded what Peter had asserted. While Peter's commitment had been founded in a motivation that was good, it was short of being the best. The ground he had planted in was the fear of the Lord and, as a result, Peter was highly concerned about what people knew about him. His motivation was built on reputation. As a result, when the heat of confrontation threatened him, Peter quickly denied that he had even known Jesus (John 18:18–27).

Larry Crabb in his book, *Inside Out,* cites the reasons why a Christian man will avoid looking at the pornography section when he enters a pharmacy. They include:

1. He avoids the magazine rack because of a *fear* that a deacon or other board member might come in and find him and his *reputation* would be ruined, or at least marred.
2. He avoids the magazines because of a *fear* that he might light a temptation fire that he will not have the power to put out. In this case he is not willing to *risk* kindling a problem he could not fix.
3. He avoids the magazine rack because of his *friendship* with Jesus Christ. His action is based on a deep desire to avoid anything that could move him away from his intimacy with Jesus Christ. In this case he does not want to risk interrupting his sweet fellowship with the Lord.

Privilege No. 4—With the *fear of God* we approach faith as a set of *rules* to keep. Through a *friendship with Jesus* we approach faith in a deeper manner—as a *relationship* to cultivate, maintain, and deepen.

In John's first epistle he goes to great lengths to reassure us of God's deep and abiding love for those who fear him. He makes it clear that our love for God is best shown by our obedience to him:

When we obey God, we are sure that we know him. But if we claim to know him and don't obey him, we are lying and the truth isn't in our hearts. We truly love God only when we obey him as we should, and then we know that we belong to him. (1 John 2:3–5, CEV)

Jesus died on a cross to set us free from the rigors and regimen of rules to keep. He wants to liberate us to live on a higher plane in the wide open kingdom of God's love. It is in this place where every act of righteousness is not a stab at brownie points or extra credit but an embrace of our heavenly Father and of his good, perfect, and pleasing will for our lives. The fear of God leads us to this place, but friendship is what we find once we arrive.

Privilege No. 5—With the *fear of God* we see him as perfect and become overwhelmed with our weaknesses and shortcomings. Through a *friendship with Jesus* we discover that our weaknesses are the stages on which the grace of God is displayed.

The perfectness of God's character is what the Bible refers to as his holiness. He is perfectly pure, perfectly righteous, perfectly trust-worthy, perfectly joyous, perfectly peaceful, and so much more. His holiness, however, is not a badge God wears to rub in our noses. Nor is it a tool he uses to upstage mankind and play out some one-upsmanship tendencies in his character. No, the essence of holiness is wholeness, being complete, fruitful, and fulfilled.

It is the will of God that each of us experience his strength, especially in the areas of our weakness.

Privilege No. 6—With the *fear of God* we become overwhelmed with a great responsibility to please and obey God. Through a *friendship with Jesus* we become overwhelmed with a great asset—the fact that we are deeply loved of God.

The fear of the Lord is the passageway to a deep friendship with Jesus:

The LORD is exalted, for he dwells on high; he will fill Zion with justice and righteousness. He will be the sure foundation for your times, a rich store of salvation and wisdom and knowledge; *the fear of the LORD is the key to this treasure.* (Isaiah 33:5–6, emphasis mine)

Diving into the deep end of friendship with Jesus, John humbly described himself as "the disciple whom Jesus loves." There was no fact more important to John than this one. This was his anchor point in life. This was the lightbulb over his head and the fire in his belly. He was the object of God's intense affection and devotion. There was no truth more essential to him than this one.

John's nineteenth-century biographer, James Culross, writes:

The fact that it was John himself who used the name [i.e.: "the disciple whom Jesus loved"], as he did again and again in his Gospel, brings into view his beautiful and childlike humility. A self-conscious man never would have ventured to do it, lest he should be charged with claiming distinction and honour for himself above his fellow disciples. With finest lowliness of mind, he uttered no disclaimer of merit, made no formal protestation of unworthiness. He did not feel it necessary to do so. To my mind, the humility of fearlessly using the name is as touching as when the Apostle Paul calls himself "less than the least of all saints," or remembers how he was "of sinners the chief." The glory of his beloved Lord lighted up and beautified his countenance, as well as penetrating his soul, and he thought no more about it than a child, unconscious of the grace of his own movements or the lustre of his eye. Like Moses, he "wist not that the skin of his face shone" (Exodus 34:29, 30, 35, KJV). All he thought of was the felicity of being loved with such a love.[4]

Privilege No. 7—With the *fear of God* we view God in his greatness as someone we must *look up to* and in judgment face. Through a *friendship with Jesus* we see God in his glory as someone we can *lean upon* and in love embrace.

As John Bevere has written:

> The fear of the Lord is the beginning, or starting place, of an intimate relationship with God. Intimacy is a two-way relationship. For example, I know about the president of the United States. I can list information about his accomplishments and his political stance, but I do not actually know him. I lack a personal relationship with him. Those in the president's immediate family and his close associates know him. If we were in the same room, I would quickly recognize the president, but he would not know me. Although I'm a citizen of the United States and know about him, I could not speak to him as though he were my friend. That would be inappropriate and even disrespectful. I would still be under his jurisdiction and authority as president and under his protection as commander in chief, but his authority over me would not automatically grant me intimacy with him…
>
> The Lord said we cannot even begin to know Him on intimate terms until we fear Him. In other words, an intimate relationship and friendship with God will not even begin until the fear of God is firmly planted in our lives.[5]

YOU CAN CALL ON HIM ALL YOU WANT

Imagine what it would be like if you called on your best earthly friend as frequently as you can call on God. Regardless of how close you are to that person, whether spouse, sister, or co-laborer, such an individual would tire quickly of hearing you call their name. Not so with Christ. You could be lying on a bed of suffering and illness straight through the night and still call his name ceaselessly. He would hear you every time and would be moved with compassion.

Privilege No. 8—With the *fear of the Lord* we are *impressed* with God's power and greatness. Through a *friendship with Jesus* we are more than impressed, we are *blessed* to discover that he, remarkably enough, has chosen to *confide* in us.

In 1875, Nehemiah Adams, an astute observer of the privileges afforded to us by the Lord, put it this way in his study, *Christ, A Friend:*

> The secret communication of Christ to John is an illustration of their intimate relations, and of the confidence which Christ felt in the character of the beloved disciple. "The secret of the Lord is with them that fear him, and he will show them his covenant." Beautiful instances do we find in the Bible of this confiding of secrets in the intercourse of God with man. "And the Lord said, 'Shall I hide from Abraham that thing which I do? For I know him, that he will commend his children and his household after him, and they shall keep the way of the Lord…'" The willingness of John to relate…his religious experience, to speak of intimate love and special favors from Christ, is one of the best evidences of the purity of his feelings, the absence from his heart and life of all those inconsistencies of allowed sin which, through the power of conscience, would have prevented these disclosures to the world of special intimacy with Christ.[6]

One hundred years later, John White described this powerful principle in his important book, *Daring to Draw Near:*

> It may seem inconceivable that the same God wants such a relationship with you. You are a creature he made. You are a sinner he redeemed. You are even his child by adoption and by supernatural new birth. Yet he calls you to a higher dignity—to that of friend and partner. "No longer do I call you servants," Jesus told his disciples, "for the servant does not know what his master is doing; but I have called you friends, for all that I have heard from my Father I have made known to you" (John 15:15, CEV). He chose you to be such.
>
> Two facts necessarily follow. If you are his friend, he will share his thoughts and plans with you. If you are his partner, he will be concerned about your views on his plans and projects. Whatever else prayer may be, it is intended to be a sharing and a taking counsel with God on matters of importance to him. God has called you to attend a celestial board meeting to deliberate with him on matters of destiny.[7]

What would you call a person who:

Knows everything about you—all your faults and shortcomings—and still loves you?

Accepts you as you are but will not let you settle for being anything less than everything you can possibly be?

Is so close you feel as though the two of you have one soul?

Wants you to be totally honest and open with him all the time?

Has overcome every kind of trial you will ever face and is eager to help you become an overcomer also?

Freely chooses to commit himself to you and to daily developing his relationship with you?

Sticks closer than a brother?

Is willing to lay down his life for you?

Wants me to call Him "friend, my very best friend."[8]

Ultimately Ray Kroc's MultiMixer produced a lot more than just five milkshakes. Three men found themselves in the mix. In the long run, they all got what they asked for. All three saw something special in the making. But, only one grasped just how special it would all become.

In the long run we find that *fear and friendship* do, in fact, mix. It is an absolute wonder that this God of wrath and judgment who is so worthy of our fear has chosen not only to forgive us in grace, but to befriend us as well. Wonder of wonders!

PART TWO

JESUS,
MY COMPANION

Chapter Nine

HARNESSING THUNDER

You do not know what manner of spirit you are of.
JESUS TO JOHN
LUKE 9:55, NKJV

For God to do an impossible work,
he must take an impossible man...and crush him.
CHARLES SWINDOLL

A soul is a brilliant diamond in the eyes of God. It takes a lot of vision to discover a diamond...and much work to mine one. When we look up at the heavens against the backdrop of night, we view the shimmering stars, which shine with splendor. I have often wondered how God views life on this planet from his throne in heaven. This Scripture gives us a peek:

> That you may become blameless and pure, children of God without fault in a crooked and depraved generation, in which you shine like stars in the universe as you hold out the word of life. (Philippians 2:15–16a)

Diamonds are the hardest natural substance known to man and one of our most valuable resources. Of all gemstones, the diamond is the most enduring because of its hardness. In settings of gold and silver, it is the traditional jewel for engagement and marriage. In industry the diamond is used for cutting, grinding, and boring other hard materials.

One reason diamonds are so expensive is because they are so rare. Only four significant fields of diamonds have ever been found in Africa, India, South America, and the Soviet Union. Africa alone produces about 70 percent of the world's supply. Many of the diamonds that grace rings and necklaces are found in rock formations deep in the earth. Amazing, isn't it, that something so brilliant and fragile is extracted from such a crude and crusty cradle?

The particular rock in which diamonds are found is called blue ground. Even in South Africa's rich mines, tons and tons of blue ground must be drawn from the deep earth, crushed, and sorted to obtain just one small diamond (about three tons of blue ground to uncover one carat of diamond). No wonder it is so valuable.

The process of preparing a diamond for display is expensive and laborious. It requires highly skilled workers and many years of refining the art. The process includes drawing the rock from the ground, carefully cutting it, intensively polishing it, and creatively placing it.

The process for preparing a diamond for display is similar to the one God takes a soul through. *He draws us out* of our earthbound stubborn state of bondage, *cuts* away the spiritual debris, *polishes* and *refines* us, and *places* us into his service. We are the diamonds he is mining "for the display of his splendor" (Isaiah 61:3b).

When Jesus found John the Beloved, he was covered with blue ground. John was soiled up and sooty, his edges rough. This guy was raw and unrefined, and yet ultimately he became the disciple who walked the closest to Christ. A closer look at John paints a vivid picture of how God makes a man into a man of God.

What do we know for certain about the raw material in John's life?

First of all, John was uneducated. Most of the men Jesus called to himself were. They were "unschooled, ordinary men" (Acts 4:13). What John knew did not come from a fraternity or a factory, but a fishery. Some would call him unlearned, unsuitable for ministry, and ill equipped. On the contrary, Jesus saw him as ripe for learning. Less educated, sure, but potentially more teachable than most.

Second, John was intolerant and controlling. Two of John's peers, Mark and Luke, recorded an incident John would probably rather have forgotten (Mark 9:38–41, Luke 9:49–50). It seems that on at least one occasion John had come upon someone outside of their group of disciples who had driven out demons in Jesus' name. Being on the inside track, John took it upon himself to tell this unauthorized minister to cool it. When, like a good Boy Scout, he brought the news to the Lord, Jesus promptly rebuked him saying, "whoever is not against us is for us." Is it any wonder that John conveniently left this particular story out of his gospel account? (Of course, who needs to repeat such a story when you have friends like Mark and Luke who'll do it for you?)

Third, John had a fiery temperament. This is clear from the surname "Son of Thunder." Despite widespread misconceptions and misrepresentations of John as some soft, milquetoast kind of character, the New Testament begs to differ. So did Charles R. Brown, a former dean of Yale Divinity School, whose book dealt with the temperament of the man:

> First, there is the John of legend and of art, who has been portrayed as a mystic, quiet and modest, gentle and tender. He has been made almost effeminate, a kind of companion-piece to Mary the Mother of our Lord. His face and his heart have been made to appear as fine and as soft as the face and

the heart of a woman. The artists have painted him almost uniformly without a beard and with a delicacy of feature quite out of drawing for a really masculine disposition.

This you might say is the conventional John, the John of the stained glass windows and of the art galleries, the John of religious poetry and of polite society...In the second place, there is the real John of the Four Gospels. He is another type of man altogether! He and his brother were called by their associates "Boanerges, the sons of Thunder." There was something powerful, electric, startling about him...

There were times when he was hot and terrible in his outbursts of feeling...There were days when he roared and was troubled. He could upon occasion show himself a whirlwind of enthusiasm or a tornado of wrath. He did just that repeatedly. So far from being a placid, passive, milk-and-water sort of man, he was a man of violent temper.[1]

The thunder rolled once again not long after John descended from the Mount of Transfiguration, where he had been privy to behold Christ in a glorified state conversing with none other than Elijah and Moses:

Now it came to pass, when the time had come for Him [Jesus] to be received up, that He steadfastly set His face to go to Jerusalem, and sent messengers before His face. And as they went, they entered a village of the Samaritans, to prepare for Him. But they did not receive Him, because His face was set for the journey to Jerusalem. And when His disciples James and John saw this, they said, "Lord, do You want us to command fire to come down from heaven and consume them, just as Elijah did?"

But He turned and rebuked them, and said, "You do

not know what manner of spirit you are of. For the Son of Man did not come to destroy men's lives but to save them." And they went to another village. (Luke 9:51–56, NKJV)

John read the scene quickly and clearly. I would gather that his thoughts ran something like this:

You, Samaritans! So, you don't want us on your land, do you? Well, you don't know who you're dealing with. And, on top of that, you have no idea what kind of power you're messing with. Why, I just came from a mountain meeting with two of the greatest prophets who ever lived. One parted an ocean with a stick. The other called down fire from heaven with a word. That does it! You've just picked on the wrong bunch one time too many! It's time to fight fire with FIRE! Lord, let me at 'em. Go ahead, God. Make 'em toast!

John saw it as boldness…Jesus saw it as boyishness.

John was freshly intrigued with power…Jesus knew he had somehow missed the love.

John was determined to do God's will…Jesus was determined it would be done his way.

If John lived in our time, you'd have to tell your friends, "Wow, don't offend *this* guy! If John ever attends your church and you forget to welcome him, watch out! If you forget to ask if he wants a refill on his coffee, look out overhead!"

Fourth, John was ambitious. At one point he, along with his brother, brought a prayer request to Jesus that seemed so high-minded and outlandish that when the other disciples heard about it they became absolutely indignant.

Then James and John, the sons of Zebedee, came to him [Jesus]. "Teacher," they said, "we want you to do for us whatever we ask."

"What do you want me to do for you?" he asked.

They replied, "Let one of us sit at your right and the other at your left in your glory." (Mark 10:35–37)

To John, and James, it seemed that being on the team itself was not enough. No, they had to be *first*. And suddenly it sounded to the other disciples, I'm sure, like they had stopped petitioning a Savior and started rubbing Aladdin's lamp.

Request Number One: "We want you to do for us whatever we ask." Now that is one all-inclusive request, isn't it? Sounds like wish number one on a magic lamp where you are only granted one wish.

"do...whatever we ask."

In asking Jesus to do whatever they asked, James and John wanted a commitment of his will before they revealed their intention. Just sign on the dotted line, Jesus. Obviously, they had forgotten about a very important consideration: the sovereignty of God.

And *Request Number Two?* "Let one of us sit on your right and the other on your left in your glory." One brother on his left and the other on his right. Great! But where did that leave the rest of the disciples?

If this had been a contract negotiation for the NBA, then James and John were the heavy-handed hot shots who expected exclusive rights, privileges, salaries, first-class airline seats, but who gave no thought to the rest of the team. As long as their contract was right, they would be fat and happy. Who cares about the other team members?

One close observer of John, Son of Thunder, summed it up this way:

There is very little evidence of humility in this youthful disciple...This was the John who first followed Jesus: "A son of thunder", electric and powerful; a man of temper liable to quick and hot resentment; capable of being intolerant and vindictive, indeed, "A child of the storm!"[2]

Sometimes the thunder of life gets too loud for us, doesn't it? We get overwhelmed and overpowered by it and we just want to cover our ears and wait for it all to stop. However, thunder never intimidates a Thundermaker. Underline that. Neither John's lack of education and tolerance nor his hotheaded temper and ambition could ever close God's ears to the deeper sounds of his soul. To God, the thunder was just a bunch of blue ground crying out for a prospector. It was all in a day's work. There were still diamonds to mine.

Before we write John off for his weaknesses, let's consider a moment. What about the John-like characteristics within us? What is it that thunders inside of your personality, your attitude, your life?

Well, sure, I have my weak points…but, I wouldn't consider myself uneducated.

Yes, but are you still learning and growing? Are you teachable today? You see, the greatest challenge Christ faces with a person is never how little he knows. It is always how much he thinks he already does know. That calls for harnessing thunder, and he's good at it.

But, I'm certainly not what I would call intolerant. Why, that's not even politically popular.

Oh yes, but do you ever find yourself labeling people around you? You know, writing them off before you really get to know them? Saying to some, at least mentally, "You are this way. You have always been this way. You will probably always be this way."

Maybe. But, I just know that I don't have a truly fiery temperament.

Of course you don't, but do you ever find yourself fighting fire with fire? Getting angry at those who are angry with you? Getting even with your critics? Fighting cold shoulders with cold shoulders, attitudes with attitudes, disinterest with disinterest?

Alright, maybe a bit of that, but I definitely know that I am not overly ambitious. No way.

How about the driving desire to have things turn out your way? Or the motivating impulse to be first, in the lead, ahead of everyone else, on the top? Have you ever felt driven to look successful, or even highly spiritual, in the eyes of others?

If I were interviewing a person wired like the John Jesus first met, I would not have hired him. Not a chance. As a matter of fact, he's more the kind of guy you would want to fire. Just think about it. The interview would probably go something like this:

EMPLOYER: So, Mr…eh…John. Excuse me, what is your last name, again?

JOHN: Uh, Thunder.

EMPLOYER: How's that?

JOHN: I said, *thunder!*

EMPLOYER: What kind of last name is that?

JOHN: Why, you got a problem with it? 'Cuz if you do I could just torch this place, you know.

EMPLOYER: No, no problem with that. Let's get right down to it. What are your qualifications for this position?

JOHN: Well, uh, I'm a pretty good fisherman.

EMPLOYER: And your credentials?

JOHN: Sorry, fresh out. But, I do have plenty of perch, halibut, and sea trout! Ha, ha!

EMPLOYER: Cute! And exactly what position are you interested in here at our company?

JOHN: Just one!

EMPLOYER: What's that?

JOHN: I want you to agree to do what I say no matter what I ask.

EMPLOYER: Wait a minute here. Now just who's interviewing whom?

JOHN: I just want to be second in command. I'll take a nice plush office right next door to the president's for starters. Got that?

No degrees. No patience. No tact. No humility. Bold. Brash. Presumptuous. This is not the kind of person you'd employ, is it?

Well, in Jesus' eyes at least, he had everything to gain and, nothing to lose. And yet, somehow, I am certain that there was more to the fact that Jesus acquired this Son of Thunder as a disciple than just that there was something to gain. By virtue of his very nature, Jesus had something to give. While many would have seen the thunder as something to avoid, Jesus saw it as something to harness. He did what few are willing to do: he saw beyond it to its very source.

Too often we seek a god of our own making, don't we? I like a Jesus who pats me on the back, who makes my dreams come true, and who overlooks my inconsistencies. I want a Jesus who will make me feel good about me, who will be on my side whatever my side of the issue is. I want a dispenser of grace, not of truth. I want someone who will calm my fears, not condemn my actions. I want the warm feelings of safety, not the agonizing emotions of shame. I want a Savior who will applaud my successes, not one who magnifies my weaknesses. And yet I discover, as John did so well, that a great chasm exists between the Jesus I want and the Jesus I truly need.

For the next three plus years, no disciple would undergo a transformation any more profound than John's. The Son of Thunder would become "the disciple whom Jesus loved." The uneducated fisherman would become one of the most prolific writers of the New Testament, giving us the most personal account of the life and ministry of Jesus. This fiery force of a follower would experience the love of God in depths previously uncharted among the souls of men. The fire within him would burn away the chaff, and out would emerge a soul profoundly tender and submitted to God. The young man so eager to be picked first on Christ's team would be privileged to view what no others would: the very revelation of Christ.

Our eyes see the man, rough and untempered. In Christ's eyes, however, everything looked so much different.

The fact that John was uneducated became a reason for amazement. In other words, what John lacked in education he would by God's grace more than make up for in spiritual knowledge, experience, and insight. And his limited academic credentials made his profound spiritual insight all the more amazing.

Underneath the layers, his quick, though often wrong, responsiveness and lack of tolerance revealed a propensity for perseverance. Even though sometimes wrong, John had proven that he could stand by his convictions and values. This seedlike quality would grow to oak proportions by God's grace and cause this disciple to weather storms and endure hardships like none other.

Jesus saw that John's fiery temperament revealed a potential for godly passion and bold commitment. With John, at least, you never had to wonder if he was hot or cold. And no other disciple would feel the depth of his faith or communicate the passion of Christ as would this one. Biographer Howard Ferrin put it well:

There was nothing halfhearted about him [John]. He was never halfinterested or halfcommitted. If the call came from the Master Teacher, "Follow Me," as it did that day on the shores of Galilee, there was no hesitancy, no delaying of deliberations, no methodical ponderings. Flinging down his nets and abandoning his boats, John followed hard, and all the way…

Yet this very enthusiasm needs instruction lest it blunder tragically. The fiery intensity which, under control, can accomplish so much for God, if not restrained makes the crude bigot and the ruthless persecutor. The word *enthusiasm* comes from two Greek words *en* and *theos* which means "in God." Let zeal be according to knowledge, let passionate emotions be under God's control, and there shall be found a worthy and fruitful servant of Jehovah. The redemption of the passionate soul is one of Christ's greatest and finest achievements.[3]

Perhaps even his awkwardly expressed ambitions revealed a deep hunger for intimacy with God. After all, he and his brother James had requested the throne right next to Jesus. He was passionate for a place of privilege. Underneath the intolerance, impulsiveness, and temper of the man beat a heart hungering for God.

Chuck Swindoll has said, "For God to do an impossible work, he must take an impossible man and crush him." For the Son of Thunder, he had just come face to face with one even greater, the Father of Thunder. And, somehow he understood the storm within John's soul as could no other. The very characteristics that would heartbreak a parent and frustrate an employer were signs of something deeper. For somewhere in there, deeply imbedded in the blue rock of his own striving and struggles was a diamond just waiting to be unearthed, cut, polished, and placed.

Take a few minutes right now to prayerfully ponder the following poem. It speaks vividly of the process through which God takes a person whom he is shaping. Do you identify with any of these images thus far in your journey with Christ?

GOD KNOWS…

When God wants to drill a man,
And thrill a man
And skill a man,
When God wants to mold a man,
To play the noblest part;
When He yearns with all His heart
To create so great and bold a man
That all the world shall be amazed,
Watch His methods, watch His ways!
How He ruthlessly perfects
Whom He royally elects:
How He hammers him and hurts him,
And with mighty blows converts him
Into trial shapes of clay which
Only God understands;
While his tortured heart is crying
And he lifts beseeching hands!
How He bends but never breaks
When His good He undertakes;
How with every purpose fuses him;
By every act induces him
To try His splendor out
God knows what He's about.[4]

DALE MARTIN STONE

MIRROR TALK

I have loved you with an everlasting love.
JEREMIAH 31:3A

I would prefer to combat the "I'm special" feeling
not by the thought "I'm no more special than anyone else,"
but by the feeling "Everyone is as special as me."
C. S. LEWIS

No two kids are exactly alike. Certainly not our two oldest daughters.

Driving on a routine journey with our girls, my wife found herself in a not-so-routine conversation. In the background, Pam and the kids had been listening to a beautiful children's song called "You Are a Masterpiece." The girls, Kristi (then 7) and Kara (5), by now having heard the song for the hundredth time or so, were singing their hearts out in the back seat, not missing a lyric. As the song ended, Kristi posed a question.

"Mom, am I a masterpiece?"

"You sure are, Sweetheart!" Pam readily replied, eager to affirm.

Before I go any further, you need to know a little something about our girls. By this point in their lives, we had clearly identified that they were as different as snowflakes. Kristi, the older, was quite sensitive, compliant, tenderhearted, and intuitive. Kara, on the other hand, was energetic, motivated, strongwilled, and a party waiting to happen wherever she went. On the downside, Kristi could at times be oversensitive and Kara sort of pushy.

"Mom, what's a masterpiece?" Kristi returned.

"Oh, a masterpiece is something that is created by a master artist; it is very valuable and something that is so special it is one of a kind."

With a big satisfied smile, Kristi soaked up the encouragement. "Mom, I'm a *masterpiece!*"

Not wanting to miss out on the action, Kara chimed in. "Mom, I'm a master!"

"No, honey. You mean a master*piece*. You see, a master is some-one who tells everyone what to do and treats people like slaves. Jesus made you a master*piece,* Sweetheart. That's what you meant to say."

"No, Mom. I'm a *master!!!*"

We have looked back at that occasion in light of the girls' unique personalities and have had to laugh more than once. We had then, and have today, high hopes for the character development of our daughters, but never did we have a better look at the raw material.

"WHO ARE YOU?"

The annual opening week of classes at the college I attended was never my favorite. Not by a long shot. One reason was because I never knew what the professors were going to call on me to do. And I was never thrilled with the idea of having to speak in front of the entire class on those particular weeks.

It could be that I got this way partially because of my Sociology 101 class.

New teacher.

One hundred plus students.

And, an assignment.

"Ladies and gentlemen, I want you to stand up and, without talking at all about your name or what you do, tell us *who you are as a person.*"

I thought, "Oh, brother! Day One and we're already expected to wax philosophical. With my luck I'll be the first one chosen to stand."

You guessed it.

I gave it my best shot.

"I am a young man who wants to pastor a church…"

"Woah! Hold it right there, Mr. Crosby," the professor asserted. "That is something you want to do. I asked you to tell us who you *are.*"

It was going to be a long day. Hey, it was going to be a long *semester*.

Identity. It is something which we often find hard to define and, yet, in all of us there is a deep longing to have our identity defined. Just who am I…as a person…as an individual? Who am I really? That question confronts us at key junctures in life: When we draw close to high school graduation, when we are selecting a college to attend, when we pick a profession, when we marry, when we face raising our own children (and their blossoming identities), when those children leave home, as we approach midlife, and when we retire.

Identity. Empty souls ignore it. Stouthearts seem to have settled it.

The best shot of identity I have ever received did not come from a book I read, from a lecture I heard, from a counseling session, or from a career evaluation. It came from a four-year-old.

INTERVIEW WITH A FOUR-YEAR-OLD

Heading home from work after a long night at the office is not exactly prime time for parental instincts. For me, this particular "long night at the office" had consisted of a full day of pastoral duties climaxing with our weekly youth group meeting at the inner city church in Rochester, New York, where I served as youth pastor. Sitting in Mom's seat next to me in our Plymouth Horizon, my just-turned four-year-old, Kristin, was used to late nights at church on Wednesdays. Rubbing my eyes and trying to stay focused enough to make the fifteen-minute ride home while keeping the car between the lines, I wasn't much company for the little bright-eyed blond. I was tired, quiet, and winding down when a little voice pierced the silence…

"So…Daddy…what did you do today?"

My first reaction was that I was tired and really didn't feel much like talking. Still, Kristin struck a chord in my conscience, conjuring the memory that this little girl and I hadn't spoken much at all since the day before. On top of that, I could tell that she was giving this bridge-building effort her best little shot. How could I resist? I ventured a response…

"Well, Sweetie…Dad studied and met with some people and made some phone calls and spoke at the youth meeting tonight!"

Suddenly, my brain was jarred by a curious notion that I found impossible to jog. A question came to mind that I had never asked my daughter before. Come to think of it, I had never asked anyone this question. And now I found myself feverishly interested in what her response might be. The question was so simple, and yet so important…so central to life, yet so overlooked. I was almost afraid to ask it, but somehow it seemed in that moment that she, of all people, was uniquely qualified to answer it.

"Kristi…what does Daddy…do?"

There. I had asked it. The question was born out of shear intrigue. I couldn't help but imagine what this young and innocently truthful mind thought about what she saw her dad doing week in and week out. My first guess was that she probably thought that, as a pastor, I am constantly talking to people, with people, in front of groups of people. Kristi probably thought that I ran my mouth all day long, all the time. I couldn't seem to shake the discouraging notion of that being all she ever saw me doing.

"Kristi…what…does Daddy…do?"

Her response was without much delay. Kristi redirected her blue-sky eyes straight ahead, scrunched up her brow a bit, and sincerely offered an answer.

"Hmmmmm…you sing…[she usually says that I sing "loud" and Mom sings "pretty"]…and you teach… kids…how to love Jesus!"

In an instant, my brain went into overdrive. My head went from ten gallons to twenty. My heart gushed what felt like gallons of adrenaline. But most of all, my soul wanted to shout, "Bull's-eye! Kristin Anne Crosby, you hit the nail right on the head!" I was absolutely beside myself with joy over what my four-year-old had just said. "You teach kids how to love Jesus!"

So much of our adult lives, it seems, we struggle to find the simple focus of what it is we want to do, or more importantly, what it is we feel called to do. Not the many "good" things, but the "this one thing I do" *great* thing. My self-esteem had just nailed a slam dunk…and the assist came from my little girl. Who would have thought it?

My four-year-old daughter did more in that moment to help me with focus and vision in my career than all the books and articles I had ever read on the subject. She articulated with clarity and force what was, in fact, my highest goal in ministry. A true sense of identity. Not just to preach, teach, host youth events, or counsel, but to "TEACH KIDS HOW TO LOVE JESUS!" I felt so affirmed…so built-up…so encouraged that my daughter saw this in her dad…so challenged to press ahead. And God's vessel of choice? A four-year-old. Her gift to me? Six little words.[1]

That was the night my four-year-old rewrote my job description and greatly boosted my sense of identity. *If I just fill a slot every day,* I want to stay in bed. *To teach kids how to love Jesus*—now that's worth getting up for.

MODELS OF IDENTITY

Paul the Apostle had a tremendous sense of identity. We find it as we read the openings of his letters in the New Testament:

In Romans, he begins...
"Paul, a servant of Christ Jesus, called to be an apostle and set apart for the gospel of God..."

In 1 Corinthians...
"Paul, called to be an apostle of Christ Jesus by the will of God..."

In Galatians...
"Paul, an apostle—sent not from men nor by man, but by Jesus Christ and God the Father..."

In 1 Timothy...
"Paul, an apostle of Christ Jesus by the command of God our Savior and of Christ Jesus our hope..."

In Philemon...
"Paul, a prisoner of Christ Jesus..."

Clearly, Paul had a tremendous sense of identity, both of who he was and of who he was called to be. This was very important to him. He prefaced every letter with a similar introduction.

Among the Twelve, no disciple possessed a more blessed sense of identity, however, than John the Beloved. On no less than five occasions, he referred to himself as "the disciple whom Jesus loved."

Isn't it interesting that John preferred to refer to himself not as...

An apostle.

A servant.

A minister.

A preacher.

A worker.

A leader.

But, as "the disciple whom Jesus loved."

That's identity. Not just *a* disciple, but *the* disciple whom Jesus loved.

In other words, the best thing there was to know about John was that he was someone God loved. From the moment John became consumed with an awareness of the love of Christ, he seemed to take that love with him everywhere he went. More than any other character in the entire New Testament, John saw and absorbed a deep understanding of the love of Jesus in his life. It was much more than an established doctrine; it was a consuming experience. John learned the secret of not just loving God, but of letting God love him.

LIVING IN THE LOVE

I am convinced that many Christians today would be quick to say they believe in God's love for them, but if they were honest, they would have to admit they are not truly living in that love. Rather, they live under a constant cloud of guilt, fear, condemnation, and doubt. They have heard about the banqueting table called salvation, but they have only nibbled at the crumbs. They are not truly free.

They have partaken of enough to sense that Jesus *can* free them, but not enough to know that he truly *has*. They feel they never have, can, or will measure up to what God expects of them. Repeatedly they say to themselves, "Something is wrong with me. This isn't working in my life like it is for others. I must be doing something wrong." In short, they know in principle that Christ loves them, but they are not letting him love them in their experience.

I don't know when. I don't know where. I don't know how. But, sometime, somewhere, and somehow John became convinced, I mean deeply convinced, that he was the object of Jesus' love. When this light turned on within his soul, nothing ever again was the same. His very nature changed from that moment on. Maybe it happened up on the mountain.

Charles Spurgeon calls us to let God love us:

Do you know, O saint, how much the Lord loves you? Can you measure His love? Do you know how great is the affection of His soul toward you? Go measure heaven with a span; go weigh the mountain in the scales; go take the ocean's water, and tell each drop; go count the sand upon the sea's wide shore; and when you have accomplished this, you will be able to tell how much He loves you.[2]

In our present delight in God we have the assurance of our endless joy in Him...Oh, the love of God! The amazing, immeasurable, incomprehensible love of the Father! Oh, to feel this till our very souls are inflamed with it, and our unloving nature is all on fire with love to the great Lover of the souls of men![3]

To hear the love of God is sweet—to believe it most precious—but to enjoy it is paradise below the skies.[4]

John hoisted the sail of his faith and captured the propelling wind of the love of Jesus in his life. It carried him and compelled him on an adventure of walking with the Savior through life. John heard and recorded the one new commandment Christ left for his followers:

> A new command I give you: Love one another. As I have loved you, so you must love one another. By this all men will know that you are my disciples, if you love one another. (John 13:34–35, NIV)

Such an important command. So central to all the rest of Christ's teachings, ministry, and example, and yet no other Gospel writer records this significant command. It seems, perhaps, that three out of four missed it. Could it be they still do today?

Years later, John reminded the faithful to remember the command.

> This is the message you heard from the beginning: We should love one another. (1 John 3:11)

John's Gospel is replete with words of Christ that the other three Gospel writers either overlooked, forgot, or felt unnecessary to include in their biographical accounts. One such passage reveals:

> As the Father has loved me, so have I loved you. Now remain in my love. If you obey my commands, you will remain in my love, just as I have obeyed my Father's commands and remain in his love. I have told you this so that my joy may be in you and that your joy may be complete. (John 15:9–11)

I appreciate the way the same passage reads in *The Message* version:

> I've loved you the way my Father has loved me. Make yourselves at home in my love. If you keep my commands, you'll remain intimately at home in my love. That's what I've done—kept my Father's commands and made myself at home in his love. I've told you these things for a purpose: that my joy might be your joy, and your joy wholly mature. (John 15:9–11)

Another man named John (Eagen), who died in 1987, came to a liberating discovery of soul in his own journey while on a prayer retreat and in conversation with a brother in Christ, who said to him:

> John, the heart [of what I believe God wants you to know] is this: to make the Lord and his immense love for you constitutive of your personal worth. Define yourself radically as one beloved by God. God's love for you and his choice of you constitute your worth. Accept that, and let it become the most important thing in your life.[5]

Once John the Beloved tasted of the love of God, he was absolutely hooked. For the rest of his life he would devote himself to considering the depth, breadth, height, and length of the love of God.

John knew that the love of God is…

…the highest goal in all of life.

…the finest motivator one can ever find.

…the greatest power on the planet.

Alexander Whyte, a nineteenth-century biographer, ponders:

What was it in John that lifted him so high above Peter, and Thomas, and Philip, and made him first such a disciple, and then such an apostle, of wisdom and love? For one thing it was his gift and grace in meditation. John listened as none of them listened to all that his Master said, both in conversation, and in debate, and in discourse. John thought and thought continually on what he saw and heard. The seed fell into good ground. John was one of those happy men, and a prince among them, who had a deep root in themselves.[6]

John was not only perceptive, he was deeply perceptive. The challenging words and confrontive love of Christ had hulled out a deep cavity in the soul of this man and he seemed eager to fill it with all the love his Lord had to offer. In the next few chapters we will consider five experiences John had that reminded him he was the Beloved, that he was "the disciple whom Jesus loved."

Most Christians certainly know about God's love for them doctrinally. They have heard it preached and taught. They have watched it reenacted in Christmas musicals and Easter pageants. They would be the first to tell you they believed the message of the first Sunday school song they ever learned: "Jesus loves me, this I know, for the Bible tells me so..." However, there is a big difference between ascribing to a doctrine and genuinely experiencing its power and freedom within your soul. When one has been bitten by a venomous snake and infused with a poison, it is one thing to keep an antidote in your medicine cabinet, but it is entirely another to ingest the healing substance. John drank, and drank deeply.

He certainly was one of the first, if not *the* first, to discover a satisfying insight that Brennan Manning describes in this way:

God created us for union with Himself: This is the original purpose of our lives. And God is defined as love (1 John 4:16). Living in awareness of our belovedness is the axis around which the Christian life revolves. Being the beloved is our identity, the core of our existence. It is not merely a lofty thought, an inspiring idea, or one name among many. It is the name by which God knows us and the way He relates to us.[7]

John heard and recorded Christ's only new commandment. No other Gospel writer recorded this. Perhaps no other remembered it or thought it important enough to record in his account. "A new command I give you: Love one another. As I have loved you, so you must love one another. By this all men will know that you are my disciples if you love one another" (John 13:34).

In other words, of all the things Jesus had taught them there was one commandment to which he gave special status: "Love one another the way that I have loved you." If they would do this, all the world would know that they were his disciples. Sitting in the room where Jesus first said these words, we know that at least one of them heard it and heard it well. He became the "disciple whom Jesus loved" and his Gospel would become known as the "gospel of love."

The beloved disciple clearly saw the main reason for the Incarnation to be our intimacy with God: "to all who received him,...he gave the right to become children of God" (John 1:12). John heard the intimate manner in which Jesus began his important discourse in the upper room, "My children..." (John 13:33). And he summed it up in this manner: "How great is the love the Father has lavished on us, that we should be called children of God! And that is what we are!" (1 John 3:1).

We are told that even in his old age, John would be carried

feebly from church to church so that he could deliver always the same message: "Little children, love one another…as he has loved you." John heard it. Three out of four gospel writers missed it. Three out of four still miss the love of God today. Three out of four Christians today miss the message of the love of God amidst the mechanics of trying to do all that we think he expects.

The biggest hurdle into the Christian faith is not us trying to measure up to all of God's rules, it is becoming humble enough to let Jesus love us.

Charles Spurgeon, the great Baptist preacher of the last century, said, "True love is intense. Its coals burn with vehement heat. It makes all things around it living."

Yes, my daughter reminded me of something very important. That life is all about love. But how could I propose to "teach kids how to love Jesus" without knowing how deeply Jesus loves me? "Jesus loves me, this I know…" That is where the plan and purposes of God begin. This is where life, *real* life, begins This is his will and this is his way.

Have you ever noticed how when a loving person walks in a room, that room comes to life? And have you noticed how when a bitter person walks in, the room grows cold? Love to God is obedience. Love is holiness. To love God and to love man is to be conformed to the image of Christ.

One day, he was John, "the Son of Thunder."

The next, he had become John, "the disciple whom Jesus loved."

That, my friend, is an identity change.

Chapter Eleven

LEANING ON JESUS

THE FIRST INSTANCE

One of them, the disciple whom Jesus loved, was reclining next to him.
JOHN 13:23

Do you understand what I have done for you?
JESUS
JOHN 13:12B

What were the events that shaped John's relationship with Jesus? What did these experiences teach him about what it meant to have Jesus as his companion? Just how did John become such a model of what a friendship with Jesus affords us?

The inside track. Everybody wants it. Brokers on Wall Street yearn for the inside scoop on a stock company and its potential performance hoping to make a great investment. Motivated couponers clip away and scan the grocery circulars in hopes of saving a few more dollars. Football fans study stat sheets with microscopic precision so they can confidently predict the outcome of a big game. Eager fishermen purchase expensive sonar equipment in order to get the first shot at a school of fish. It is amazing to see the lengths we will go to, to find out what we really want to know.

I thought I had heard it all until I found out how far one grocery store owner would go just to get the recipe for a great tasting cookie. Rochester, New York, has a grocery store chain (Wegman's) that we absolutely love shopping at. More than half of the city shops at the Wegman's stores. I know men aren't supposed to like grocery shopping, but these places are more than stores, they are an adventure. Not only do they have a good selection of food items, they also include pizza restaurants, European-type market displays, and all kinds of fun stuff. But the real treats are their bakery items—the very best—with some items obtained at no small cost.

Apparently, a few years ago Danny Wegman, son of the grocery store founder, was on vacation in France when he came across a cookie that he found irresistible. He enjoyed it so much that he made up his mind that his store bakeries back in Rochester just had to have it. He met the original chef and complimented him on the delicious dessert. The creator was flattered over his interest but absolutely unwilling to part with his recipe. Even though money was offered and the cookies would be baked in ovens thousands of miles away, far from any competitive threat, the chef said no. Nonetheless, Danny tried everything he knew to get what he wanted.

What follows is rather hard to believe. Operation Cookie Recipe began to read like a case right out of *Mission Impossible*. In his first covert move, Danny went for the insider information. He found out the name of the chef's girlfriend, met with her, and did his best to get her to divulge the recipe. All of this effort for a cookie.

Eventually, by hook or crook, Wegman got his coveted recipe. He sought out the information he wanted and found a way to get it.

John the Beloved knew what it was like to carry privileged information. Anyone who sits closely to someone of great importance knows about that.

On five occasions and amidst five distinct experiences John

was profoundly reminded that Jesus loved him deeply. In this chapter, and in the next four, we will look closely at these intimate and life-impacting encounters. Let's walk these paths together with John into the presence of Jesus and find ourselves to be "the Beloved" as well.

Few scenes in all of Scripture are as rife with dramatic tension as that which unfolded around the Last Supper. Every month as I prepare to distribute the elements of communion to our congregation, I am naturally brought back to the scene. It is once again mine to ponder and consider.

The atmosphere must have been absolutely electric. Jesus' men knew that intolerance was sharpening its sword all around them and that their critics were no longer merely scrutinizing doctrine; they were preparing to draw blood. On the one hand, these ordinary men Jesus had called alongside himself—James, John, Peter, Andrew, and the lot—had seen their Master perform powerful acts: healing bodies, raising the dead, calming violent storms with a word. On the other hand, Jesus' popularity had peaked and many who had once gravitated toward him were now clamoring against him. Political pressures were threatening on every side. It was getting difficult to be associated with him and still breathe freely.

To make matters worse, they had seen Jesus strike at disease; they had watched him lash out at poverty and hunger. They had beheld him choking the surging winds of a driving storm; they had heard him speak confrontively and boldly against the hypocrisy of the religious spin doctors of his day. Yet, there was one thing they had never seen him do. They had never seen his fingers form a fist or strike a blow.

At the Last Supper the disciples sat with their captain, knowing that danger was imminent but certain that he would have a battle plan. Why surely, a seized crown and a reestablished throne—the throne of David—were only a matter of days away. And certainly it would not be long now before James and John would have their wish and get to sit on thrones at Jesus' side ruling in Jerusalem. After all, hadn't these disciples' eyes watched as the Lord's miracles grew in breadth and power? From *water changed into wine* to *blind eyes opened* to *paralytics parading* to *meals multiplied* to *walking on water* to *storms stilled* to the pivotal *raising of Lazarus* from the dead. And what would be next for such a miracle man? Surely an opposing horde of bourgeois traditionalists posed no real threat. What would be Jesus' next miracle-of-choice to wipe out their unenlightened regime?

Pensive and curious, Jesus' men were never more riveted on his every word than they were at this moment. The Last Supper had just ended. For now, they were safe in this hallowed room, but the social and spiritual tensions were mounting. Jesus' enemies, the religious establishment, were losing what little patience they possessed. Something was about to break. A plan was desperately needed. Their very lives depended on it.

So, what would it be? Would Jesus, like Elijah, call fire out of heaven to consume their resistors? Like Daniel did, would he shut the mouths of these vicious lions? Or would he, like Saul, allow them to take up swords and to slay a thousand Philistines in a day? They waited for Jesus' directives to come, but it was not a sword he chose to brandish before them, but a towel.

A towel?

Making his way around the room, Jesus did what slaves were supposed to do: he washed soiled foot after soiled foot. With his loyal followers looking on, he shunned the scepter and became a servant. They had hoped that he might reveal more of his glory. What they didn't know was that he, in fact, was revealing that glory. He was revealing that the greatest power available to them was the power of love, and the greatest way to demonstrate love is to serve one another.

All the while, Jesus' beloved disciple, John, was watching and weighing it all in his heart and mind.

As if the air was not already tense enough, Jesus dropped another bombshell on them, informing them that there was a notorious character seated among them…the devil himself. In fact, one of them was poised, even as they shared these intimate moments, to break rank and to betray him.

> "I am not referring to all of you; I know those I have chosen. But this is to fulfill the scripture: 'He who shares my bread has lifted up his heel against me.'
>
> "I am telling you now before it happens, so that when it does happen you will believe that I am He. I tell you the truth, whoever accepts anyone I send accepts me; and whoever accepts me accepts the one who sent me."
>
> After he had said this, Jesus was troubled in spirit and testified, "I tell you the truth, one of you is going to betray me." (John 13:18–21)

This monologue conjures up a common scene in many movie and dramatic television episodes: The lead character, whether cowboy, sheriff, outlaw, or gangster, is talking to his posse or his team. Suddenly someone says something suspicious and the boss gets an angered look in his eye sensing a traitor in the midst. Then everybody gets a little shifty and on edge. "Who is it?" "Does he think I did it?" "Who would be so stupid?" "Can I trust anyone in this room?" The atmosphere is injected with anxiety and the boss begins to speak in very concrete terms. He doesn't mince words. He

doesn't veil his threats. He is determined to isolate the problem.
Here's how the Bible described that moment:

His disciples stared at one another, at a loss to know which
of them he meant. (John 13:22)

The disciples "stared at one another." Notice, the word is not
glanced. The word is stared. Twenty-four eyeballs scanning the
room, twenty-two of them anxiously wondering. That moment
must have seemed like an eternity. Their close camaraderie was suddenly contaminated by a traitor in the midst. It was enough to cause
their Lord to be "troubled in spirit." Jesus knew a dreadful truth, a
harsh reality, and they wondered as they never had before.

Interestingly at that moment, Peter, who generally prided himself on being the one in the know, seemed at a loss. He just didn't
get it. Remember, he is the one who *knew* that though all the others
would forsake Jesus, he would not. He is the one who on one occasion thought he *knew* more than Jesus, daring to rebuke him over a
matter of faith. And it was Peter who *knew* not much earlier that
evening that Jesus did not need to wash his feet. It seems as if Peter,
at times, thought he *knew* how to carry out his Lord's mission better
than the Lord did.

Suddenly Peter found himself searching for some insider information of his own. After all, this revelation of an imminent betrayer
in the midst was a vital piece of intelligence. Most interesting at this
point is not *what* Peter asked, but *of whom*. It is obvious that Jesus
was intentionally concealing the identity of the betrayer, so who
could Peter go to or through to get the lowdown? The answer to this
question seems automatic to Peter; a no-brainer. If you wanted
some inside info you went to the disciple who was the closest to

Jesus, his confidant: "the disciple whom Jesus loved."

> One of them, the disciple whom Jesus loved, was reclining
> next to him [Jesus]. Simon Peter motioned to this disciple
> and said, "Ask him which one he means." Leaning back
> against Jesus, he asked him, "Lord, who is it?" (John
> 13:23–25)

TOUCHING JESUS

John is sitting at the table in ancient Jerusalem. If it was like most
tables, it set only a few inches above the floor. What is John's posture? He is reclining or leaning against Jesus. It is very possible that
they reclined shoulder-to-shoulder or back-to-back almost to create
a type of back to a chair for their support and comfort. And who sat
right next to Jesus?

I can imagine John walking in the room, scoping out the set
table and asking "Where's Jesus sitting?" When you want to sit next
to a certain person, you find where that person will be and you put
your stuff right next to them. Remember, this was the guy who asked
the Lord to allow him to sit at his right hand when he entered into
his kingdom. He was still a bit persistent about that because he
wanted to be close to Jesus. He saw more than a chance to be a part
of the team that would overthrow Rome. He saw that God was in
that room and a seat was available right next to him.

That is the same seat that is available to us when we recognize
that the Lord has beckoned us to come to his table and sit by his side
and pray:

> The eyes of the LORD are on the righteous and his ears are
> attentive to their cry. (Psalm 34:15)

Everyone who calls on the name of the LORD will be saved. (Romams 10:13)

Ask and it will be given to you; seek and you will find; knock and the door will be opened to you. (Matthew 7:7)

Until now you have not asked for anything in my name. Ask and you will receive, and your joy will be complete. (John 16:24)

John saw the privilege and he took full advantage of it.

The enemy of your soul wants you to miss the high privileges. For instance, he wants you to believe that prayer is just hard work. The Holy Spirit wants you to see the real truth—that prayer is, instead, a place of high privilege where we can lean on Jesus as John did. Oswald Chambers clearly experienced that in his friendship with Jesus:

What is the sign of a friend? Is it that he tells you his secret sorrows? No, it is that he tells you his secret joys. Many people will confide their secret sorrows to you, but the final mark of intimacy is when they share their secret joys with you. Have we ever let God tell us any of His joys? Or are we continually telling God our secrets, leaving Him no time to talk to us? At the beginning of our Christian life we are full of requests to God. But then we find that God wants to get us into an intimate relationship with Himself—to get us in touch with His purposes. Are we so intimately united to Jesus Christ's idea of prayer—"Your will be done" (Matthew 6:10)—that we catch the secrets of God? What makes God so dear to us is not so much His big blessings to us, but the tiny things, because they show His amazing intimacy with us—He knows every detail of each of our individual lives.

...As we grow spiritually, we live so fully aware of God that we do not even need to ask what His will is, because the thought of choosing another way will never occur to us. If we are saved and sanctified, God guides us by our everyday choices. And if we are about to choose what He does not want, He will give us a sense of doubt or restraint, which we must heed.[1]

Although Jesus touched and ministered to the masses, there are only three times in Scripture where we see people touching him. A closer look at these instances reveals the touch of faith, the touch of hope, and the touch of love.

Faith dared reach out to touch Jesus one day in the form of a woman with an issue of blood (Mark 5:25–34). So set was the focus of her belief in his ability to heal that she was determined that all she needed was to touch the hem of his garment amidst the throng of followers. Faith said, "If I can get only close enough to feel his presence brush by, that will be enough."

Hope took hold of the soiled feet of Jesus one day. Overwhelmed to be in the presence of the Grace Giver himself, a brokenhearted Mary cast caution to the wind, broke beyond the rules of propriety and washed Jesus' feet with her tears. So absorbed was she in the moment that she held his soiled feet and wiped them clean with her tresses.

Then we come to John the Beloved, who in *love* never hesitated to place his full weight against the back of the Sin Bearer. Peter's request to know the identity of the present betrayer seemed to pique John's curiosity, as well. John and Peter's responses here paint a picture of the difference between a casual acquaintance and a close friend of Christ's. When an acquaintance's (i.e.: Peter's) curiosity is enlivened, he only wonders. From a distance, he tries to calculate what the Lord is thinking. Yet, when a friend's (i.e.: John's) curiosity emerges, he does something different. Something more. He does far more than wonder. He asks.

Not only did "the disciple whom Jesus loved" ask, first he *leaned*. You see, that's how it works. We tend to get it reversed. When we are faced with a problem, we tend to want God to provide us with satisfactory explanations of the *whys* and *how comes* of life before we lean, trust, and depend. But until that moment comes, we worry or, at the very least, wonder.

John was a leaner. In his mind leaning was synonymous with believing. As a matter of fact, the word he uses for *believe* in his Gospel, translated, literally means "to lean upon, to place one's full weight upon." The picture of John just casually leaning against Jesus' back is one of the most relaxed and at-ease images in the entire New Testament. John seemed so at home around Jesus, so disarmed and comfortable in his company. This speaks volumes about the kind of relationship they must have shared.

Brennan Manning writes:

> "The disciple Jesus loved was reclining next to Jesus…He leaned back on Jesus' breast" (John 13:23, 25). We must not hurry past this scene in search of deeper revelation, or we will miss a magnificent insight. John lays his head on the heart of God, on the breast of the Man whom the council of Nicea defined as "being co-equal…to the Father… God from God, Light from Light, True God from True God." This passage should not be reduced to a historical memory. It can become a personal encounter, radically affecting our understanding of who God is and what our relationship with Jesus is meant to be. God allows a young

Jew, reclining in the rags of his twenty-odd years, to listen to His heartbeat![2]

Max Lucado has described John this way:

I like John most for the way he loved Jesus. His relationship with Jesus was, again, rather simple. To John, Jesus was a good friend with a good heart and a good idea. A once-upon-a-time storyteller with a somewhere-over-the-rainbow promise. One gets the impression that to John, Jesus was above all a loyal companion. Messiah? Yes. Son of God? Indeed. Miracle worker? That, too. But more than anything Jesus was a pal. Someone you could go camping with or bowling with or count the stars with. Simple. To John, Jesus wasn't a treatise on social activism, nor was he a license for blowing up abortion clinics or living in a desert. Jesus was a friend. Now what do you do with a friend? [Well, that's rather simple too.] You stick by him. John teaches us that the strongest relationship with Christ may not necessarily be a complicated one. He teaches us that the greatest webs of loyalty are spun, not with airtight theologies or foolproof philosophies, but with friendships; stubborn, selfless, joyful friendships. After witnessing this stubborn love, we are left with a burning desire to have one like it. We are left feeling that if we could have been in anyone's sandals that day, we would have been in young John's and would have been the one to offer a smile of loyalty to this dear Lord.[3]

Back-to-back, John discovered that there is a great difference between knowing about someone and knowing them personally and intimately. That night in the upper room was the defining moment in

John's life. Some sixty years after Christ's resurrection, the apostle—like an old gold miner panning the stream of his memories—recalled all that had transpired during his three-year association with Jesus. He made pointed reference to that holy night when it all came together, and he affirmed his core identity with these words: "Peter turned and saw that the disciple whom Jesus loved was following them. [This was the one who had leaned back against Jesus at the supper]" (John 21:20).

If you asked John, "Who are you as a person? What is your core identity? Your deepest sense of your self?" his reply would be different than Paul's. He would not say "an apostle, a disciple, a prisoner, or a servant," but "the disciple whom Jesus loves."

Peter knew who to go to when looking for the identity of the traitor Jesus had alluded to. When you want to know what the Master is thinking, you don't approach his most prominent follower, nor the wealthiest. You don't necessarily seek out the most intelligent, or the most credentialed disciple. No, when you really want to know what is on the Lord's mind you seek the company of the disciple who is the closest. You go to his companion and confidant. That would be John. Peter never had to think twice about it.

John learned that letting God love you involves learning to lean on Jesus. J. I. Packer captured the essence of this in his classic book *Knowing God:*

> What matters supremely, therefore, is not, in the last analysis, the fact that I know God, but the larger fact which underlies it—that He knows me. I am graven on the palms of His hands. I am never out of His mind. All my knowledge of Him depends on His sustained initiative in knowing me. I know Him because He first knew me, and continues to know me. He knows me as a friend, one who

loves me; and there is no moment when His eye is off me, or His attention is distracted from me, and no moment, therefore, when His care falters. This is momentous knowledge. There is unspeakable comfort…in knowing that God is constantly taking knowledge of me in love and watching over me for my good. There is tremendous relief in knowing that His love is utterly realistic, based at every point on prior knowledge of the worst about me, so that no discovery now can disillusion Him about me, in the way I am so often disillusioned about myself, and quench His determination to bless me.[4]

Perhaps knowing himself all too well, Peter might have thought Christ would not trust him with such volatile information. But he never wondered if Jesus would trust John with it. So he asked John to ask Jesus. And John asked Jesus. And Jesus did answer…immediately.

What we do not know from the passage is whether John passed that much-coveted piece of insider information on to Peter.

Jesus answered, "It is the one to whom I will give this piece of bread when I have dipped it in the dish." Then, dipping the piece of bread, he gave it to Judas Iscariot, son of Simon. As soon as Judas took the bread, Satan entered into him. "What you are about to do, do quickly," Jesus told him, but no one at the meal understood why Jesus said this to him. Since Judas had charge of the money, some thought Jesus was telling him to buy what was needed for the Feast, or to give something to the poor. As soon as Judas had taken the bread, he went out. And it was night. (John 13:26–30)

Something about John and his approach to Jesus was unique.

The disciple Thomas, when he later doubted the Resurrection, in essence said, "*Show me.* Prove it. Then I will believe."

Peter would say things like, "*Watch me.* Hear my words. See my swordsmanship. Look as I walk on water."

John said, "Teach me. Lead me. But, most of all, *love me.*"

John felt the strength of Christ as did no other disciple, because he leaned more upon Jesus. John experienced the steadfast encouragement of Jesus in his soul, because he asked more. Are you leaning fully and asking boldly?

Dawson Trotman's words in this regard have challenged me more than once:

> Do you know why I often ask Christians, "What's the biggest thing you've asked God for this week?" I remind them that they are going to God, the Father, the maker of the Universe. The One who holds the world in His hands. What did you ask for? Did you ask for peanuts, toys, trinkets, or did you ask for continents? I want to tell you,...it's tragic! The little itsy-bitsy things we ask of Almighty God. Sure, nothing is too small—but also nothing is too big. Let's learn to ask from our big God some of those big things he talks about in Jeremiah 33:3 (KJV)—"Call unto me, and I will answer thee, and shew thee great and mighty things, which thou knowest not."

John invites us to get to know the touchable Jesus. He not only heard Jesus' words in his ears and saw his miracles in his eyes, John felt Jesus' back against his very own.

How powerfully can God use people who recognize how deeply God loves them? And when you come to the place where

you have accepted that you, like John, are Beloved, something powerful will occur. Your striving will cease. Your fears will diminish.
Your tensions will ease. You will find the seat closest to Jesus. You
will learn to lean.

Chapter Twelve

HOW FAR?

THE SECOND INSTANCE

Near the cross of Jesus stood his mother…
and the disciple whom he loved…

JOHN 19:25–26

We are called to an everlasting preoccupation with God.

A. W. TOZER

I only wanted to *look* at the airplanes.

Walking through the aero-repair shop was a fascinating experience. When my wife and I were first beginning to date, Pam kept her promise and took me to visit a friend of her family's who was an airplane mechanic. His shop was a museum of sorts, replete with a couple of restored World War II planes, a first-generation hovercraft, and other assorted flying machines. I had heard about this gentleman's great shop and I was not disappointed.

Especially interesting was getting a look at several older planes in various levels of repair. It was a treat just hearing this man's stories about his work and the various planes, projects, and experiences that had accompanied it over the years. No doubt, he was a master at his craft and just getting to look a bit closer was enough adventure for one afternoon. Or so I thought.

Then something unexpected happened. The mechanic invited

me to go up in a three-passenger Cessna with his nineteen-year-old son. If you're like me, your initial thought may have been, *Alright! I'm going to get to go up for a spin with a master pilot and his son.* Then I discovered that the old man had work to do and his son was going to be at the controls. I was not too sure about this arrangement, but I thought, *What can one little spin or two hurt?*

I learned something over that twenty minute flight. I found out how nineteen-year-old pilots fly. *The same way nineteen-year-old drivers drive!*

We took off smoothly and landed nicely. It was everything in between that made my lunch look for an eject button. We dipped, we surged, we dove, we looped. Most of the time I felt my face pressed up against the window like a sardine.

And to think—I only wanted to *look* at the airplanes. I never intended to go as far as I did.

I want to ask you a vital question right now. Let it sink down deeply, because I believe it is the question the Holy Spirit desires to ask us—you and me—individually, personally, piercingly: *How far are you willing to follow Christ? How far will you really go with him?*

Of all the thousands upon thousands of people Jesus touched, taught, healed, fed, and ministered to as he walked this planet, how many went with him and stayed true all the way to the cross? Of his twelve disciples, how many were at his side all the way to that point?

This question is unparalleled in its importance. After all, Jesus' direct call to his disciples was "follow me" (John 1:43). And the command came with no prepositional phrase, no reducing qualifiers. It was not "Follow me…as long as it's comfortable" or "Follow me…as long as it's convenient." He did not say "Follow me…as long as you see fit" or "Follow me…until things get difficult."

Two words. Simple and straight. Unequivocal. Irrevocable. Undeniable. *"Follow me."* No *ifs,* no *ands,* no *buts* included. Jesus' expectations were clear. "I am walking this way. Walk with me. And never look back again." Jesus made it clear that his call was toward a deeper and more intimate walk and relationship with him. Discipleship is the means, but intimacy is the end.

For certain we know that twelve disciples dropped their nets, left their careers, and began that demanding journey. The question remains: How many completed it?

THE FIVE THOUSAND

We know that five thousand followed Jesus to the place of healing and feeding (John 6:1–15). John records the miraculous feeding of the five thousand in his illustrious gospel account. The masses had followed the Master "to the far shore of the Sea of Galilee" (John 6:1) because of the miracles they had seen him perform. The hour was getting late. The people were hungry. The only food available belonged to a boy who had a sack lunch of five loaves of bread and two fish. All the while, John the Beloved was there, and he was watching. With a word, Jesus multiplied the food and fed the masses, with basketfuls left over.

So ecstatic and inspired were these followers that they intended to make Jesus king by force. And who wouldn't want a king who had the cure for all your diseases and the ability to turn one boy's meal into a veritable grocery store full of goods?

We would willingly follow him to this place. To "the far shore of the Sea of Galilee." To the place of healing and feeding.

"Lord, please heal this headache I have. And, dear God, I ask you to open the door for us to purchase that new house. I really need your help with all these bills we're facing, Father. Please help me get that new job, Lord. You know how much we can use that raise right now!"

Consider the following story from John's account:

Jesus answered, "I tell you for certain that you are not look-ing for me because you saw the miracles, but because you ate all the food you wanted. Don't work for food that spoils. Work for food that gives eternal life. The Son of Man will give you this food, because God the Father has given him the right to do so."

"What exactly does God want us to do?" the people asked.

Jesus answered, "God wants you to have faith in the one he sent."

They replied, "What miracle will you work, so that we can have faith in you? What will you do? For example, when our ancestors were in the desert, they were given manna to eat. It happened just as the Scriptures say, 'God gave them bread from heaven to eat.'"

Jesus then told them, "I tell you for certain that Moses wasn't the one who gave you bread from heaven. My Father is the one who gives you the true bread from heaven. And the bread that God gives is the one who came down from heaven to give life to the world."

The people said, "Lord, give us this bread and don't ever stop!"

Jesus replied:

"I am the bread that gives life! No one who comes to me will ever be hungry. No one who has faith in me will ever be thirsty…" (John 6:28–36, CEV)

The good news is that we have a Savior who invites us to the places of healing and feeding. He welcomes us with his own words:

"Come to me, all you who are weary and burdened, and I will give you rest." (Matthew 11:28)

"I have come that you might have life, and life to the full." (John 10:10b, CEV)

Certainly God loves to give, but he is not some cosmic vending machine. He is God. And the Bible does not instruct us to "Taste and see that his *gifts* are good," but to "Taste and see that *the LORD* is good" (Psalm 34:8, emphasis mine). In like manner, we are not urged to seek the hand of God, but rather, to seek his face (Psalm 27:8).

Feeding and healing are God's blessings to us. He delights to do so to this day. The truth we must not miss is that at this juncture, the journey has only begun. The question?…"How far are you willing to follow Christ?…To the place of *feeding*? To the place of *healing*?" These are all important steps in a beginning process of experiencing intimacy with Christ.

THE SEVENTY

Seventy followed Jesus to the place of working and serving (Luke 10:1–24). This was an exciting time in Jesus' ministry. Things were really coming together. A major leadership team had been trained and was being commissioned. Jesus "sent them two by two ahead of him to every town and place where he was about to go" (v. 1). John was a part of one of those teams that day. These were the front men for Jesus' ministry. They were to go ahead of him and break ground for his arrival.

The stakes were high. The promises grand. The results astounding. Just read the headlines!

"The harvest is plentiful…" (v. 2)
"Go! I am sending you out like lambs among wolves." (v. 3)

"Do not take a purse or bag or sandals" (v. 4)

"Heal the sick" (v. 9)

"Tell them, 'The kingdom of God is near you.'"(v. 9)

"He who listens to you listens to me" (v. 16)

"He who rejects you rejects me" (v. 16)

"Lord, even the demons submit to us in your name." (v. 17)

"[Jesus] replied, 'I saw Satan fall like lightning from heaven.'" (v. 18)

"I have given you authority…to overcome all the power of the enemy." (v. 19)

"Nothing will harm you." (v. 19)

This is the second major step in a disciple's journey with Jesus. He brings us first through the place of *receiving*, where we are fed, healed, and nourished by His Spirit. Then, he calls us into the place of *service*. Into the place of investing our gifts and energy in the works that matter the most to him.

This is the place where, by God's grace, we begin to shed more of our selfishness and get involved in blessing others. It is here that the Christ who has served our needs so powerfully bids us to serve the needs of those around us by getting involved, by discovering what we have in our hearts to do for him, and by doing it. He changes us from reservoirs of his blessing into rivers!

And the significance of that service only he describes best:

"For I was hungry and you gave me something to eat, I was thirsty and you gave me something to drink, I was a stranger and you invited me in, I needed clothes and you clothed me, I was sick and you looked after me, I was in prison and you came to visit me.

…"I tell you the truth, whatever you did for one of the

least of these brothers of mine, you did for me." (Matthew 25:35–36, 40)

The question confronts us today. It confronts me. It confronts you. "How far are you willing to follow Jesus Christ? To the places of *feeding* and *receiving*? To the places of *working* and *serving*?" It is important to repeat that following Jesus in this way is not the end, but the means to intimacy with God.

THE TWELVE

Twelve followed Jesus to the place of leaving all (Matthew 10:2–42). Right in the midst of their developing careers Jesus found them. Surrounded by fishnets. Making a living, and yet somehow missing the life. So compelling was this man to them that they left their livelihoods, their gainful employment, to go his way. They not only laid down their nets, they were beginning to lay down their lives, as well. These were the first steps of faith.

Jesus' fame certainly preceded his invitation to his newly called disciples. They had observed him from afar. John the Beloved was probably a primary disciple of Jesus' cousin and forerunner, John the Baptist. So, when the call came, he like many of the others knew quite a bit about the man who was calling. But, it is one thing to be fond of Jesus or interested in his philosophies. It is another to drop your vocation and join his traveling band. That is exactly what their call involved.

As Jesus was walking beside the Sea of Galilee, he saw two brothers, Simon called Peter and his brother Andrew. They were casting a net into the lake, for they were fishermen. "Come, follow me," Jesus said "and I will make you fishers of men." At once they left their nets and followed him.

Going on from there, he saw two other brothers, James

son of Zebedee and his brother John. They were in a boat with their father Zebedee, preparing their nets. Jesus called them, and immediately they left the boat and their father and followed him. (Matthew 4:18–22)

"At once they left their nets and followed him." *At once*. There is an absolute sense of immediacy here, don't you agree? The Christ who called the Twelve called them to drop everything—their careers, their resources, their hobbies, their "thing"—and to do an about–face and fully follow him.

About now some may be thinking, *Yes, but that was for the Twelve. God doesn't expect that kind of commitment from the average guy like me.* Oh, but he does. Remember his words:

"If *anyone* would come after me, he must deny himself and take up his cross and follow me. For whoever wants to save his life will lose it, but whoever loses his life for me and for the gospel will save it. What good is it for a man to gain the whole world, yet forfeit his soul?" (Mark 8:34–36, emphasis mine)

Remember the rich young ruler who approached Christ claiming to have kept all of the commandments and asking how he could make it to heaven? Jesus placed his finger on his spiritual pulse by calling him to sell all of his possessions and to follow Christ. You know the story. He left discouraged, physically wealthy, and spiritually impoverished. His commitment was no commitment because it was halfhearted.

When we give our lives to Christ, we give *our lives* to Christ. We say to him, "All that I have and am are yours. I bow my knee to your throne and I submit my entire life to your will." One practical way to consider this total commitment is to empty your pockets. Go ahead: Take out your purse or your wallet. Don't worry, I'm not asking for some mail-in offering. What I would like you to do is to set a few things in front of you—let's say your car keys, your own business card, pictures of your family, your ATM card, and whatever else you have that represents some significant part of your life. Pray a prayer along these lines:

"Lord, I give my life, I mean *my whole life,* to you right now. I ask for your complete forgiveness of my sins and my sinfulness. And I commit the remainder of my years on this planet to following Jesus Christ as my Lord. Lord, guide and direct the course of my life (car keys). Help me to realize what you've designed me to do (business card) and help me to work as unto you. Help me to be faithful first of all to you and also faithful to my relationships and family (picture). Take care of my needs, Lord, and help me to bring glory to you in how I spend and use my God-given resources (ATM card). All that I have and all that I am are yours, Father God. I commit myself, my family, and my resources to you. Do with me and with them as you desire. In the great name of Jesus. Amen."

Once again, the question lingers, *"How far are you willing to follow the Lord? To the places of feeding and receiving? To the places of working and serving? What about to the places of leaving all to follow him?"*

John remembered a time when many disciples deserted Jesus. He was the only Gospel writer to record, or possibly to remember, this fallout that came after Jesus described himself vividly and quite controversially as the very Bread of Life.

From this time many of his disciples turned back and no longer followed him. "You do not want to leave too, do you?" Jesus asked the Twelve. Simon Peter answered him,

"Lord, to whom shall we go? You have the words of eternal life. We believe and know that you are the Holy One of God." Then Jesus replied, "Have I not chosen you, the Twelve?" (John 6:66–70a)

Peter's discourse with Christ really says it all:

Peter said to him, "We have left everything to follow you!" "I tell you the truth," Jesus replied, "no one who has left home or brothers or sisters or mother or father or children or fields for me and the gospel will fail to receive a hundred times as much in this present age (homes, brothers, sisters, mothers, children and fields—and with them, persecutions) and in the age to come, eternal life." (Mark 10:28–30)

THE THREE

Three followed Jesus to the place of prayer, the Garden of Gethsemane (Matthew 26:36–46).

But, even though they followed to the place of prayer, once they arrived they failed to pray. Certainly, the disciples in retrospect after the crucifixion and resurrection of Christ must have felt shame over this. It is interesting to note that every Gospel writer records the Gethsemane occurrence except the one who was a part of it, John. Perhaps the memory was too deep, too personal or too painful to recite.

Matthew's account portrays it vividly:

Then Jesus went with his disciples to a place called Gethsemane, and he said to them, "Sit here while I go over there and pray." He took Peter and the two sons of Zebedee along with him, and he began to be sorrowful and troubled. Then he said to them, "My soul is overwhelmed with sorrow to the point of death. Stay here and keep watch with me."

Going a little farther, he fell with his face to the ground and prayed, "My Father, if it is possible, may this cup be taken from me. Yet not as I will, but as you will."

Then he returned to his disciples and found them sleeping. "Could you men not keep watch with me for one hour?" he asked Peter. "Watch and pray so that you will not fall into temptation. The spirit is willing, but the body is weak." (Matthew 26:36–41)

Deep within Jesus' heart in this, his darkest hour, was a desire for something that he would not receive. It was truly the one thing he asked from his followers, the one thing he most coveted, and, apparently, the last thing they were prepared to give fully. He wanted to pray together with them. Jesus did his part—he called them to prayer. But they failed to pray.

The questions confront us hard and direct. They penetrate more deeply. *How far are you willing to follow Christ? To the places of feeding and receiving? To the places of working and serving? To the places of leaving all for his sake? Or to the places of prayer, and prayer together?*

One Confederate soldier prayed this prayer as the battles intensified:

I asked God for strength, that I might achieve;
I was made weak, that I may learn humbly to obey.
I asked God for health, that I may do greater things;
I was given infirmity, that I might do better things.
I asked for riches, that I may be happy;

I was given poverty, that I might be wise.
I asked for power, that I might have the praise of men;
I was given weakness, that I might feel the need of God.
I asked for all things, that I might enjoy life;
I was given life, that I might enjoy all things.
I got nothing I asked for but everything I hoped for.
I am, among all men, most richly blessed.

THE ONE

Finally, one disciple followed Jesus all the way to the cross. Only one. Over the preceding three years leading up to this fateful day, thousands had clamored to receive his gifts of healing, teaching, and comfort. Now, when the tables were turned, and Jesus was the one in need, in pain, in agony, only one disciple stood by him.

Consider the contrasting ways in which John and Peter followed:

Near the cross of Jesus stood his mother,...and the disciple whom he loved standing nearby... (John 19:25–26)

But Peter followed him at a distance, right up to the courtyard of the high priest. He entered and sat down with the guards to see the outcome. (Matthew 26:58)

As John, the lone disciple, stood at the cross observing all the shame, the agony, and the suffering of his Lord and friend, he must have felt the words of Jesus echoing in his memory:

"Anyone who does not take his cross and follow me is not worthy of me.

Whoever finds his life will lose it, and whoever loses his life for my sake will find it." (Matthew 16:24, CEV)

As the *Pulpit Commentary* cites:

It was one thing to stand by him [i.e.: Jesus] in his hour of joy and triumph, in the day of his power and the exploits of his loving strength, when heaven opened and streamed upon him its glory; when Divinity encircled his brow, and made his word omnipotent and his very gaze or touch almighty; when at his bidding diseases fled, and demons quit…their dark haunts; when the storm was hushed, and the waves crouched at his voice; when food increased under his hands, and even Death gave up his prey when he spoke. But it was another thing to stand by him on a cross, when hell besieged him with its torments, heaven seemed closed to his breathings, and Divinity itself seemed to have deserted him.…It is one thing to follow him with faithful disciples and a jubilant crowd; but it is another to stand alone by his cross. Where were zealous and good-hearted Peter, James, Andrew, and Philip, and others? They had all left, with the exception of the disciple of love and these loving women. Others may be among the crowd, or on the outskirts, beholding from afar; but they stood by his cross when all had left him…They were helpless, and could render no assistance. They could make no progress; still they stood their ground, and manifested their undying and unconquerable attachment. They clung to Jesus for his own sake apart from circumstances.[1]

Surely no moment filled John with such despair as this one, when we find him at the side of Jesus' mother Mary, looking with her at her tortured and emaciated son.

Near the cross of Jesus stood his mother, his mother's sister, Mary the wife of Clopas, and Mary Magdalene. When Jesus saw his mother there, and the disciple whom he loved standing nearby, he said to his mother, "Dear woman, here is your son," and to the disciple, "Here is your mother." From that time on, this disciple took her into his home. (John 19:25–27)

Peter would be called eventually to watch over Christ's church, but John was being called right now to watch over his mother. John's responsibility was a high one and mattered much to Jesus in this moment of greatest need. Mary's womb had been the cradle of his incarnation. Heaven touched that cradle before it ever set foot on earth. No woman before or since has known such high responsibility. Surely no soul has known such joy, or such sorrow. Simeon had prophesied this moment at Jesus' dedication as an eight-day-old baby: "A sword will pierce your own soul too" (Luke 2:35b). The care required now for Mary called for someone who would best represent Jesus' grace to her. "The disciple whom Jesus loved" had been readied for the great task all along the way.

In this high moment, Jesus not only entrusted his beloved mother to John's care, he welcomed John into his family. And now, he no longer called him "Son of Thunder," "disciple," "servant," "cousin," or even "friend" for that matter. In a real sense, Jesus saw him as his brother. He said to Mary, "Woman, here is your son." He said to John, "Here is your mother." What kind of a man would it take to care for such a pierced soul as Mary's? Knowing John's heart, the assignment was not made in the form of a task, but in the form of a relationship. Jesus did not say, "John, you will serve as the custodian or legal guardian." He did not say, "Mary, will you watch after this young associate of mine?" He invited them to form a family, a covenant bond, a relationship. Isn't that the way we are to approach our ministry to Jesus? Not as a task to perform, but a relationship to fulfill.

John was the sole disciple who did not just hear that Jesus had been crucified…his eyes saw "the one they [had] pierced" (John 19:37). John learned that loving Jesus meant walking with him through life and death, from dropping nets on a shore to facing a cross on a hill.

John showed us that we are not only called to rejoice with Christ at the Resurrection, we are called to stand with Christ at the cross. We are called to stand with Jesus Christ at the cross points of life. Even though John wasn't there preaching or heralding his own righteousness, he was there. But close enough for Jesus to see him. Close enough for Mary to gain comfort. Not saying a lot, perhaps, but he was standing. That's what faithfulness is like. It may not say a lot, but it always stands.

These words from Tozer say it best,

The life that halts short of the cross is but a fugitive and a condemned thing, doomed at last to be lost beyond recovery. That life which goes to the cross and loses itself there to rise again with Christ is a divine and deathless treasure. Over it death hath no more dominion. Whoever refuses to bring his old life to the cross is but trying to cheat death, and no matter how hard he may struggle against it, he is nevertheless fated to lose his life at last.[2]

We must do something about the cross, and one of two things only we can do—flee it or die upon it.[3]

From five thousand to one. The odds were stacked against John. No other disciple would follow Jesus as far as he. To our knowledge,

John followed to the cross not shouting protests as a loyalist, not shedding blood as a zealot, not lecturing as a teacher, but simply standing and serving as a companion and friend.

My airplane repair shop tour started out nice and easy. I watched a bit. Learned a little. Asked a few questions. Contemplated and considered. And then…I followed the son of the repairman into the cockpit. That is when the adventure really began. That is when my faith took wings, literally.

How far are you willing to follow Jesus Christ? To the places of feeding and receiving? To the places of working and serving? To the places of leaving all? To the places of prayer? Or all the way…to the places…of the cross?

Letting Jesus love you includes a compelling desire to stand with him through the crosses and the crowns of life.

"The disciple whom Jesus loved" was the only disciple who followed all the way to the cross.

Howard Ferrin gives this account:

We must conclude that there was something about John which made Jesus love him deeply. There must have been something peculiar to his character that was not so prominent in the other disciples. What was it? We believe it was John's deep capacity for love, and especially for love of Christ. From the first day that John followed Jesus, his Lord filled, absorbed, and entranced his soul. John's chief delight was to be in the company of his Master. Only for one brief moment, when sudden panic seized him at the flash of the lantern in the Garden, only for one brief moment did John leave Jesus. But love soon cast out fear, and he followed his Lord to the Judgment Hall, unmindful of what might befall him if he were discovered. He stood as close to his Lord as possible. And finally when Jesus was hanged upon the tree, he it was who was there at His feet—a witness of His dying.

If John was "the disciple whom Jesus loved," it was probably because John was the disciple who, more than any other, loved Jesus.[4]

John made one thing clear. He was interested in more than just the tour. Following Jesus through each important stage of this obedient journey is the path to greater intimacy. If John were here right now I think his words to us might be, "The Pilot's waiting, the engines are warm, and there's a seat with your name on it."

Whatever you do, don't miss it.

Chapter Thirteen

OUTRUNNING PETER

THE THIRD INSTANCE

*But the other disciple…the one Jesus loved…
outran Peter and reached the tomb first.*

JOHN 20:4, 2

*The man that has the most of God is the man who is seeking
the most ardently for more of God.*

A. W. TOZER

I was determined that she was not going to get ahead of me again. After all, I was the male and she the female. It was important for me to win. Was it pride? Probably. Did I have something to prove? Most definitely.

Growing up across the street from your cousin is not always easy. Especially when your cousin is a girl. When you're a ten-year-old guy and you're growing up across from a cousin who is a year older than you, and a tomboy to boot, it can be torture.

Nancy and I were actually pretty good friends growing up. She played kickball, whiffle ball, and the outdoor stuff I enjoyed. That was great. The tough part was that she was usually better at those games than I. On one particular spring afternoon in my backyard, I was determined that this trend had to be stopped. With typical competitive invitation, Nancy said, "Hey, Robert, betcha' I can beat ya' to the swing."

"No way!" I protested. And the race was on.

Trying to think on my feet, I spotted a peach tree I could cut under to break into the lead. A handy shortcut.

Well, the shortcut turned into a long afternoon. The plan had failed miserably. Not only did Nancy win again, but I ended up in the hospital with a face laceration. My shortcut under the peach tree? Well, let's just say there was a branch and a limb, and I forgot to duck.

Several stitches and protective bandages could not put back together my ripped-open ego and frustrated hopes. Once again, she outran me. Once again, I came up short. Once again, I lost.

John the Beloved was accustomed to Peter being the disciple who led the way, not as much perhaps by popular demand as by self-assertion. Peter seemed to be first at just about everything. First to *speak out* when Jesus asked a question, as if it were intended just for him and not for all of them. First to *step out* of the boat when Jesus walked on the water. First to *bow out* when Jesus was washing all of their feet at the Last Supper, as if he were somehow different from the rest. Oh yes, and who could forget the time when he had been the first, and only, one to *spout off* in front of Jesus, "Though all forsake you, yet will I serve you."

But after the cross, after that dreadful Friday and that eternally long Saturday, something was now different about Peter. He was more subdued, even quiet. He bore a certain grief. Sighs were frequent. His countenance was dejected, his will nowhere to be seen.

Dreadful Fridays. Eternally long Saturdays. Resurrection Sundays. This seems to be the pattern of life so often, doesn't it?

Life is so full of dyings and of new awakenings, of chapters closing and new ones opening. There is almost a rhythm to the process: dark Fridays and bright Sundays, shattered dreams and hopes fulfilled, things dying and others coming to life.

I am convinced that God gives us grace for the seasons of dying and for the seasons of awakening. He calls us to "rejoice with those who rejoice and to weep with those who weep." Certainly he is present in our seasons of loss. He is there to comfort and hold us. And surely, he is with us in our seasons of new birth and new life. Rejoicing. Celebrating. Exulting with us. He is there and his grace is there.

And yet it is neither the dark Fridays nor the bright Sundays that require the greatest grace. The greatest grace is most needed during the eternally long Saturdays of life.

Saturday exists right between our deaths and our new births. It is where we seek to get through our grief and disappointments, and to get on with life.

Saturday can feel like a vacuum or a time warp that just refuses to end.

Saturdays are timeless. They refuse to be relegated to twenty-four-hour slots. Other days begin with sunup and end with sundown. Not Saturdays. They begin with sundown and end only when the sun is beginning to rise.

Saturday is that place in our lives where we long for hurts to turn into hope, for loss to turn into life, and for disappointments to turn into determination.

On Sunday, we rest. On other days, we work. But on Saturday, we *wait*. And we find that the waiting is the toughest work of all.

And if we fail to wait God's way, Saturdays become our maximum stress producers. For when our expectations and our realities are miles apart, what fills the chasm is stress. When a man's new job position was going to be "an exciting challenge" but has become a constant pressure, stress measures the gap between his hopes and his experience. When a woman's marriage was going to be "the road to happiness" but has become the gateway to her despair, stress measures the gap. When disciples dream of prestigious positions in earthly messianic utopias and find themselves bolting the doors and drawing the curtains because their Master is dead and their enemies are hunting them, stress measures the gap.

We can wait or we can worry. If our hopes are grounded in the consistent character of a God who never fails, we wait. If our hopes are built on the way *we* think he will move, we worry. Peter, John, and the other disciples endured the longest Saturday in history. That Friday, they lost everything they had lived for. Their hopes were not wounded; they were annihilated. Their dreams were not shattered; they were utterly stripped. The epitome of their plans, beliefs, desires, ambitions, and pursuits in life had been ripped open on a bloody instrument of execution. Everything they had seen, heard, and embraced the past three years had just gone up in smoke.

Had they, for these three years, been full of faith or just naiveté?

Had they walked with the Messiah or a masquerade artist?

Had they missed something, or were they just blind?

God only knows how much torment filled the souls of the eleven on that Saturday. The self-doubt. The questions. The anguish. The confusion. The fear. The wondering. The bewilderment.

Wasn't it just yesterday that Jesus walked into our lives?

Didn't the crowds swarm to him?

Didn't the demons flee?

Didn't the miracles flow?

Wasn't it just yesterday that our hearts were full of faith? That nothing was too difficult to face? That we felt right on the brink of a coronation and within arm's reach of the glory of God?

What happened to this organization? What will become of us? What were these last three years all about? Have we been hoodwinked?

Look at what they did to Jesus. What will happen when they get hold of us?

We left all to follow him, and now look at where we are—Christ-less, hope-less, help-less.

On that Saturday, I believe John understood something that Paul also later understood by divine revelation—that the Saturdays of life are intended to teach us how to die to ourselves as God, the engineer of our circumstances, shapes us.

I believe John saw and Paul saw too—God showed it to them—that repeatedly in our human experience, there is a walking with Christ to the Cross and a walking with Christ to the Resurrection. But what about that in-between place? We go through experiences in life in which we are dying to self. God, the engineer of our circumstances, allows circumstances to come our way, some so difficult we cannot understand them. But God allows them because he is helping us to die to self.

> "If anyone would come after me, he must deny himself and take up his cross daily and follow me." (Luke 9:23)

Life contains far more Saturdays than it does Fridays or Sundays. Have you discovered that yet? Far more *waiting* days than *dying* days or *rising* ones. And if we aren't careful, Saturdays can erode the intimacy we feel with Jesus.

After studying hundreds of married couples for over twenty years, Dr. John Gottman discovered a few key habits of strong and lasting marriages. The first among them is the habit of remembrance. He observes that when a husband and wife intentionally remember the good times and positive experiences they have shared, their sense of intimacy and closeness is refreshed. Remembrance, or rehearsing God's faithfulness, can get us through life's Saturdays.

Crucifixion needs to be a *daily* part of the Christian experience. These are times when events feel like they are killing you—problems with your children or your finances or your health. Events in your career or circumstances of which you say, "There is such a sense of death in them." Albert Schweitzer said, "The most tragic thing about man is not that we die, but it is that which dies within us while we yet live."

Living in the body but having no life in the soul is the most tragic thing in the world. A man who can tell you all about his career, pursuits, and aspirations, but he cannot tell you about the richness of his relationship with his God, his wife, or his kids—that is tragic.

We know that there are Saturdays in our experiences of life. They are difficult, they are deep, and they are dark. Why are there Saturdays? I'm sure John asked that. I'm sure Mary did too. After all, things had been going so well. Wasn't it just yesterday that Jesus rode into Jerusalem heralded by the people? Why are there dying experiences in this thing called life?

Eternally long Saturdays are all too familiar, aren't they? They strike at the soul of the forty-five-year-old company man who just got offered an early retirement program or else. They seize upon the mother who becomes unexpectedly pregnant with her fifth child, as well as the childless woman whose obstetrician has just phoned that the test results once again are negative. They wear on the mind of the young bride whose husband is working late at the office for the fifth time this week, and the widow who forlornly waits for the telephone to ring, just once.

Maggie McKinney, an eighth-grade Spanish teacher in the western North Carolina mountains, faced a long Saturday herself twenty years into her marriage.

> When my husband of 20 years and I separated, people
> called, wrote letters, came visiting. Some promised, "You'll

marry again soon—and next time your marriage will last."
Others said, "You're better off single." Almost everyone
encouraged me, "Go for it!"

Eighteen months later, when my husband and I
decided to try our marriage again; the support was subdued, often nonexistent. "I heard you two are back
together," said one caller. "I hope…it isn't true." Another
asked: "Are you sure you want to risk going through this
again?" "When something is dead," a minister told me, "you
need to bury it."[1]

Perhaps Peter, James, Bartholomew, and Andrew were pondering similar thoughts that Saturday, the kinds of thoughts that come
after a dream or a hope has fallen flat on its face or just died:

"It's over. I just have to accept it."
"What's the use in crying over it anymore?"
"It's time to buck up and just get on with life."
"Maybe it will just never be the way I had hoped and dreamed."
"It is time to abandon the dreams and just deal with the realities."
"When the going gets tough…"

Surely John heard these voices of bewilderment and discouragement throughout his eternally long Saturday. Surely they challenged the words of Christ that he had so fully heard and pondered.

Yet that Saturday was different for John than it was for the
others. He retained the words of Jesus as did no other. He caught
what others missed, and I am convinced that he carried within his
soul the very thing that is designed to get us through the Saturdays
of our lives—the hope that comes from remembering the words of
Christ.

Alexander Whyte asks an important question:

What was it in John that lifted him so high above Peter, and Thomas, and Philip, and made him first such a disciple, and then such an apostle, of wisdom and love? For one thing it was his gift and grace of meditation. John listened as none of them listened to all that his Master said, both in conversation, and in debate, and in discourse. John thought and thought continually on what he saw and heard. The seed fell into good ground. John was one of those happy men, and a prince among them, who had a deep root in themselves.[2]

Could it be that the following words, which John would later uniquely place in a permanent gospel record, already coursed through his heart and mind on that long, long Saturday? Is that where he found the endurance? Did these words bring some sense to the desperate Friday? Did they create some hope for a Resurrection Sunday?

I tell you the truth, unless a kernel of wheat falls to the ground and dies, it remains only a single seed. But if it dies, it produces many seeds. (John 12:24)

But I, when I am lifted up from the earth, will draw all men to myself. (John 12:32)

You are going to have the light just a little while longer. Walk while you have the light, before darkness overtakes you. (John 12:35)

I am the resurrection and the life. He who believes in me will live, even though he dies; and whoever lives and believes in me will never die. (John 11:25–26a)

Succeeding at giving it a second shot was something that few people in Maggie McKinney's life had any hope for. Deep into the Saturday of her separation, she found herself caught amid a mixture of thoughts and emotions. The day her husband came back into her life, she was contemplating the freedom she was about to enjoy, the trips she would take, and the projects she could tackle. The divorce papers were expected to arrive any day, and she was becoming more and more comfortable with the idea of being single again.

While sweeping up cat litter in the basement, Maggie heard a familiar sound as a car pulled into the driveway. Without a word, her husband slowly entered the basement and invaded the silence as he walked over and gently hugged his wife. He came this time not with papers, but with a question: "Could we try again?"

In a millisecond all kinds of questions flooded Maggie's mind: Should she toss two decades of marriage in the trash along with the cat litter? Or should they give it another go? Did she want to have to answer to someone again? Did she want all the cooking and laundry that went with it? The meals? The sharing? What about the complaints she would hear about her shortcomings? And yet, what about the good times they had known together before everything went sour?

Maggie was torn. Yes, for better or for worse, vows had been made. She had made a promise. She wondered about the kids. Wouldn't they be better off with both parents at home? Still, that seemed an insufficient reason for moving back in together. As she walked the valley of decision, Maggie's hopes were paper-thin. Still, she felt more positive about the idea of giving it a try again together than going it alone.

She felt the risk of either decision. Reenter the marriage and it might blow up in her face. Leave it and she might regret having given up so soon.

Amid her long Saturday, Maggie's soul was starting to *remember*. Is it any wonder that Jesus left us with an important component to our spiritual walk with bread and wine and the words "Do this in remembrance of me"?

Faith is never more needed than on the Saturdays we face. Something has gone. Something has left us. Something has died. Something or someone that once filled a great place within us has left us just as empty as we were once full, just as lonely as we were once befriended, just as uncertain as we were once sure.

Faith is the radar system that alone can detect a resurrection. When our eyes can see nothing but what we've lost, faith is the inner prompting that something else is drawing near. Something bright. Something new. Something different than we have ever known before. And then came Sunday:

> Early on the first day of the week, while it was still dark, Mary Magdalene went to the tomb and saw that the stone had been removed from the entrance. So she came running to Simon Peter and *the other disciple, the one Jesus loved*, and said, "They have taken the Lord out of the tomb, and we don't know where they have put him!"
>
> So Peter and the other disciple started for the tomb. Both were running, but the other disciple outran Peter and reached the tomb first. He bent over and looked in at the strips of linen lying there but did not go in. Then Simon Peter, who was behind him, arrived and went into the tomb. He saw the strips of linen lying there, as well as the burial cloth that had been around Jesus' head. The cloth was folded up by itself, separate from the linen. Finally the other disciple, who had reached the tomb first, also went inside. He saw and believed. (They still did not understand

from Scripture that Jesus had to rise from the dead.) (John
20:1–9, emphasis mine)

In his own Gospel account, John wanted us to know that Jesus
had risen from the dead. He also wanted us to know that his eyes
had seen the empty tomb. He was not only a witness, but also an
*eye*witness. But there was something else he wanted us to know.
Something no other Gospel writer recorded or saw a need to record.
Something perhaps overlooked by others but absolutely vital to
John. To him, the record would be incomplete without it.

John outran Peter. He got to the tomb *first.* This was such a switch
that John wanted the moment forever marked in history. To John, it
wasn't some inconsequential item of trivia. It was significant. John
had outrun the lead man. He had come in first for the first time. It
was a picture of passion, an explosion of faith.

John went to great lengths in his Gospel to paint the picture
clearly and set the record straight:

"The other disciple [John] *outran* Peter…"
"[John] reached the tomb *first*…"
"Simon Peter, who was *behind him* [John]…"
"Finally the other disciple, who had reached the tomb *first*…"
(John 20:4, 6, 8, emphasis mine)

So frequent in the space of only five verses are John's assertions
of the finishing line order that he sounds almost redundant. He had
something vital to emphasize. His faith had drawn him to the finish
line. His passion had pushed him several lengths ahead of Peter.

John's life drove home the principle that *letting Jesus love you
incites a pursuit in your soul…the pursuit of God.*

What pushed him over the edge? What propelled him past

Peter? I am convinced that it was the words of Christ that so filled his heart and his mind. His intimacy with Jesus had faltered, but it had not failed—all because of remembrance. Mary's assertion that Jesus' body was gone was all it took. Her message was the match that set ablaze the faith fuel that had poured over John's soul. He had not only *meditated* on the words of Christ, he had *marinated* in them. And when the voice of encouragement and hope came, his passion erupted, and his faith lifted him and led him to the place of resurrection.

I love the story about the young boy who walked up to his dad's chair and proclaimed, "I love you, Dad!"

From behind the newspaper the preoccupied man mumbled, "Uh huh, me too, son."

The boy tried again, "Dad! I said I love you."

"Mm, hmm," he replied, even more engrossed in the sports section now.

Suddenly the boy jumped right up on his father's lap, ripped the paper in half, slapped a big hug around him and shouted, "I love you, Dad, and I've just got to do something about it!"

Brennan Manning observes the way people responded to Jesus:

I [am] struck by [John's] choice of verbs and adverbs in narrating his own perception of Jesus and that of others.

Upon being told by her sister Martha that Jesus had arrived in Bethany and wanted to see her, Mary got up quickly and went to Him (John11:29).

Mary of Magdala is heartbroken and tearful when she finds the tomb empty. At the moment of recognition when Jesus calls her name, she clung to him—"Do not cling to me, because I have not yet ascended to the Father" (20:17, CEV).

As soon as Peter and John received word of the empty tomb, they ran together to the garden, but the other disciple, running faster than Peter, reached the tomb first (20:3–4).

Peter, the first denier of Jesus, a failure as a friend in the hour of crisis, a coward in his soul before the servant-girl in the courtyard, jumped into the water almost naked once John told him Jesus was on shore. "At these words 'It is the Lord,' Simon Peter, who had practically nothing on, wrapped his cloak round him and jumped into the water" (21:7). John notes that the boat was about a hundred yards offshore.

These biblical characters, however clean or tawdry their personal histories may have been, are not paralyzed by the past in their present response to Jesus. Tossing aside self-consciousness they ran, clung, jumped, and raced to Him. Peter denied Him and deserted Him, but he was not afraid of Him.

John seems to be saying that the disciples of Jesus ran to Him because they were crazy about Him.[3]

As he approached the empty tomb, not only did his pace pick up, but something began to bubble within John's soul. Life was being formed right in the midst of his dying experience. He was thinking along these lines: "You know, I believe that God's hand is behind all of this. Not the hand of man, but the hand of God. God has a purpose and he sees the day of Resurrection, and he wants to get me to that place."

And what propelled a struggling wife named Maggie to give it another shot? What pushed her over the edge and gave her the courage to do something difficult? It doesn't sound like it came from the words of her friends or even her minister. Amid all of her struggles, she didn't forget *to remember*.

> Our separation taught us a little about what is and what isn't important. Forgiveness, we've learned, is essential. And we've avoided (at least so far) the anger and bitterness that can come from divorce.
>
> Our marriage is far from perfect...But the marriage is better than it was before...We walk nearly every day, eat out more frequently, talk more. Both of us have learned to pay more attention to each other than we did in the past.
>
> The minister wasn't wrong. At the time I talked to him the marriage was dead. But hasn't he heard about resurrection?[4]

John and Maggie had something in common. While others, deeply discouraged by their devastating Fridays, elected to throw in the towel, these instead picked up a lantern, dusted off their disillusionment, and found their way to a resurrection.

Chapter Fourteen

AN UNMISTAKABLE
CALL

THE FOURTH INSTANCE

Then the disciple whom Jesus loved said to Peter, "It is the Lord!"
JOHN 21:7A

*I*t is amazing what happens when Jesus gets in your eyes.

Growing up and going to Sunday school as a youngster, I learned many songs that dealt with getting Jesus into your heart.

"I've got that joy, joy, joy, joy down in my heart…"

"Into my heart. Come into my heart, Lord Jesus…"

"You ask me how I know he lives. He lives within my heart…"

Heart songs permeated my earliest years of theology. And yet, the older I get, the more I feel the need to get God not only into my heart, but also into my eyes.

You see, my heart *feels,* but my eyes *analyze* both the events of my day and the situations of my life. My heart *emotes,* my eyes *scrutinize.* My heart is *moved,* my eyes are *drawn.* Jesus did not say, "If your *heart* offends you, pluck it out" but "If your *eye* offends you, pluck it out (Matthew 18:9, CEV, emphasis mine)."

It was John the Beloved who penned the most colorful account of Christ sometimes referred to as the Gospel of Belief. And John was the only Gospel writer to record the significant discourse the Lord had with Nicodemus on being born from within. But, the much-loved disciple knew Jesus as more than the heart changer, he knew him as the eye opener.

If Jesus was ever a sight for sore eyes, he was on Easter morning. The eyes of the weary fishermen were sore indeed. Their very corneas that had ingested so many images of majesty in the ministry of Jesus and miracles in the things he said and did were now faced with blinding realities. Their champion had been crucified and publicly humiliated. Their king defrocked, dethroned, and destroyed.

These disciples' lives that had been so filled with constant adventure and direction were now on hold. Before that dark day of the cross they had awakened every morning for three years with an eagerness to engage the day, with a curiosity to discover what the Master had planned. *What would he do today? What glory would he reveal? What miracle would he work? What heavenly insight might he impart? What lives would he transform? What grace would he display? What challenge would he extend?*

John and his comrades had developed an appetite that none else had ever known. Their souls had tasted and seen what no others thought possible. For three years they had walked with God. For well over a thousand days they had looked into his face and listened to his words. Life could never be the same after that.

But now…now that he was gone…everything had changed. If their sails had lost their wind, surely their eyes had lost their fire and focus. What had happened to them happens all too often to us. Discouragements and disappointments do more than take hope from our hearts, they take it from our eyes. So much so that we miss God even while he is standing on the shore and calling our names.

So how was it that John on Sunday morning saw what others missed? Why did he recognize the voice that others overlooked?

Take a close look at the passage that describes this encounter with Jesus on the beach after his resurrection:

Early in the morning, Jesus stood on the shore, but the disciples did not realize that it was Jesus.

He called out to them, "Friends, haven't you any fish?"

"No," they answered.

He said, "Throw your net on the right side of the boat and you will find some." When they did, they were unable to haul the net in because of the large number of fish.

Then the disciple whom Jesus loved said to Peter, "It is the Lord!" As soon as Simon Peter heard him say, "It is the Lord," he wrapped his outer garment around him [for he had taken it off] and jumped into the water. The other disciples followed in the boat, towing the net full of fish, for they were not far from shore, about a hundred yards. When they landed, they saw a fire of burning coals there with fish on it, and some bread.

Jesus said to them, "Bring some of the fish you have just caught."

Simon Peter climbed aboard and dragged the net ashore. It was full of large fish, 153, but even with so many the net was not torn. Jesus said to them, "Come and have breakfast." None of the disciples dared ask him, "Who are you?" They knew it was the Lord. Jesus came, took the bread and gave it to them, and did the same with the fish. This was now the third time Jesus appeared to his disciples after he was raised from the dead. (John 21:4–14)

John sets the scene of Jesus' post-Resurrection reappearance to the disciples by the Sea of Tiberias by making two things quite clear:

One, Jesus was about to *show* himself (ie: "After these things Jesus *showed Himself* again to the disciples…and in this way he *showed Himself*" [John 21:1, NKJV, emphasis mine]). There is in these words a sense of a revelation. Even after all the time he had spent with them, there was something more of himself that Jesus wished to convey to Peter and John.

And, two, John was the first to recognize him (ie: "Therefore that *disciple whom Jesus loved* said to Peter, 'It is the Lord!'" [John 21:7, NKJV, emphasis mine]). Among all the disciples who had returned to the net, John was the first one to recognize that the stranger on the shoreline was indeed no stranger at all.

John not only possessed what it takes to recognize God in life, he used those gifts constantly and consistently. Somehow John had exercised his spiritual senses much more than the other disciples. When you read his record of the life and ministry of Jesus and compare it to the others, it is almost like comparing a line drawing to a colorful masterpiece. His memories are full of hundreds of shades of emotion, definition, and detail. Such specifics flow not merely from a mind that simply reports, but from a soul that deeply ponders.

The use of John's extraordinary and perceptive gifts are within his account. You might not have caught them the first time around, but they are present. One need only to ponder and perceive. Let's consider a few of the insights:

First of all, recognizing Jesus takes a watchful eye. When Jesus first arrived on the shore this particular morning, the disciples did not know who he was ("Jesus stood on the shore; yet the disciples did not know that it was Jesus" [John 21:4b, NKJV]). Apparently, by this point after his resurrection his appearance had changed somewhat. Perhaps his clothing was different. It could have been that a fog was present or they were at a significant distance. Regardless, we know two things: It *was* Jesus and they *could not* tell.

The Christ of the Bible is the one who says to his followers, "I will never leave you nor forsake you" (Hebrews 13:5, NKJV). Once we become Christians, he is with us all the time and everywhere we go. On our brightest days, he is there. In our deepest darknesses, he is just as much present. Most of Jesus' disciples at this point could not see this important truth. John was beginning to.

David, reminding himself of that ever presence, wrote:

Where can I go from your Spirit?
Where can I flee from your presence?
If I go up to the heavens, you are there;
    if I make my bed in the depths, you are there.
If I rise on the wings of the dawn,
    if I settle on the far side of the sea,
even there your hand will guide me,
    your right hand will hold me fast.
If I say, "Surely the darkness will hide me
    and the light become night around me,"
even the darkness will not be dark to you;
    the night will shine like the day,
    for darkness is as light to you. (Psalm 139:7–12)

John had the eyes of an eagle. He saw what others missed. He captured the details, understood things significant, and embraced the insights that just flew right by others.

As Culross has written:

In the ancient church he was symbolized as the flying eagle, "kindling her undazzled eyes at the full midday beam." He rises to loftier heights spiritually than any other of the New Testament writers…As Augustine says, speaking of the four Gospels, "While the three evangelists remained below with the Man Christ Jesus, and spoke but little of His Godhead, John, as though impatient of treading the earth, rose from the very first words of his Gospel, not only above the bounds of earth and air and sky, but above the angels and celestial powers, into the very presence of Him by whom all things were made."[1]

While others looked, John saw. While some considered, John perceived. And while many simply watched, John weighed, pondered, explored, and meditated.

No one else saw what John saw. Consider these examples: So precious and personal to him was the moment he began to follow Jesus that he records the hour of the day when it occurred (John 1:39). He alone among the Gospel writers recorded the moment when Jesus was pierced with the lance at his crucifixion evidencing a heart literally broken ("bringing a sudden flow of blood and water" [John 19:34b]). With an awe-filled and almost investigative faith, John tells us that he stooped down and looked inside when he arrived at the empty tomb.

Second, recognizing Jesus requires a yielded heart. When Jesus arrived on the scene, if he had found a note from the disciples it would have read: "Gone fishing!" In the wake of their Lord's absence, they reverted to what they had known before they met him: their trade, their occupation, their fishing.

The only thing they caught, however, was probably a good dose of impatience. A long night of casting the nets in several places and reeling them in gained them nothing but net. Again and again, they were doing what they knew best and still coming up empty–handed.

The first word the stranger spoke from the shore said it all. "Friends…"

Just seeing him had left them all wondering who this stranger might be. But when John heard *that* voice speak *that* word at *that* moment, his mind registered a possibility that his heart perhaps thought too great to be true. In a nanosecond John's memory banks erupted into overload with an ocean of treasured moments and memories. Intimacy was reawakened by a word.

"Friends…"

John is the only man in the Bible ever to record Jesus saying: "I no longer call you servants, because a servant does not know his master's business. Instead, I have called you friends, for everything that I learned from my Father I have made known to you" (John 15:15).

The greeting of the man on the beach was warm and the concern immediate. John felt it. He not only knew the sound of that voice, but the feelings the sound evoked.

After all, there were few, if any, people who would even speak to the disciples these days, much less associate with them. They had kept their distance from crowds and strangers of late, not only out of despair but out of fear. The brand, the label of having been the followers of the one crucified had weighed heavier with each passing day.

If ever a word sounded foreign to their ears now, it was the greeting "Friends!"

Rebels? Perhaps.

Deceived? Maybe.

Traitors? Probably.

But, "Friends!" Hard to imagine.

And yet, the stranger wasted no time zeroing in on their most immediate need. Hadn't he always done just that?

"Friends, haven't you any fish?"

No fish!

"Throw your net on the right side of the boat and you will find some" (21:6).

The greeting was warm, the concern immediate, and the command crystal clear. In the space of two sentences, he had used an affectionate name, asked a pointed question, and given a direct command. Who else could pack love, compassion, *and* guidance into his first paragraph? Surely by this point John's heart had swelled with anticipation.

As Ferrin explains:

[Matthew, Mark and Luke] have given the outward history of the Master; but John presented its inward and eternal meaning. Love is the best interpreter of the Spirit. The secret of John's deep spiritual insight is love; love is "full of eyes." It sees far, far beneath the surface…Love always gives the clearest vision.[2]

Third, recognizing Jesus involves a faith-filled step. Not only was Jesus calling these men to cast a net out once again, he was casting his own. And John was about to get caught in it.

First, Jesus set the bait.

"Friends…"

Then, he threw out the net where the "fish" were the hungriest.

"…haven't you any fish?"

Next, he drew them in.

"Throw your net on the right side of the boat and you will find some."

And, he knew when they were caught.

"Then the disciple whom Jesus loved said to Peter, 'It is the Lord!'"

"As soon as Peter heard him say, 'It is the Lord,' he…jumped into the water."

I suppose you could say, John was the first to take the bait;

Peter, second. John responded with a shout, Peter with a jump. John allowed his spirit to be reeled in from the moment he heard the stranger say "Friends," but Peter made a beeline with his body to Jesus' side.

Without a doubt, John saw what others missed. James Stalker offers these insights:

> St. John's writings…show what he was as a thinker…No doubt they are inspired and the glory in them is due to the Spirit of God; but inspiration did not override or overlook the individuality of the human agents whom it employed, but made use of it, allowing them to speak with their own accent and to think in accordance with the peculiarities of their minds. Now, of all the New Testament writers St. John is the most peculiar. He cannot make a remark, or describe a scene, or report a conversation or a speech, without doing it as no one else could. His peculiarity has been described by calling him a mystic: he does not deal much with the outsides of things, but lays hold of everything from within. A scene or an occurrence is only interesting to him on account of the idea which it embodies. His thinking is intuitive: he does not reason like St. Paul or exhort like St. Peter, but concentrates his vision of the object, till it opens to his steady gaze. His ideas are not chains of argument, united link to link, but like stars shining out from a background of darkness. He often appears to speak with the simplicity of a child, but under the simple form are concealed thoughts which wander through eternity.[3]

For John, faith was a word…a shout! Once the lightbulb went off in his soul, he had to let everyone know. His faith spoke right up.

For Peter, faith was a step closer...or, in this case, a jump! When he realized whose company he was in, he just had to get his feet wet.

Faith is like that.

Chapter Fifteen

EAVESDROPPING!

THE FIFTH INSTANCE

*Peter turned and saw that the disciple whom Jesus loved
was following them.*
JOHN 21:20

*Difficult as it really is to listen to someone in affliction, it is just as
difficult to know that compassion is listening to him.*
SIMON WEIL

A remote control is an interesting device. With it in hand, I am in full control. I can turn things on, I can shut them off. If I get tired of looking at one person, I can change to another with just one click. If I get bored with listening to someone, I can cut them off with one touch of a button. I get to see just what I want to see, when I want to see it, and for just the amount of time in which I remain interested…no more, no less. With a remote control, I can control things as long as I want to, and, best of all, it requires no commitment from me whatsoever. I can hear what I want to hear, and I never have to respond. I can make people move ahead at my will. I can make them stop, rewind, fast forward…even pause…at my command.

Listening in. We have all been tempted to do so, haven't we? There are just some moments too good to miss. Whether as the proverbial fly on a wall or bug on a phone or a hidden camera on the scene, there are conversations, situations, and confrontations that we would be willing to purchase box seats for if only given the chance.

There are three moments I would have loved to listen in on so that I could answer some burning questions:

...What sights were the most astounding to Lewis and Clarke on their landmark journey across the western American wilderness?

...Just what went on in FDR's mind for the twenty-four hours after discovering that Pearl Harbor had been hit?

...What thoughts coursed through Neil Armstrong's mind right after he took "one small step for man"?

John seemed to have, whether knowingly or not, eavesdropped on the remote-wielding Peter from time to time. His Gospel records his memories of Peter...

...reassuring Jesus of his undying commitment the day that many others turned their backs on him (6:67–69).

...overreacting when Jesus proceeded to wash his feet at the Last Supper (13:6–11).

...cutting off a soldier's ear at Jesus' arrest (18:10–11).

...denying outright that he knew Jesus the night before the Lord's execution (18:25–27).

...showing up at the empty tomb right behind John (20:4).

...carrying on a difficult and humbling conversation with Jesus after his resurrection (21:15–23).

EMBRACING THE MOMENT

John the Beloved had a penchant for making the most of the moments he lived, every one it seemed. He was tuned in to the significance of the occurrences around him as few men ever have been. He not only looked, he perceived. He not only heard, he listened…and deeply. What intrigues me the most about his Gospel account is not simply what each line includes, but what seems to be written between them. In the truest sense of the word, John had eyes to see and ears to hear.

Orin Crain scripted a prayer that embodies the values John embraced:

Slow me down, Lord.
Ease the pounding of my heart by the quieting of my mind.
Steady the hurried pace with a vision of the eternal reach of time.
Give me, amid the confusion of the day,
the calmness of the everlasting hills.
Break the tension of my nerves and muscles
with the soothing music of the singing streams
that live in my memory.
Teach me the art of taking minute vacations—
of slowing down to look at a flower, to chat
with a friend, to pat a dog, to smile at a child,
to read a few lines from a good book.
Slow me down, Lord,
and inspire me to send my roots deep
into the soil of life's enduring values,
that I may grow toward my greater destiny.
Remind me each day that the race is not always to the swift;
that there is more to life than increasing its speed.
Let me look upward to the towering oak and
know that it grew great and strong
because it grew slowly and well.

James Culross summed it up well:

> As our life in God deepens, we begin to perceive that, while the image of the Lord mirrors itself in him, as the sky mirrors itself in the depths of the Galilean sea, [John] is no mere passive and idle recipient of light, no mere cold reflecting surface, but a great, loving, deeply spiritual soul, all aglow with adoration, and enthusiasm, and delight, and ever living wonder, absorbed with the Lord, and resting in the calm assurance of His favour. As when one gazes with speculative eye into the starlit heavens, piercing far into their deep immensity, so [spiritually] does this man gaze into the depths of Christ, with the gaze of love. He exhibits no sign of doubt and conflict and struggle, of suspicion or cloudings of fear; these [if they ever were] lie behind him; the darkness is past, and the true light now shineth…He does not dispute or reason; he "shows," "testifies," "bears witness," "declares what he has seen and heard." There is nothing obscure in his thoughts; while fathomlessly deep, they are always crystal clear and untroubled. It is their clear depth that baffles us.[2]

One of the lives John seemed the most interested in was that of Peter. His Gospel paints a vivid picture of key events in Peter's encounters with Christ and follows them with almost novel-like interest and intrigue.

The king of the remote control. The title surely fits Peter. On more than one occasion the man who would eventually lead the church proceeded to do so almost by force. Consider these episodes:

When introduced to Jesus. Our Lord spotted his stubborn streak right up front. John the Beloved in the introduction to his Gospel paints a picture of Jesus meeting Simon and immediately bestowing upon him a new name. Although Peter would prove to have Simon-ese tendencies throughout his tenure as a disciple, Jesus took him on as a project. Certainly Jesus saw the holstered remote strapped to his side from the day he met him. Regardless, there would come a day when Simon Peter would lay it down once and for all. In essence, the Savior saw beyond the mere man Simon and viewed something solid within his soul just waiting to be uncovered, polished, and placed in an appropriate setting. Thus, he bestowed on him that day of their introduction the name Peter or *Petros,* meaning rock.

When first finding out that Jesus expected to die. On the very heels of his pivotal profession of belief in Jesus' Messiahship (Matthew 16:13–20), Peter rejected the added insights vehemently. After acknowledging that Jesus was "the Christ," it seems the Lord felt it safe to confide further in Peter, even telling him about his looming crucifixion. But Peter not only resisted such dialogue, he proved absolutely intolerant of it. One moment, Peter had hailed the very character and person of Jesus as the Gift of God to man. The next, he treated Jesus as inept, uninformed, misguided, and in need of instruction.

> Peter took him aside and began to rebuke him. "Never, Lord!" he said. "This shall never happen to you."
>
> Jesus turned and said to Peter, "Get behind me, Satan! You are a stumbling block to me; you do not have in mind the things of God, but the things of men." (Matthew 16:22–23, CEV)

As soon as Peter heard something he did not want to hear, he whipped out his remote, aimed it at Jesus, hit the pause button, and then proceeded to record over what he had just heard. Rather than investigating, asking, discussing, and seeking out the truth, Peter chose the path he was more familiar with. It went something like this, "Hey, I don't like that. Shut up. Sit down, and listen to me."

At the Last Supper. In the moment when all surely expected Jesus to wield a sword or, at the very least, a coup strategy for establishing his earthly throne, Jesus chose to brandish a towel. Instead of displaying battle plans and political ploys, Jesus saturated his approach with acts of servanthood. Circling the table, our Lord displayed for the disciples what they would most need to complete his mission and touch their world for God—a gracious heart of servanthood. Yet even here, Peter resisted.

If the scene of the Last Supper had been written according to the disciples' notions, I'm sure it would have looked more like a putsch than a prayer gathering. After all, the plot had thickened and the heat was on. The Jewish officials and the Pharisees were moving in for the kill. The disciples' lives were in greater peril than ever before. If they'd ever needed the power that this revolutionary they had chosen to follow could offer, they needed it now. What would his strategy be? When would he launch the attack? When would Christ's miracles shift from healing the blind to gouging out the eyes of the Romans? How long before Jesus would mount his rightful throne and reestablish the Davidic legacy with his loyal disciples powerfully placed at his side? The disciples waited at the table, perhaps pensively, perhaps eagerly, for Christ to roll out his battle plans.

But the power tool of Christ's choice? A towel. Jesus picked up a towel and a basin of water and made his way around the table, washing feet. Washing Peter's feet, despite his impulsiveness. Washing Thomas's feet, despite his doubts. Washing James's feet, despite his brashness. Even washing Judas's feet, despite his betrayal. Just when they thought he would take up a sword, Jesus marshalled a power more formidable than the world had ever before known—the power of love. The power tool Jesus so freely imparted in that room drilled right through the stoney shields covering those men's hearts, and it touched them. It planted something within them that power alone can never plant.

Our lives are constantly filled with opportunities and challenges that call upon us to act with power or with love. Power seeks to control. Love seeks to influence. Moment by moment, every one of us must decide what will motivate our actions, reactions, and responses. Those moments occur when your wife reminds you that it's your turn to change the diapers, when the kids spill their milk at the dinner table for the third time in one night, when your oldest son has borrowed the tool you desperately need only to forget to put it back where it belongs. It happens when your authority is questioned, your will challenged, and your hopes interfered with. Power or love. Force or influence. In the home, the choice is between being master or father. On the job, the decision is to boss or to lead. Jesus chose to love and to lead. He knew that wielding a weapon could pierce the flesh, but that washing feet would open up the soul.

Pivotal events in the lives of world leaders are usually somewhat similar in type: A throne. A coup. A speech. An act of power of some sort. But not so with Christ. The pivotal event of his life and ministry was a cross. What could have possibly made him appear any more power-less than the cross...an execution device of the most humiliating sort. And yet, the cross *was* a power act...in the sense that Jesus knew that it wasn't merely the surroundings of man that bound him (political climate, financial status, government in power, etc.), but rather that it was what was within man that bound him…and it would take more than power to break that.[3]

When Jesus first slid the basin of water up alongside Peter's feet, the impulsive disciple picked up the remote yet again and hurriedly pressed the stop button.

"You will never wash my feet!" (John 13:8a, CEV)

To which Jesus asserted…

"If I don't wash you…you don't really belong to me." (v. 8b)

Peter reluctantly conceded to the kind act and yet drew the remote again, this time choosing the fast forward button insisting that Jesus do even more.

"Lord, don't wash just my feet. Wash my hands and my head."

"Jesus answered, 'People who have bathed and are clean all over need to wash just their feet.'" (v. 9–10a)

There Peter goes again. Always the controller. Ever the king of the remote.

When Jesus revealed that one of the disciples would deny him. "Peter replied, 'Even if all fall away on account of you, I never will'" (Matthew 26:33). Peter wielded his trusty remote and cranked up the volume, proclaiming that "I never will." Jesus prophesied, while Peter pontificated.

Especially in the latter months of Jesus' earthly ministry, Peter and John the Beloved make quite a study in contrasts.

Peter was visible and vocal; John, inconspicuous for the most part, and quiet.

Peter was impulsive and forceful; John, ponderous, yet influential.

When Jesus spoke, Peter heard what he *wanted* to hear; when Jesus spoke, John generally heard what Jesus said (and we, thankfully, have his unparalleled record of those words today).

Peter was determined to do Christ's will, but only his way. John had a spirit that seemed to discern not just the Lord's strong will but his loving ways.

Ever since the death of Christ and Peter's prophesied denial, Peter had regressed in every way. Surely depression, discouragement, and embarrassment had filled the soul of Peter. Since his reprehensible and cowardly denials during Jesus' trials, the once self-avowed most devoted of all of Christ's followers had drifted away from the edge. The passion that once burnt red hot had diminished. The boldness had withered. And the confident words had long since waned.

Not only had Peter's zeal been watered down, he had drifted back so far that he was now where Christ had first found him. On a boat. Fishing. Out at sea. At his old job. And doing quite poorly, at that.

Consider what John's eyes had seen:

Second only to Jesus, Peter had been the unofficial leader of the pack.
Peter had been quick to assert his loyalty to Christ.
But, when the going got tough, Peter failed...and failed miserably.

Carefully pore over this account of Peter's life along with me as we find it in John 21:15–25. Surely it was one treasured by Christ and unarguably pondered by John, who would never forget it. Few could have felt the natural tension that was tapped when the resurrected Jesus showed up on the same shoreline as the man who had promised to stay by him when all others left and, yet, who proved to be one of the first to not only forsake him, but to deny him as well.

John had been so close to Jesus and Peter. He surely felt Peter's tension at meeting the Lord once again. He certainly sensed some of the struggle going on within Peter's soul. *Could Peter's depression be overcome? How would Jesus receive the one who had so vehemently denied him in his moment of suffering? Could Jesus forgive him? Could Peter forgive himself? Could Peter even look up past those nail-scarred hands and back into the face he once knew so well? Would grief ever allow him to smile again? Would brokenness ever allow him to lead again? And if he could look and if he could speak, what would the conversation consist of? What would Peter say? What could he say? And what would Jesus ask, if anything at all?*

Consider the climactic moment of tension that Jesus chose to prelude with a home-cooked breakfast:

> When they had finished eating, Jesus said to Simon Peter, "Simon son of John, do you truly love me more than these?"
>
> "Yes, Lord," he said, "you know that I love you."
>
> Jesus said, "Feed my lambs."
>
> Again Jesus said, "Simon son of John, do you truly love me?"
>
> He answered, "Yes, Lord, you know that I love you."
>
> Jesus said, "Take care of my sheep."
>
> The third time he said to him, "Simon son of John, do you love me?"
>
> Peter was hurt because Jesus asked him the third time, "Do you love me?" He said, "Lord, you know all things; you know that I love you."
>
> Jesus said, "Feed my sheep. I tell you the truth, when you were younger you dressed yourself and went where you wanted; but when you are old you will stretch out your hands, and someone else will dress you and lead you where

you do not want to go." Jesus said this to indicate the kind of death by which Peter would glorify God. Then he said to him, "Follow me!"

Peter turned and saw that the disciple whom Jesus loved was following them. (This was the one who had leaned back against Jesus at the supper and had said, "Lord, who is going to betray you?") When Peter saw him, he asked, "Lord, what about him?"

Jesus answered, "If I want him to remain alive until I return, what is that to you? You must follow me." Because of this, the rumor spread among the brothers that this disciple would not die. But Jesus did not say that he would not die; he only said, "If I want him to remain alive until I return, what is that to you?"

This is the disciple who testifies to these things and who wrote them down. We know that his testimony is true.

Jesus did many other things as well. If every one of them were written down, I suppose that even the whole world would not have room for the books that would be written. (John 21:15–25)

Just as John might have expected, the moment was rife with tension. It was the stuff movies are made of. It was not at all unlike other climactic moments of confrontation in the Bible…Jacob finally facing his offended brother Esau…Nathan squaring off with the fallen King David…the Prodigal Son approaching his estranged father…

The central issue for Jesus in dealing with his repentant disciple was love. Pondering his three questions makes it clear that Peter had somehow never made the connection between loving God and loving God's people.

"Simon son of John, do you truly love me?" (John 21:15).

What John the Beloved had come to embrace early, Peter had somehow missed. He had been much more intrigued with the potential power of a kingdom than with the priority of a Savior's love. As a result, while Christ chose the path of loving influence, Peter was determined to maintain control.

Here he sat, Peter, the self-proclaimed leader of the pack, back at square one. Not only had he failed to recognize the Master (unlike John), he was now being asked a question that seemed more suited for new converts than for a seasoned follower such as he.

"Simon son of John, do you love Me?"

To make matters worse, Jesus had gone back to calling him by his former name, Simon. That is the name he used before he began to follow. Why?

Was it because he had drifted so far away from the Master's path?

Was it because he was no longer worthy to be called Peter, "the rock"?

Was it a concession? Was Jesus giving up on him?

Had every solid thing Jesus had seen in him faded? Was it lost forever?

Was there no more hope?

Could deniers not find forgiveness?

Was there no real reason to go on?

"Simon son of John…"

Three times he had to endure hearing that old name from Jesus' lips. Each one stung with the searing edge of a knife that penetrated his scorched soul. The truth hurt. It always does. It was forcing Peter to face facts.

Three times Jesus asked if Simon loved him.

Three times Peter had denied that he even knew him.

PITY PARTIES

I believe Jesus called Peter by his old name not to offend or embarrass him. He did so because the man he was sharing breakfast with was not Peter— not in his attitude and approach to life at least. No, Peter had left the new identity Christ had given him and reassumed the old. Three years earlier on the same shoreline, Simon had laid down his old identity and been given a brand new one. Jesus had called him by name...by his new name—Peter, the rock.

When you and I fall into our pity parties, whether by failure or erosion of attitude, we lay down the new identity Christ gave us and fall into our old ones. D. L. Moody once said, "God cannot use a discouraged man." This principle rang true that day.

Jesus was intent on restoring Peter. Three times Peter had denied. Three times he had failed. Three times now he was answering, "Lord, you know I love you!" Serious damage had been done, but the bitter tears were turning to brokenness. The process of restoring was in motion.

Once before, when Peter had first acknowledged that Jesus was the Son of God, Jesus confided in him sharing that he would soon have to die. Peter had wielded his remote and, in that instance, actually rebuked the Lord.

Now Simon Peter was acknowledging in triplicate his renewed devotion to Jesus. Only after he did so did Jesus risk revisiting the subject of death with the disciple again. Not the Lord's death this time, however, but Simon's.

> Jesus replied, "Feed my sheep. I tell you for certain that when you were a young man, you dressed yourself and went wherever you wanted to go. But when you are old, you will hold out your hands. Then others will wrap your belt around you and lead you where you don't want to go."

Jesus said this to tell how Peter would die and bring honor to God. Then he said to Peter, "Follow me!" (John 21:18–19, CEV)

Sobering words, especially for the king of the remote control. Just how would these phrases sound in the ears of a control freak?

"Others will wrap your belt around you"

"Others will…lead you where you don't want to go"

The King of Glory was calling the king of the remote control once and for all to lay it down and follow—to truly follow. From now on, Jesus would call the shots. It would not only involve doing God's will, but doing God's will *God's way*. From the day they first met on that shore, every day had been leading to this one. Every invitation and call was a mere foreshadowing of the deep call that now poured from Jesus' lips and into the stubborn disciple's heart. The chips were down. The stakes were high. The moment was filled with everlasting implications.

Jesus was calling Peter, but into something apparently quite different than he had ever expected. Jesus was calling Peter into a relationship not based on some earthly title or powerful position. He was extending a relationship based on love. "Simon, do you love me?" He was beckoning the failed follower into a friendship.

The very fact that Jesus had to ask the question of him three times (always an emphatic literary method in Scripture) makes it clear that he wanted a heartfelt answer to the question. Jesus wanted a sincere affirmation from this disciple that he would walk in the deep personal companionship of soul and spirit the Lord was calling him toward. Nothing else mattered next to this. Jesus had prepared much more than breakfast for him that day.

But Peter at first did not understand what the Lord meant. He was clearly perplexed.

WITH FRIENDS LIKE THIS

To make matters worse, not only was Simon facing the loving confrontation of the one he once said he would never fail, but he discovered that he also had an audience.

> Peter turned and saw Jesus' favorite disciple following them. He was the same one who had sat next to Jesus at the meal and had asked, "Lord, who is going to betray you?" When Peter saw that disciple, he asked Jesus, "Lord, what about him?"
>
> Jesus answered, "What is it to you, if I want him to live until I return? You must follow me." (John 21:20–22, CEV)

The last time Jesus had talked to Peter about the kind of death the Messiah would die, Peter went ballistic. He proceeded to set God straight. This time Jesus had talked to Peter about the kind of death the disciple would die. Instead of an assault, Peter merely asked a question. John recounts the moment:

> When Peter saw that disciple, he asked Jesus, "Lord, what about him?" (21:21, CEV)

Even in his dying moments, the persona better known as Simon was not going to go down without a fight. By this point most of the fight was already knocked out of him, but not all. You can almost hear the remote control still at work although the batteries are clearly beginning to fail. He was probably worried that his words were on John's record button (they were). This last-ditch effort was not some sincere curiosity on Peter's part; Simon was still prying. You can tell by the way Jesus responded.

"What is it to you, if I want him to live until I return? You must follow me." (v. 22)

As subtle as it might have seemed, in this episode the king of the remote control showed that he still had growing to do. This time he was not trying to tell the Lord how to live, or how to serve, but how to direct the life of another one of Jesus' followers…and not just any follower, but "the disciple whom Jesus loved."

I can almost hear Peter's next words, had Jesus not cut them short:

"Wait a minute. That's not fair!"

While reading this passage, it occurred to me to ask just what the Lord might find most repulsive about the remote controls we carry. As wrong as they are, it's not the pushiness, the abruptness, or the manipulation that he finds most offensive. It is not what the controller does, but what he touches. Ultimately, the controller invades more than circumstances; he toys with the sovereignty of God. And that's a line God won't allow any man to cross.

The people who followed after Noah tried it when they erected the Tower of Babel. God knocked it down.

King Saul tried it when he consulted with a witch. God brought him down.

Ananias and Sapphira would try it years later when they would lie to Peter. God took them out.

No man had ever crossed that line and lived to tell about it. And Simon was not about to be the first. No, Peter still did not understand the demands of a relationship based on love, something John had long since learned.

PART THREE

JESUS,

MY COMFORTER

Chapter Sixteen

FINDING CHRIST IN YOUR CONFLICT

STORM LESSONS

All the troubles of a Christian do but wash him nearer Heaven;
the rough winds do but hurry his passage across the straits of life
to the port of eternal peace.
CHARLES SPURGEON

It takes a world with trouble in it to train men for their high calling as
sons of God, and to carve upon the soul the face of Christ.
J. S. STEWARD

on't let the bus break down here of all places."
Driving in an old school bus full of young people in the middle of July through a rural area with no air conditioning was about the worst possible situation for a breakdown. It was in *my* mind at least.

Our old rattle-trap used school bus, affectionately known as the "Blue Bomb," was the best transportation we could afford to get our Rochester youth group down to a Christian youth festival in Virginia. This was our first major trip with this group. I was a new youth pastor with a bus full of teens, full of sponsors, and full of responsibilities. I wanted my first adventure to be a good one. After all, this was my big chance to establish trust with this bunch and with their parents back home.

We were no more than fifty miles out of our city, and that big blue bus decided to conk right out. I couldn't believe it. Only fifty miles into a five-hundred-mile trip and we had already broken down. The junior high leader and I popped up the hood and tried to fix it. But it was no use.

We waited until a patrolman came by and then got ourselves towed to a little gas station. I believe it was the only one in the little town called Wayland, New York. Our teens ventured down to what appeared to be the only restaurant in town and got a snack while they waited. After the mechanic gave the engine an initial look, he told us that he had a good bit of work to do and that he couldn't promise us anything. *Great,* I thought. *Just what I need. Eight hours to spend in a tiny little town with a bus load of teens with nothing to do.* I could just imagine the complaints I would be hearing before long. All I could think was "Lord, why? Why *me?* Why *us?* Why *here?* Why *now?* Why *on our first trip?*" On the outside, I was working overtime to maintain my cool. On the inside, however, a storm was rising swiftly.

Over the next few chapters we will take a closer look at how intimacy with Jesus is cultivated in a believer's life. One of the most intimate words in the New Testament is one that describes a precious gift we have been given in Christ: *comfort.* Paul's words to the Corinthians expressed it well:

> Praise be to the God and Father of our Lord Jesus Christ, the Father of compassion and the God of all comfort, who comforts us in all our troubles, so that we can comfort those in any trouble with the comfort we ourselves have received from God. For just as the sufferings of Christ flow over into our lives, so also through Christ our comfort overflows. (2 Corinthians 1:3–5)

The effectiveness of our walk with Jesus is directly related to the maintenance of a deep intimacy with him. A deep sense of closeness with the Lord is what we crave. Paul goes on in the Corinthian passage to further describe this comfort as *the refreshment of our spirits* (2 Corinthians 7:13).

In this chapter we will consider what hinders us from receiving the comfort God wants to give us. Then, in the following chapter, we will explore what affords that comfort, what draws it in our direction. And, following that, we will discover how to more fully experience the Comforter in our daily walk of faith.

Jesus' disciples faced their share of unexpected storms. But none stand out as much as this particular experience:

> That day when evening came, he said to his disciples, "Let us go over to the other side." Leaving the crowd behind, they took him along, just as he was, in the boat. There were also other boats with him. A furious squall came up, and the waves broke over the boat, so that it was nearly swamped. Jesus was in the stern, sleeping on a cushion. The disciples woke him and said to him, "Teacher, don't you care if we drown?"
>
> He got up, rebuked the wind and said to the waves, "Quiet! Be still!" Then the wind died down and it was completely calm.
>
> He said to the disciples, "Why are you so afraid? Do you still have no faith?"
>
> They were terrified and asked each other, "Who is this? Even the wind and the waves obey him!" (Mark 4:35–41)

REACTIONS TO STORMS

Storms are a part of all our lives. They are simply a fact of life. And, more often than not, we don't see them coming: One day we are drifting along minding our own business, then—BAM!—out of the blue a storm seizes upon us…unexpected, uninvited, and certainly unappreciated.

What differs among us when storms hit is how we react to them. Like you, I have been through my own share of storms. As a matter of fact, I am in a couple right now. And, I expect they won't be the last. Maybe you have reacted to storms in some of the negative ways that I have:

"Everything just feels out of control!"
"This is so frightening."
"I have to find someplace to hide…to get away from it all."
"I just want it to stop."
"I can't wait for the sun to come back out again."
"How long will this last?"
"Have we already gone through the worst of it?"
"This ruins all of my plans!"

Storms come in all kinds of shapes and sizes. An unexpected illness. Family squabbles. Unemployment lines. Haunting memories. Abuses. Harsh words. The loss of a mother, a dad, a spouse, a child, or a friend. Mounting debts. Nagging fears. Life-controlling addictions. Tough-to-get-rid-of anxieties.

Storms are epidemic in people's lives. If we could get a meteorological peek at the turbulence around us in a given day, it would often be off the charts. Storms are the sources of countless maladies, psychosomatic illnesses, traumas, phobias, and stresses. Storms have produced a mass of weather-beaten souls. They have made counseling a big business in America: I am told that some forty billion plus dollars is spent on treatment for depression in America annually.

When I first became a Christian, I suppose I had a sneaking notion that maybe now that I had God in my life he would spare me from having to deal with storms. In my mind, then at least, the idea of deliverance *out of* storms was much more intriguing than the thought of perseverance *through* them.

THE PERFECT STORM

Instead of pulling me out of storms, however, I soon discovered that God usually had another plan in mind. Angrily asking *why* when in the midst of a raging storm won't get you any further along your journey. A better question to ask of God is *what*. *What do you want to teach me through all of this? What spiritual muscle are you strengthening within me, Lord? What do you want me to do in the midst of this storm?*

The motivation to ask *what* instead of *why* comes when we embrace what I call the First Storm Principle:

Storm Principle #1: "Storms" can serve to propel us forward in the direction of God's will.

Spurgeon said that "all the troubles of a Christian do but wash him nearer Heaven."

At this instance recorded in Mark 4:35–41, the disciples were aboard the very boat that Jesus had been teaching from all day. Everyone thought that he had finished the lessons for the day. Earlier a great crowd had gathered on land—and also in an accompanying fleet of boats—to listen to Jesus teach. After this storm blew in, this group of boats and sailors would eventually view Jesus calming the storm. First, however, this great host of witnesses would watch the disciples suffer and cry out in fright. Everyone was full of anxiety, even, apparently, Peter and John. No one knew that the violent wind and waves were there to serve as God's outboard motor designed to hurry them on toward their destination, toward the next places of God's will.

When I first began reading Oswald Chambers's classic devotional *My Utmost for His Highest,* I was not many weeks into the book before I noticed a theme that threaded throughout his teaching. Put simply, it goes something like this: *"God is the Engineer of our circumstances."* More and more, this scriptural principle became real to me, and it has greatly affected the way I view my life. Life is not just a random set of circumstances. God has his hand not only on my life and yours, but mysteriously he has his hand on the very circumstances of our lives. Chambers's insight caused a strand of verses to breathe with new life as I read them:

> And we know that in all things God works for the good of those who love him, who have been called according to his purpose. (Romans 8:28)
>
> All the days ordained for me were written in your book before one of them came to be. (Psalm 139:16)
>
> Joseph to his brothers after they sold him as a slave: "You intended to harm me, but God intended it for good to accomplish what is now being done, the saving of many lives." (Genesis 50:20)

That means that even what we would consider limitations can be used to God's glory. Whether the limitation is an extreme or slight one, God can pour through the broken places in your vessel—your life—like a precious perfume. God heals today. I am convinced of it. However, when his glory is not displayed in the kind of healing we would expect, it is often displayed in other ways. I never cease to marvel at the grace of God that pours through Joni Erickson Tada whenever I hear her speak, read her works, or see her drawings.

Despite her tragic teenage storm of a deep dive in shallow water, which left her paralyzed, she beams with the glory of God. And now she ministers regularly to the disabled. The limitation has served as a divine guidance system and has led her in the path of God's will.

When I lost my voice for a year and a half, my first reactions were quite natural: *Why me, Lord? Why did you call me to be a preacher and then take my voice away? When are you going to remove this problem? How long can people put up with listening to my weakened voice?* Well, I am pleased to report that God chose to heal in his own way, but not on my timetable. The long wait, however, served to create an insatiable desire within me to write again. Out of that slow birth has come a number of books, including this one. God used that limitation to guide me in a path I never imagined possible.

Comfort comes amidst our conflicts when we walk in the companionship of Christ. Even if my boat is rocking, once I remember that Jesus is with me in the storm, my soul can be still once again.

Sitting outside that gas station watching our old bus being tinkered with, I began to notice something. A couple of our youth workers were having a long conversation with the mechanic while he worked. My first thought was, "Leave the guy alone and let him do his job. You're slowing him down." Several minutes later I found out that the young man was in tremendous spiritual need. His brother, who was a pastor, had died not many months previously of cancer. Ever since that tragic event, this mechanic had struggled terribly with anger and bitterness toward God. By the end of the day, however, our leaders were able to pray with him to commit his life to Jesus Christ. Suddenly and unexpectedly, a reason for our detour had emerged. What had appeared limiting, even restricting, had become absolutely liberating to one soul who mattered much to God.

—∞∞∞—

Bill and Kathy Peel, two popular conference speakers, say that our limitations become God's chief sources of direction and focus in our lives. In other words, without limitations we tend to spread ourselves too thin, like water in a low-lying swamp. The water just sits and stagnates. Our limitations, struggles, and weaknesses, however, become the walls that turn swamps into rivers. The water ceases to spread all over the place and begins to flow in a specific direction. Without the limitations of the walls and banks there would be no focus and no flow. Thus, the Second Storm Principle:

Storm Principle #2: "Limitations" can provide guidance and focus in our lives.

The secret is learning to find Christ within your storm, within your conflict. He is there and he's never overwhelmed by the waves or the water. He's the one always walking on them. You can find him if you'll look.

When the disciples' storm blew over them, Jesus was not far off; he was right there with them in the boat and in the midst of the storm. We tend only to want to associate God with the *blessings* that touch our lives, but not the *difficulties*. He, however, has chosen to utilize both the mountains and the valleys in his process of molding us into the image of his Son (Romans 8:29). Remember, he is in the midst of your storm this very moment. Have you found him yet? Are you looking for him in it?

Nobody likes to be the last to be picked when a backyard ball game is about to begin. No one enjoys getting turned down after a job interview they eagerly wanted to work out. It can be humiliating and discouraging. And no one enjoys being overlooked and ignored by their spouse, their parents, their children, or their coworkers. The experience can be painful and wearing. However, Jesus knew what it was like to be "rejected by men" (Isaiah 53:3). As a matter of fact, the cross is the ultimate emblem of rejection. It symbolizes the whole world's rejection of Christ. This leads to another principle.

Storm Principle #3: "Rejection" can actually be God's direction.

One of my fattest files is my writing projects rejection file. I do my best to save all of my rejection letters. Over the years, I have received from publishers several rejection letters for every acceptance letter. For the first several years after I started writing, most of my work was rejected by many publishers before being accepted.

I remember when I received my first couple of rejection letters as a writer. It was agonizing. There were moments when I wondered if I would ever want to try again. However, try I did, and, thankfully, doors began to open.

Rejection letters are still less than pleasant, but I don't dread them as I once did. More often than not now, God has helped me to view them as doors he has closed and motivation to set my prayerful focus toward the ones he will open (Revelation 3:7).

FOUR ESSENTIALS FOR NAVIGATING LIFE'S STORMS

When you are out in a boat and a storm sets in, it suddenly becomes easy to distinguish the true sailors from the joyriders. The experienced mariners move into action; they become focused and deliberate, leaning heavily on their tools of navigation. The joyriders panic and tend to turn green. The Bible provides you and me with tools for navigating the storms of life. Consider these:

1. Remember…He is the Christ who always beckons us to go with Him "to the other side" (Mark 4:35–36).

God's people have faced many storms throughout the years and have gotten through them as they have heard him calling them to follow "to the other side." Just think about it. He called…

…Noah to build a great boat and, in the face of the storm to beat all storms, to sail with him to "the other side."

…Abraham to leave the land of his father and to go with him to a land that he knew not.

…Moses to leave his safe pasture on the back side of the desert and to journey with him "to the other side."

…Joshua to devote his life to leading his people to the Promised Land.

…David to leave the safety of the Israelite soldier camp and face a nine-foot-tall "storm" by the name of Goliath.

…a young single mom in the midst of a famine to share her last meal with the prophet Elijah and to walk with him to "the other side" of God's provision.

Jesus himself called…

…Twelve common men to lay down their personal pursuits and to follow him to "the other side" of a brand new life.

And today, Jesus is calling…

…you to go with him to "the other side." Remember, he has already been there. He is not afraid of what it holds, even if you sometimes are. And he will be your personal tour guide the whole way through.

2. Remember…Journeying with Jesus often involves unexpected "storms" (Mark 4:37).

Gary Gulbranson has written: "It's not the magnitude of the mess that matters; it's the measure of the man in the midst of the mess."

When a physical therapist designs a recovery plan for an athlete who has been injured, it includes a certain number of repetitions of special exercises. There is usually a bit of pain in the process. The result, however, is a strengthened muscle and a place back on the field. We are quick to consider the difficult dynamics of the struggles and trials we face. Have you stopped to consider what things this process is strengthening within you? How will enduring trials strengthen the faith muscle in your soul?

More often than not, it seems, storms come unannounced and suddenly. The Sea of Galilee was considered dangerous by some because of the high frequency of sudden storms. They would often seem to come right out of the blue. The journeys were never dull.

3. Remember...Disciples tend to forget just who is in their boat (Mark 4:38).

Jesus was apparently wearied physically by the day full of teaching the multitudes. The trip over the lake would have allowed him a much needed opportunity to rest, but he was abruptly awakened by the sounds of distrust and unbelief.

"Teacher, don't you care if we drown?" (How often do we cry out the same thing in our conflicts and storms?)

The disciples became impatient, perhaps even irreverent. They weren't remembering, they were remoting.

They had a day of miracles behind them. Then, with just one conflict, they question the motives of God. Though weak and dispirited, they at least showed enough faith to call on Jesus for help. Perhaps their underlying confusion and frustration could be summed up as..."How could you let the struggle go this far? How could you let the storm get this big?"

Their panic gave them away. And our attitude and spirit reveals much about our confidence in the Lord or lack thereof. Maintaining what I call a right spirit involves not allowing ourselves to be given over to doubt or despair, but by God's grace maintaining our joy in the Lord. This becomes a litmus test of our Christian growth.

It is all about this important life principle: Our confidence in the character of God, no matter the circumstance of life.

4. Remember…He's the Christ who longs to reveal himself in the face of our conflicts (Mark 4:39–41).

There are at least a few ways in which the Bible promises that Christ will reveal himself to us in the face of our sufferings and struggles:

- *Jesus' glory will be revealed* (Romans 8:18). Somehow the glory of Christ within our lives is polished and drawn out by the struggles we endure.
- *Good will be accomplished* (8:28). Even the bad situations and the evil attacks we face will ultimately work toward a good end as we yield our trust fully to Christ.
- *Jesus' love for us will be reaffirmed* (8:37–39). Children tend to hold the hand of their parents a bit tighter when storms hit, don't they?

Augustine challenged us to trust in our Friend's character during the soul storms we face: "When we allow temptations to overcome us, Christ sleeps in us. We forget Christ at such times. Let us, then, remember him. Let us awake him. He will speak. He will rebuke the tempest in the soul, and there will be a great calm."

THE BUS RIDE THAT WAS NOT

Well, that big old blue bus never moved another inch that day or the next. By the middle of the afternoon we had to fork out extra money and hire a rental bus to complete the trip. I was just thankful to be on any bus and get on our way. At least we were moving. Finally, a chance to complete what we first set out to accomplish—a successful youth retreat.

As we headed down the highway, a couple of the young people

came up to me and said: "Hey, Pastor Bob. Guess what we think?" I was all ears. "We think that it is cool the way God let our bus break down right next to where that mechanic was who prayed to receive Christ. And now, we bet this hired bus driver is gonna give his heart to the Lord too."

My first thought, I'll admit, was *Okay, guys, don't push it! Just be happy for what already happened. Don't expect too much. You may be disappointed.* Right away I felt chastened in my spirit by the Lord who said, "Where is your faith?"

You guessed it. In one of our devotional studies the next morning, some of the young people shared their faith with our hired bus driver and he, too, prayed with them that God would change his life.

Oh yes. The old bus was fixed and we picked it up on the way home. Our old bus did finally complete the journey we set out on. We just ended up going places I never dreamed possible.

PLAYING
FAVORITES?

Jesus' favorite disciple was sitting next to him…
JOHN 13:23, CEV

You are the Beloved…all I hope is that you can hear these words as
spoken to you with all the tenderness and force that love can hold.
My only desire is to make these words reverberate
in every corner of your being—You are the Beloved.
HENRI NOUWEN

*J*esus seemed to favor John. Somehow God playing favorites
doesn't jibe with the theology I was raised on. The God I
learned about in Sunday school is one who shows absolute equality in his expression of love toward men. He doesn't have favorites.
God loves everyone the same. Right? The Jesus I learned about on
the front pew is one who would never think of playing favorites.
"Jesus loves the sinner on skid row just as much as he loves the
pastor. He loves us all the same." That's what I was told.

Still…the Jesus I read about in the Bible did have a favorite—a
favorite disciple, that is.

On five occasions, John described himself as "the disciple
whom Jesus loved" (John 13:23; 19:26; 20:2; 21:7, 20).

Clearly, if Jesus did not have a favorite disciple, John thought otherwise. Yes, we all know that there was a select three: Peter, James, and John, the triumvirate in whom Jesus confided more than the other nine. But John was clearly his closest follower.

Howard Ferrin explains it this way:

> If Peter and James were first among the twelve, John was first in the affection of his Lord. [Five times] in his Gospel he is designated as "the disciple whom Jesus loved." Did not Jesus love all of His disciples? Indeed He did, but it does seem that John was more beloved by our Lord than were the other disciples. At first this thought is quite startling, but if we think deeply we have here an argument for the complete humanity of our Lord. Is it not a familiar fact that as human beings we love some more than others? We may argue against it, but even among our most intimate friends, we find those with whom we are more spiritually akin than others. If our Lord was fully man, sharing with us in all of our experiences, we should not be surprised to learn that Jesus found his "kindred soul" in John. Perhaps another reason for this lies in the fact that if Jesus was to be known as fully as possible by mortal man, there had to be one among the disciples to whom Jesus would more fully disclose Himself than to any other.[1]

John the Beloved was that man. He held a place of high privilege in relationship to Christ. He had a level of showing openness and sharing with Jesus that none of his peers ever tasted. Was that because no one else ever aspired to such a close walk? Or was it ordained to be just that way? Was John just incredibly diligent and devoted, or did he possess a unique God-given grace? I believe the answer is yes to all of the above. John had a spiritual predisposition to being incredibly absorbent and open. And yet, this was a God-given grace. Did others possess it as well? Perhaps. The difference with John is that he did something about it. He followed. He responded. He learned to sit at Jesus' feet. While others talked and made idle promises, John listened. He pondered. He grew. And Jesus took notice.

THE PAINTER IS PLEASED

When God paints his image upon the soul of a man, he dips his brush deep into the reservoir of his Spirit and comes up with colors rich in character that seek a suitable canvas. Any soul will do. Perhaps one of the reasons Jesus was so drawn to John is the way in which John allowed the Holy Spirit to paint the heart of God upon the canvas of his own. I am convinced that Jesus felt somehow closer to his Father in the company of John, due at least in part to the fact that the character of God was growing powerfully within the young disciple. Jesus found his companionship absolutely refreshing.

James Culross writes an important insight:

> These qualities were of Divine creation in him, ripening through his intercourse with the Holy One. This is fully true; the very love that was showed him made him lovable; beholding the glory as of the Only begotten of the Father, he was changed into His likeness; he could say as fervently as the Apostle Paul, "By the grace of God I am what I am:" but nonetheless was his lovableness real and attractive to the heart of Jesus. Just as the painter who expresses on canvas some vision that has risen up before his inner eye, or as the musician who hears in his soul some grand piece of music,…and sings it forth with his own voice, and in his own hearing only, has delight in it altogether apart from the

thought of its being his own creation, so could Jesus love this man, although the lovableness was due to himself.[2]

John entered Jesus' life like the month of March: He blew in like a lion and out like a lamb. The stormy spirit that Jesus dubbed "Son of Thunder" obviously somehow heard Jesus speaking peace. It seems that not many months into their acquaintance John rounded a corner because of God's grace and traded in a hard head for a tender heart. This bristly, headstrong fisherman met his match in the form of a carpenter's son. And not long after the dark night of rolling thunder expired, a ray of daylight dawned and fresh dew appeared on the landscape of one man's surrendered soul.

"YOU'RE WEARING ME OUT!"

Like every man, there were people in Jesus' life who built him up and others who wore him out. Although he served the needs of the masses, he closely associated with a carefully selected set of friends. Jesus approached many people with an agenda to minister and meet their needs, but there were others whose company he simply seemed to enjoy. There were even times when the barrage of people and their needs drained Jesus emotionally, and he departed to a place of solitude with his friends to be renewed and refreshed, to get his batteries recharged.

I can see at least three different types of relationships in my life: *requiring* relationships, *reciprocal* relationships, and *replenishing* relationships. Some relationships are personally demanding and consistently so. Others are give-and-take arrangements. And a few, sometimes too few, are refreshing and renewing to me personally. I believe Jesus knew all three.

Jesus frequently visited the home of Lazarus in Bethany. It seemed to be a city of refuge for him. He was often renewed there among his friends. Not only did it fit into several journeys, but Jesus was apparently also quite fond of his friend Lazarus and his two sisters, Mary and Martha. Interestingly enough, John was the only Gospel writer who left us a specific record of Jesus' friendship with Lazarus and his sisters. John apparently was close enough to Christ to know what they meant to him.

Let's take a look at some of the characteristics of the three different primary types of relationships just described:

1. *Requiring (i.e.: Draining) Relationships.* These are the ones in which something is usually demanded or expected of me. By virtue of their nature, when I am in these relationships, I am generally on guard, cautious, and careful. I watch my words, body language, and responses more closely. These relationships are hard work. There is generally an agenda in process and a goal in mind. In these relationships I am usually a caregiver, counselor, or, at the very least, a sounding board.

Bill Hybels suggests that one way you might know you are in a draining relationship is that when you and your spouse have been invited over by such a couple or individual, you begin dinner at 7 P.M. and the first time you check your watch you discover that it is only 8 P.M. You cannot believe that more time has not passed. It sure seems like it has.

In Jesus' world, the first person from a requiring relationship who comes to mind is, you guessed it, Peter. Peter was what some might consider an EGR (Extra Grace Required) person. It is clear that Peter wanted Jesus' attention. His eagerness was often several steps ahead of his better judgment. This relationship required much of Jesus. Peter was one tough nut to crack.

On one occasion Peter proudly boasted that even if all the other disciples deserted Jesus he would remain bravely faithful (Luke

22:33). On another, he even took it upon himself to rebuke his leader and to correct his seeming misconceptions about his future (Matthew 16:22). Molding planets into shape was perhaps an easier task than changing the set-in-his-ways heart of this self-willed disciple. This relationship required much of Jesus, day in and day out.

2. *Reciprocating relationships.* These relationships are usually pretty much an emotional wash. In other words, you give some and receive some. When you leave the company of a reciprocating relationship you are generally not overly drained or deeply replenished. There is a give and a take to such acquaintances, a mutual respect and support.

I believe this was the type of relationship Jesus had with his cousin, John the Baptist. It is interesting to me that, by virtue of their concurrent heavenly callings, these two were not closer. At least the scriptural record does not reveal more than one or two encounters shared by these two daunting leaders. Certainly, John pointed the way to Christ via repentance, and yet once Jesus entered his ministry, we do not see John following Jesus himself.

Still there was an incredible sense of mutual respect between the two men. They affirmed and supported one another to those around them:

> **John the Baptist said of Jesus:** "But after me will come one who is more powerful than I, whose sandals I am not fit to carry. He will baptize you with the Holy Spirit and with fire" (Matthew 3:11).
> **Jesus said of John the Baptist:** "I tell you, among those born of women there is no one greater than John" (Luke 7:28).

3. *Replenishing relationships.* These are the relationships that are characterized by grace. They produce an atmosphere in which

nothing is expected of me. I am free to be myself. I don't have to mince and guard my words because I am not under a scrutinous eye. I am among friends. There is no agenda, no presupposed set of expectations. The purpose is just being together and sharing a piece of life. The goal is to relax, have fun, and just talk.

Grace flows freely in the company of a replenishing relationship. Such a person says to me, in essence, "I am what I am by the grace of God and you are what you are by the grace of God. I accept you. I just enjoy spending time with you. What would you like to talk about?" John certainly did not start out as this type of relationship in Jesus' life, but he soon found himself there.

Dinah Craik has described it well:

Oh the comfort, the inexpressible comfort
of feeling safe with another person.
Having neither to weigh thoughts nor measure words,
but pouring them all right out just as they are,
chaff and grain together
Certain that a faithful hand
will take and sift them, keep what is worth keeping
and with a breath of kindness blow the rest away.[3]

Lazarus was probably another truly replenishing friend to Jesus. The Master often routed his journeys intentionally to allow for a stopover at a particular home in Bethany. Certainly this was a treasured place in Jesus' world. It was here that he shared rich fellowship with his close friend Lazarus (whom the Bible says Jesus loved, John 11:36), and his sisters. This too was the blessed dwelling in which Mary sat at Jesus' feet and absorbed his every word, choosing "the better part" while an anguished Martha sweated it out in the kitchen. And it was in this precious place where Mary, too, sacrificed her much-prized alabaster jar of perfume only a few nights before Jesus' crucifixion and poured it over his feet, unknowingly anointing him for burial.

The events that took place in the Bethany home were different from every other event in the New Testament because they are pictures of people ministering to Jesus. Virtually every other picture in every other locale is of the Savior ministering to needs, not receiving ministry himself. So this place was unusually graced and blessed, because herein dwelt the replenishing relationships that brought Jesus the man much encouragement. Perhaps this is why when faced with Mary's grief over her deceased brother, Lazarus, Jesus found himself overcome: "Jesus wept" (John 11:35).

Perhaps the love that Lazarus and Mary offered to Jesus was special because it reached beyond what would be expected of the Son of God, their Messiah. It saw Jesus the man in his incarnate need to be accepted, encouraged, and affirmed. They dared to do what perhaps others thought impossible...they ministered to Jesus.

MINISTERING TO JESUS

John caught something I am convinced the other disciples missed. It was this secret that gave him the strength to follow Jesus all the way to the cross. He learned that his first ministry, his foremost duty, and his highest privilege, was ministering to Jesus. Too many Christians today have bought into what I call the Martha mind-set of service (Luke 10:38–42). Someone has said that we become so focused on the work of the Lord that we forget the Lord of the work. How sad, but how true.

If I walked in the front door after getting back from a long trip, how would I feel if I heard the following from my wife?

"Oh, hi again. Listen, I need the light replaced on the garage door, the garbage taken out, the front lawn mowed, and the disposal fixed. Do you think you could get that done tonight? I'm under a great deal of pressure and I really need your help."

Wait just a minute, I might think. *What was that? I have a few questions:*

Where's the love?
Where's the "welcome home"?
Where are the hugs and kisses?

And, yet, isn't that exactly what we do in prayer all too often? We bypass praise, adoration, and worship and go right to our laundry lists and honey-do lists. We make God into some kind of bank account or hired hand, instead of the object of our absolute honor and worship. This is not what Jesus shed his blood for. He had something much greater in mind.

We are made with a high purpose in mind: "the people I formed for myself that they may proclaim my praise" (Isaiah 43:21).

When I look into the faces of my four children, I do not love them because of their skills, talents, interests, or abilities; I love them because of who they are and because they belong to me. Did you know that absolutely nothing you do can make God love you any more than he does right now? Certainly there are steps of obedience you can take that allow you to experience more of his love, but his heart is already full of desire to bless you and share in a transforming friendship with you.

Expressing praise and worship to the Lord begins as we draw close to him in prayer and as we deeply consider the attributes of his wonderful character and how they impact and guide our lives continually. Serving the Lord is important, yes, but it is empty if it does not flow from an ever-deepening relationship with him. Prayer involves sharing our needs, yes, but so much more. It includes seasons of praise in which we rehearse his faithfulness to us in the past and present. It involves seasons of worship in which we get lost in our adoration over who he is and what he means to us. Worship means *worth-ship*. It is the place in which we ascribe the highest value to him above everything and everyone else.

John knew how to do more than just serve Jesus out of duty; he ministered not just *for* him, but *to* him as well. Is it any wonder that he was "the disciple whom Jesus loved"?

John also dared to do what others would not. When the other disciples sat around the table at the Last Supper, John dared to lean his back against the Savior's. He came close to Jesus. When everyone else fled the impending scene of Calvary's cross, John dared to journey down the Via Dolorosa to the bleeding side of his Lord. While the others were worried about their own skin, the "disciple whom Jesus loved" dared to care for Jesus' mother, Mary.

Culross continues:

He never puts himself forward in the sight of others, challenging observation, but yet is ever found by his Master's side in the hour of danger, quietly, and as of course; one of those who willingly offered themselves, and who did not turn back in the day of battle. Thus, on the night of the betrayal, he closely follows Jesus from the garden, goes in along with Him to the place of trial and judgment, and never for a moment falls away from Him. Peter, too, follows, but afar off, and takes his place with the officers and servants, as if he belonged to their company; and there lay his weakness and danger. John goes in with Jesus, quietly, and as a simple matter of course; and in this very cleaving to the Lord lay his safety. Again, at the crucifixion, he held his station near the cross of his Master all day, a witness of

His dreadful sufferings; exhibiting that rarest form of courage, which so few even of strong men are capable of the courage to stand still and look upon the sufferings of a beloved friend, protracted and intensifying from hour to hour, which we can do nothing whatever to relieve. Ah, it takes courage of the loftiest order for that![4]

What man could ever have a friend who would follow so closely and completely in the hour of blessing and the hour of devastation and not recognize how highly favored that friendship was? If expectation and requirement had been on John's mind that day, then the sight of a Savior bloodied and humiliated would have turned John away. If reciprocity—tit for tat—was the goal, the risk would be far too high and the benefit to John precarious. But if undying loyalty and the emotional replenishment of a friend who sticks closer than a brother were the motives, then the picture suddenly makes sense. Was Jesus' friendship with John one most highly prized and favored? Did John share a place of privilege? *I would think so.* And I can see why.

Chapter Eighteen

BREATHING LESSONS

If anyone is thirsty, let him come to me and drink.
Whoever believes in me,
as the Scripture has said, streams of living water
will flow from within him.

JESUS

JOHN 7:37–39

The Church has tragically neglected this great liberating truth—that
there is now for the child of God a full and wonderful
and completely satisfying anointing with the Holy Spirit.

A. W. TOZER

*P*amela had been told that if the baby weighed more than six
pounds she would need a C-section. Because of her small
frame, the doctor was certain that my wife would not be able to
deliver a large baby naturally. If she were to have a natural birth, she
was going to need some help to do so. That's where I came in.

Lamaze classes are an interesting experience for expectant
couples. One comedian has said, "I'm confused by these breathing
classes. I just don't get it. You can't just breathe an eight-pound
object out of your body."

The first time Pamela and I attended the classes, I wondered much the same. Little by little, however, I became convinced that such a feat was quite possible. The first thing I encountered when I entered the classroom was the sounds of lots of strange breathing.

La-ho, la-ha.

La-ho, la-ha.

To my amazement, these weren't chants, nor sounds of laughter. These were people practicing their breathing. Basically the classes taught us two things—to relax and to breathe. The promise made to us was that if we would work on relaxing and breathing then my wife's potential labor pain would be greatly reduced. It was even possible for her to deliver our baby without the use of pain-killing drugs.

Still, something about taking a class on how to breathe seemed a bit preposterous. Breathing is as natural as eating, isn't it? Perhaps even more so. After all, the first thing we all learn to do in life is breathe, right? Before a baby is even placed on her mother's breast, she first expands and contracts her lungs. There is no home study course, no website to peruse, and no instruction tapes to listen to. Who needs a course in something so automatic?

I had a few lessons to learn.

It wasn't long before I was discovering that the breathing I had been used to was different from what we were learning. By the first night of class, our instructor began to take us into the higher realms of Breathology. We studied *deep breathing, pant breathing, slow breathing, exhaling, cleansing breaths,* and all sorts of other types.

At one point, the wives were instructed to grab the husbands (or coaches, as we were called) by the tender area around the knee and steadily apply greater pressure until they were giving it all they had. The men, in turn, were to use one of the breathing techniques to focus and to lessen the pain (or should I say, heighten our pain threshold). This was quite a sight—a bunch of guys pinned down by their wives and hyperventilating. To my amazement, it worked like a charm. Breathing focused the mind and actually lessened the pain.

The Holy Spirit is the breath of God to the body of Christ, to every believer. Without him we cannot breathe spiritually, and without breath we cannot truly live. However, to live as overcomers and not merely survivors, in God's world God's way, we must learn to inhale the Spirit of God daily and to breathe deeply.

> And the LORD God formed man of the dust of the ground,
> and breathed into his nostrils the breath of life; and man
> became a living soul. (Genesis 2:7, KJV)

One of the most intimate occasions Jesus spent with his disciples after his resurrection, but prior to his ascension, involved breathing. While meeting with the Twelve, he "breathed on them and said, 'Receive the Holy Spirit'" (John 20:22). At the beginning of the Old Testament we see God taking dust from the earth, shaping the clay, and breathing into it the breath of life. When that happened, the Bible says that "man became a living soul" (Genesis 2:7, KJV). At the beginning of the New Testament church era, in like manner, Jesus breathed upon the clay again (now hardened by sin and rebellion) to bring it into life in the Spirit.

Jesus was focused on setting souls free, truly free. Free from sin, free from fear, free from themselves. Free to know God, free to serve God, free to share God.

It was during his earthly ministry, before he was crucified, that Jesus began to reveal his greatest wish for his followers. The first bold declaration of what he desired to impart to the souls of men took place one day at the Feast of Tabernacles in Jerusalem, in the face of a company of supporters and skeptics (John 7:25–44).

HITTING A GUSHER!

To set the scene, Christ had just told dozens of his followers that he would ultimately have to die. This came as a shock. Many were overwhelmed by such news and turned away. At this same time, the Jewish leaders were hot on Jesus' trail, determined to take his life. In order to gain more followers, Jesus' own brothers urged him to reenter Judea and do some public relations work. They told him, "No one who wants to become a public figure acts in secret. Since you are doing these [miracles], show yourself to the world" (John 7:4).[1]

It is clear what Jesus' brothers wanted him to do at this point in his ministry. *Bring in* CNN, CNBC, Larry King Live, *and* Nightline. *Get the cameras. Set up some photo ops. Line up the talk shows. Get a good publicist.*

Jesus, however, was not about to follow their counsel. Remember, he was breathing air much fresher than they. While they went on to Jerusalem, he chose to stay in Galilee. Not long after, however, he journeyed to the holy city on his own timetable—as John says, "not publicly, but in secret" (John 7:10). The city was abuzz with controversy. Everyone wanted to know, "Where is that man?" If there had been a "Twenty-Five Most Intriguing People" issue out that year, Jesus would have topped the list. Many wanted to welcome him and to learn from his teaching. Many more wanted to ridicule him, to reject him lock, stock, and barrel. Either way, he was the talk of the town. People watched every move he made and listened to every word he spoke. After all, when you're in the company of a man who heals blind eyes one day and commands storms to stop another, you don't know what he will do next.

Ultimately, on his own timetable and amid the annual feast, Jesus showed up. Everyone had wondered if he would come. He did. He came teaching right in the middle of the temple courts. Many were amazed at his authority, his teaching, and his insight.

The Jews asked, "How did this man get such learning without having studied?" (John 7:14).

Jesus responded readily:

My teaching is not my own. It comes from him who sent me. If any one chooses to do God's will, he will find out whether my teaching comes from God or whether I speak on my own. He who speaks on his own does so to gain honor for himself, but he who works for the honor of the one who sent him is a man of truth; there is nothing false about him. (John 7:16–18)

The man of truth confronted his critics even more clearly as the day went on:

Has not Moses given you the law? Yet not one of you keeps the law. Why are you trying to kill me? (John 7:19)

In order to appreciate the power and significance of what Jesus said and did that day, we need to consider a little more background of the Feast of the Tabernacles. This major celebration on Israel's worship calendar took place about six months before the Crucifixion that year. This annual autumn feast was designed to commemorate Israel's forty-year journey through the wilderness. The last day in particular climaxed a week of celebration, a week of high feasts. During this period, tents and little shelters were built from branches to house families in order to remember the Lord's leadership of their ancestors through the wilderness.

Tradition tells us of a climactic event called the Great Outpouring ceremony, which was a part of this festive week. At a decided time during the annual Feast of Tabernacles, the priests would take huge urns filled with water and simultaneously pour them from the top of the temple steps. Gallons and gallons of water would beautifully cascade out of the temple, down the steps, and toward the people. Remembering what a significant provision water was in the barren wilderness makes one appreciate this event all the more.

On the last day of the feast, probably just as the priests began to pour out their urns of water, joy would erupt among the people. When they poured the gallons of water from high atop the temple steps, the drama ran high as the Israelites lifted up praises to God. Imagine the excitement that even the children surely felt. It must have been a powerful and visual moment full of spiritual significance and imagery. The combination of bold vocal praise to God and the river-like flow of water from the temple was significant. It was apparently at this moment that Jesus raised his voice amid the crowd and forecasted a spiritual breakthrough:

> On the last and greatest day of the Feast, Jesus stood and said in a loud voice, "If anyone is thirsty, let him come to me and drink. Whoever believes in me, as the Scripture has said, streams of living water will flow from within him." (John 7:37–38)

It seems tremendously strategic, effective, and timely to me that he would prophesy this overflowing of the Holy Spirit in the lives of his followers at such a culturally significant moment. Viewing Jesus on a human level, I envision him surrounded by the Feast events, all have led up to this tremendously exciting and visual moment when the priests poured out gallons and gallons of water right down the steps of the temple. As the water flowed down the steps of that house of worship, it is as if the Lord saw the potential of having not just one structural temple, but millions and millions of spiritual temples all over the world. Out of their spirits ("inner-most beings") would flow, gush, and pour "rivers of living water." Such a thought was not meant to be whispered, but shouted loudly.

This was the joy and purpose of Christ—to release the hearts and souls of men, which were so accustomed to hindrances, chains, and sins, to the power and high purposes of God. Of all the Texas and California oil men who have ever struck oil, none of them saw in those moments what Jesus saw in this one. In this moment, Jesus could see that his life and ministry would ultimately tap a flow of life that would cover the planet and pour from the souls of men.

No religious leaders asked Jesus to take part in the Great Out-pouring ceremony that day. He had not been commissioned by man to do so. His name was not on the order of worship written out by the scribes and Pharisees. He asked no one for permission; he simply lifted his voice. He was on heaven's agenda that day. When you con-sider the significance of that moment and the vivid object lesson sur-rounding it, there was no more appropriate or meaningful moment for Jesus to prophesy the powerful coming work of the Holy Spirit than then and there. Just as John the Baptist had heralded the coming of the Messiah in the wilderness bold and unhindered, so now Jesus was heralding the coming of the Spirit in a liberated and authoritative manner.

No other Gospel writer records this epic moment; only John the Beloved. Surely it must have made an indelible impression on his mind and soul. But, then again, John was that disciple who was captivated with the fullness of what Jesus offered to his followers. This powerful event surely reemphasized for him the power and the joy afforded to the man or woman who would walk in intimate fellowship with Jesus. This was the work of the Holy Spirit, indeed. No other writer gave us a record of the most intimate promises of the coming Holy Spirit as he did. He must have often pondered this event in the years that passed between its occurrence and his writing.

RUNNING ON EMPTY

I'm convinced gas tanks are designed to go from half full to empty in a moment's time. Especially when you're stuck in rush-hour traffic, which happens often in Boston. When you're in a mad rush to get someplace fast, or when you're just flat out lost and motoring somewhere between Podunk Hollar and Timbuktoo, it is a tough time to run out of gas. Gas tanks just have no consideration whatsoever for daytimers, do they?

Years back my family and I were on our way to a church event when I realized that the red needle on the gas guage of my car had collapsed. Already pressed for time, I thought out loud, "Oh, boy, I'd better get some gas soon. We're running on fumes!" In an instant, our then eight-year-old, Kristin, came to the rescue with a sincere snap recommendation...

"Dad, just cover up the empty sign!"

"What did you say?" I replied.

"You know," Kristi echoed, "just put a piece of paper or something over the empty sign. That's all you need to do, Dad! Just cover up the empty sign!"

As quickly as my mind registered *ludicrous* to the suggestion, my heart signaled *indicted*. The sudden absurdity was overshadowed by a stunning profundity.

"Just cover up the empty sign!"

How often do we do just that in our life experience? Someone asks, "How's it going?" An urge to unload a bag full of honesty is subdued by a rhythmic response..."Just cover up the empty sign!" After all, how does an honestly empty heart express itself to a culture where synthetic fullness is fashionable? A friend asks, "How's the family?", "How's the job going?", "How is everything?" Do we answer honestly? I'm afraid that all too often we give a choreographed comeback…"Oh fine! Just fine!"

What exactly does *fine* mean, anyway? Could someone please tell me? Can we define *fine?* Is *fine* better than *good,* but not as good as *great?* Is it a synonym for *mediocre* or *semi-good?* Or is "Fine!" just another way of "covering up the empty sign"?

INTIMATE PROMISES

If the Sermon on the Mount (Matthew 5–7) is considered Jesus' best known discourse and his most theologically significant one, then the one recorded in John 14 through 17 is his most intimate and personal. These four chapters contain a flowing message from Jesus to the hearts of his followers, interrupted only by four questions he was asked.

This discourse took place at his most climactic meeting with his disciples—the Last Supper. Much happened at this table.

Jesus confided in his disciples more than ever before.

The Lord washed the soiled feet of his followers, even those of Judas.

He revealed the identity of his betrayer.

He revealed the identity of a three-time denier.

This was Jesus' last chance to speak to all of his followers together. After this he knew they would fall apart, at least temporarily, as his passion unfolded. So, Jesus revealed much in these four chapters, none more significant than what he told them about the coming Holy Spirit.

There are at least ten promises to behold in the sacred words of these chapters. Any follower of Christ wanting to grow in intimacy with Jesus would be wise not only to read, but to ponder, these promises.

Promise No. 1.—*Jesus was going to his "Father's house" to get heaven ready for us; The Holy Spirit would be soon coming into our houses to get us ready for heaven (John14:1–2, 16).* Jesus was concerned not for himself but for his disciples as he prepared for his final day. He seemed to be focused on assuring his devoted followers that even though he would be leaving them for a while, they would not be alone. The scene reminds me of the many times we have had to leave our children with a trusted baby-sitter, and of the conversations that have coincided with those moments:

"You guys are gonna' be just fine."

"We'll be back very soon."

"You are really going to like the sitter we've selected."

"Don't worry."

"We will be just a phone call away."

The difference is that Jesus' departure was not "to get a break from the kids for a while." And the "sitter" was not sent just to keep everyone in a holding pattern. No, once again he would be doing what he did best—not only saving us, but serving us. While Jesus is preparing every believer's dwelling place in heaven, the Spirit is tidying up the Lord's dwelling place in our souls.

Promise No. 2.—*Having faith in Jesus would cause us to do the works of Christ, and even greater works (John 14:12).* It is important that we ponder God's view of what "greater" is and means. Certainly in our world and mind-set, bigger is better. Perhaps a portion of the greater would be that no longer would the fullness of the Godhead at work on earth be limited to the one incarnate body of the Messiah, but to the multiplied millions of members of the Spirit-filled body of Christ. The multiplying influence and potential of the Holy Spirit was explosive, as the early church proved.

Promise No. 3.—*Jesus loves to answer our prayers because it brings glory to the Father (John 14:13).* The Bible describes Jesus and the Holy Spirit as intercessors (Romans 8:27, 34). It seems they are always petitioning heaven on our behalf. This intimate promise reminds us that when the Spirit indwells us, Christ is greatly motivated to answer our prayers. Too often, we seem to feel that God looks at us reluctantly as we pray. Our limited use of prayer demonstrates that we view God as a stingy and restrictive tyrant, not as a gracious and loving Father. In this intimate moment, Jesus not only told them he could answer prayer, he told them he would and exactly why. The Holy Spirit wants to help us pray...and to pray in the Spirit.

Promise No. 4.—*Our love for Jesus is best shown not by our words, but by our obedience to him (John 14:15, 23–24).* Remembering the promise given by Jeremiah, that a day would come when the law of God would be written in our hearts (Jeremiah 31:31–33), helps us to add significance to Christ's words recorded here. The Holy Spirit would place the will of God within us and write it upon the intent and motive mechanisms of our souls. What had been duty would now become desire. Rock tablets would turn into righteous tendencies. The true followers of Jesus would be marked by bold and willing obedience. This would be the guarantee and authenticator of our love for him.

Promise No. 5.—*Jesus will ask the Father to send the Holy Spirit to us, to help us and to always be with us (John 14:16).* That day Jesus assured them that he would not leave empty the places that he had earlier occupied in the disciples' lives. By his Spirit, he would enter into an even more personal and intimate relationship with his people. Before, as he walked the earth and made disciples, he had by choice limited his presence to the confines of one human body. The stakes of his tent went no further, in a human sense, than yours and mine. His return in the person of the Holy Spirit would increase his potential influence in our lives exponentially. As he had taught, now he would not just be *with* them, he would be *in* them. When temptation came, they would not have to wait for him to arrive (as did Mary when Lazarus died); he would be in a relationship in which he would never leave them nor forsake them (Hebrews 13:5). He would be not only their life, but their very breath.

Promise No. 6.—*One of the Spirit's primary purposes in our lives is to show us the truth (John 14:17; 16:13).* The Scripture makes it quite clear that the Christian's greatest enemy is not the world, the flesh, or the devil...it is his own evil heart. For this is the weakened place within us that the world finds so *adoring,* the flesh finds so *appealing,* and the devil finds so prone to *yielding.*

> The heart is deceitful above all things and beyond cure ["desperately wicked", KJV]. Who can understand it? (Jeremiah 17:9)

The words of a well-known hymn say it well: "Prone to wander. Lord, I feel it. Prone to leave the God I love." The man or woman who would walk with God in this world must learn to desire more than the grace of God, as wonderful as that is. He must desire, and solicit, the truth of God. All the truth. That is, the truth about God and his will for me, the truth about myself and my weaknesses and struggles, and the truth about the world in which I live. The wise Christian will not only wait for the Spirit to show him the truth, he will offer to it a daily invitation.

Promise No. 7.—*The Holy Spirit will teach us and remind us of what Jesus has said (John 14:26; 16:14–15).* A Christian is someone who studies the Word, the Bible, but he is more than that. A Christian is someone who has the Teacher within. Our eyes read the words of God emblazoned upon paper; the Holy Spirit breathes the living Word of God within our souls. There was a day in history when the written Word of God did not exist as we know it. Today you can go into a bookstore and pick up almost every type of Bible or study Bible conceivable, but that has not always been the case. However, even before the printing press was invented, the Word of God was alive and well.

As Tozer has written:

> The Bible is the written word of God, and because it is written it is confined and limited by the necessities of ink and paper and leather. The Voice of God, however, is alive and free as the sovereign God is free. "The words that I speak unto you, they are spirit, and they are life." The life is in the speaking words. God's word in the Bible can have power only because it corresponds to God's word in the universe. It is the present Voice which makes the written Word all-powerful. Otherwise it would lie locked in slumber within the covers of a book.[2]

Promise No. 8.—*The Holy Spirit will convict the world of "sin and righteousness and judgment" (John 16:8–11).* This promise lets us know that evangelism, or leading people to Christ, is not some type of sales job. We are the communicators; the Holy Spirit is the Convincer and the Convicter. Jesus promises us that the Spirit will convince the world of "sin", or of what we have done wrong. He will convince them of "righteousness," or of what he says is right. And, ultimately, he convinces of "judgment," or of the day when he will settle accounts. The Spirit-filled follower of Christ can live out his faith with confidence and boldness knowing that as he or she communicates the good news of Christ, the Spirit will make it real within the hearts of the willing hearers. Ours is a partnership with the third person of the Trinity, in which we work together to call others into intimacy with the Savior.

Promise No. 9.—*The Spirit will enable us to tell others about Jesus Christ (John 14:26–27).* God wants us to naturally and effectively share our faith in Jesus Christ with people who don't know him. It was never meant to be artificial, automated, or in any way synthetic. Jesus promised his followers that the "Spirit will come and help you...The Spirit will teach you everything and will remind you of what I said" (John 4:26, CEV). He was making clear that our experience of intimacy and closeness to Christ, enabled by the Holy Spirit, will cause us to want to express this marvelous gift to others. The ability to do so powerfully and authentically will come because of our cultivation of friendship with Jesus. Acts 1:8 says: "But the Holy Spirit will come upon you and give you power. Then you will tell everyone about me" (Acts 1:8, CEV).

Promise No. 10.—*The Spirit will lead us to a joy that no one will ever be able to change (John 16:22).* At the end of Jesus' promises regarding the Holy Spirit he brings us back into the birthing room:

> When a woman is about to give birth, she is in great pain. But after it is all over, she forgets the pain and is happy, because she has brought a child into the world. You are now very sad. But later I will see you, and you will be so happy that no one will be able to change the way you feel. (John 16:21–22, CEV)

Birthing a baby is precipitated by wells and roller coasters of emotion. The feelings a woman walks through in the months and in the hours that precede a baby's birth are tumultuous indeed. Mountains of joy. Valleys of indifference. Deep feelings of attachment. Shattering feelings of detachment. Preparations to make. Priorities to adjust. Pain to endure. Through it all, life appears. And that life puts it all into perspective. Purpose is added to the pain. It was important to Jesus in this intimate discourse to leave his disciples with a higher hope. He knew that in the days that would soon follow, they would scatter and their emotions would shatter. A cross was coming. Their tight community was on the brink of crisis. Their hopes would diminish, but out of the debris his hopes for them would emerge. Their vision of Jesus would be erased, but the Spirit would paint one much more vivid. The pieces to the parabolic puzzle he had given them would start to come together and a kingdom would emerge. As they prepared to step onto the emotional ride of their lives, Jesus knew that the first length of track was a deeper drop than any of them could imagine. He hoped they would first take a deep breath. And so, he took them to a mountain, to Calvary, to a place of promise where joy would strike a high chord and never let go.

Oh yes, by the way, Pamela did have that baby. Bigger than expected. Eight pounds, thirteen ounces. The birth: natural. No pills. No saddle-blocks. No epidurals. Just lots of breathing.

PART FOUR

JESUS.
MY CONSUMING
DESIRE

Chapter Nineteen

ONCE YOU'VE SEEN
THE GLORY

[They] went up onto a mountain to pray and they saw his glory.
LUKE 9:28B, 32B

Grace is glory in the bud.
C. H. SPURGEON

What goes up must come down, right? On one cool September day in Colorado Springs, a dozen first-time rock climbers staked their lives on it.

I was attending a church evangelism conference called Reaching the Unreached with pastors and lay leaders from all over the country. During a free-time late-morning stroll, I was admiring the huge rock formations called glens. As I drew closer, I recognized a group of people who were climbing high, laughing, and seemingly having the time of their lives. The closer I got the more I realized how incredibly steep the pitch of the mountain was, a virtual wall. As I panned to the top, I recognized the lead man. It was one of the pastors attending the event and, man, he was on the move! Get the picture? Here's this pastor and these sheep climbing behind him...up the mountain. And you could hear comments amid the chuckles:

"Piece of cake!"

"This is a lot easier than I thought."

"Nothing to it. No problem."

This group was motivated. To listen to them you would never know they were in any danger. After all, the guy at the front was their pastor. Surely he would take care of them. What was there to worry about? By now, however, they were a hundred and fifty feet up, and I wondered how they were going to get down.

Before long the brisk climb turned to a snail's pace and the confident climbers did not look so confident any more. The reason? Someone had done something none of them had yet attempted: He'd looked down. It was becoming clear to them, as it had to the growing bunch of us watching them from the ground, that they were not going to be able to get back down. The cliff was too steep, they were too far up, and the footings were too hard to spot.

The only word I could hear the climbing pastor muster for his frightened flock was "uh oh." Not very reassuring. Not particularly inspiring.

We reasoned that surely the guide could get them down. No doubt such a group would not have ventured up without a skilled leader. As it turned out, the pastor leading the pack had left faith far behind and had ventured far onto the path of presumption. He was, in fact, pretty inexperienced at climbing...but he was the only guide they had.

Then I heard the fear set in:

"What are we going to do?"

"How are we going to get down?"

"I can't believe this is happening!"

I kept waiting for the complaints to fly.

Within minutes the news teams began to arrive: ABC, CBS, and

NBC. The local reporters had seized upon what would be the lead human interest story that night. The onlooking crowd grew in size. Not far behind the media was the local rescue climber squad. The rescuers were climbing up by rope and rappelling each of the frightened sheep down one by one.

In the interviews that followed, the reporters' favorite question was: "How did you get into this fix?" The response was always: "Well, our pastor told us we could do this. He thought we could handle it."

Now, does that sound like your idea of a relaxing retreat?

If you're like me, you're thinking…"No, thanks. Give me a warm beach, a nice chair, and a great novel, instead."

Well, despite our aversion to the idea, many would opt for climbing in strange and difficult places. For some reason they see something in this kind of adventure that I just do not. It seems that their eyeglass lenses carry a far different prescription than mine.

What I see is…

Risk.
Foolhardiness.
Fear.
Stress.
Struggle.

What they see goes something more like…

Challenge.
Adventure.
Daring.
Boldness.
Compulsion.
Purpose.

The question arises: How can two people made by the same God and living on the same planet have such diametrically opposed perspectives?

The answer?

In a word...*passion*. The only difference is the nature of their inner compelling drive, a hunger in the heart of one which the other has never known and may never know, nor understand. To some, the mountain must be climbed because it is there; they are compelled to feel it under their feet. To others, there is a contentment to simply have that mountain in their view. While one is completely unsatisfied until he or she fully experiences its enormity, the other is perfectly happy to simply ponder its majesty.

MEETING GOD ON A MOUNTAIN

Mountains have played a significant part in the lives of men in the Bible. It almost seems that when God wanted to speak to a man, he brought him to a mountain. Even the psalmist wrote, "I lift up my eyes to the hills—where does my help come from?" (Psalm 121:1). Certainly mountains had a prominent part in the life of our Lord. Jesus preached a famous sermon from a mountain. He often returned there to pray. In fact, he died on a mountain called Golgotha. After his Resurrection, he met his disciples on the Mount of Olives. He actually ascended to heaven from that spot and, as the Scripture prophesies, he will one day touch down on that mountain at his Second Coming.

Moses met God on a mountain. It was on Mt. Sinai that God gave the leader of Israel the Ten Commandments. On at least one occasion when Moses descended from the mountain, his face was physiologically aglow. It actually shone with the very glory of God (Exodus 34:29–35).

Something happened on Mt. Sinai. Something weighty. Something between God and man. Something earth shattering and soul shaking. Something was imparted from the heart of heaven to the soul of a man. A transformation took place. In Moses' case, God radiated his glory to a fallen planet, from the face of a man to the faces of mankind.

CAPTURING THE GLORY

Surmounting Mt. Everest is an achievement that rides high among the glories of man. Ascending the hill of the Lord is a process essential to sharing in the greater glory of God. When Moses took this journey in response to God's call, his very countenance changed as he drew closer to God. The look on his face was different. His eyes brightened. His face shone. It was as if a part of the veil had been pulled back from the Holy of Holies.

The same thing happened when Stephen faced an angry mob of religious intolerants. The glory he received impacted his behavior. It touched the way he looked ("his face was like the face of an angel," Acts 6:15). It transformed what his eyes beheld (he saw "Jesus standing at the right hand of God," Acts 7:55). And it affected what he by grace did not see (his enemies, their accusations, and their stones). In short, the glory made the difference. And perhaps the brightest glory that radiated from a bloodied and bruised Stephen was his intense love for and awareness of Jesus. Even as his hateful persecutors pelted his body with stones, a deep love opened his eyes wide to see Jesus amid the storm.

But it seems that Jesus' transfiguration was the highest expression of God's glory on earth. If Jesus' glory was normally subdued by the veil of his human flesh, then the veil was lifted on the mountain that day as three men watched: Jesus' confidants—Peter, James, and John.

We find the account of this event in Matthew 17:1–13, Mark 9:2–13, and Luke 9:28–36.

Glory Days!

God called John to a mountain one day. And not just any mountain, but the mountain upon which Jesus would be transfigured. The cloak of the Savior's humanity would be temporarily peeled back so that he could more fully commune with heaven. The majesty of his Sonship would shine as never before and, most amazing of all, the eyes of John would behold the sight. Matthew says of this event that the face of Jesus "shone like the sun" (Matthew 17:2). Mark records that "his clothes became dazzling white, whiter than anyone in the world could bleach them" (Mark 9:3). Luke asserts that "as he was praying, the appearance of his face changed, and his clothes became as bright as a flash of lightning" (Luke 9:29).

All three of the synoptic writers record that at this mountain meeting, Moses and Elijah appeared and talked with Jesus.

My, oh my, what John must have seen! Most interesting is the fact that although being the only Gospel writer who was invited to join Jesus on that mountain, John is the only one who chose not to report the event in the Gospel bearing his name. Perhaps some things are too holy to describe. Too precious to pen. Too sacred to transport on the temporal river of human dialect. After all, how can one describe the very glory of God? Certainly, however, John held this experience ever precious to his soul.

God's glory to man has been revealed as the perceived presence of Christ. The actual Hebrew word for "glory" is *kabod*, which means "weighty," "heavy," "impressive," or "worthy."

Without a doubt, John saw the glory of God.

He said it all in just a few words: "We have seen his glory, the glory of the One and Only, who came from the Father, full of grace and truth" (John 1:14b).

As Jesus walked the planet, the unbelieving saw only a carpenter from Nazareth. The believing, however, saw in Jesus' person and in his actions the ultimate unveiling of God himself. It was he, after all, who said, "Anyone who has seen me has seen the Father" (John 14:9b).

As Jesus proceeded to climb the mountain with the triumvirate (Peter, James, and John), the moment was more than significant; it was climactic and pivotal. The cross was soon approaching. The plot against Jesus was thickening. The air was tensing. The approaching conflict held cosmic implications.

Peter had just confessed that Jesus was the Messiah (Luke 9:18–20).

Jesus had just confided that he would soon face death (Luke 9:21–22).

And Christ had just spelled out the parameters of discipleship...the specifics of what it would mean to walk with him:

> Then he said to them all: "If anyone would come after me, he must deny himself and take up his cross daily and follow me. For whoever wants to save his life will lose it, but whoever loses his life for me will save it. What good is it for a man to gain the whole world, and yet lose or forfeit his very self [own soul]? If anyone is ashamed of me and my words, the Son of Man will be ashamed of him when he comes in his glory and in the glory of the Father and of the holy angels." (Luke 9:23–26)

These moments on the Mount of Transfiguration were like none other. In the valley, Jesus had faced ridicule and rejection; on the mountain that day, he received support and encouragement. In the valley, Jesus had worked at building the men who would follow him; on the mountain, he rested in the company of the men who had gone before him. In the valley, he had been putting the wraps on his earthly mission; on the mountain, he was eyeing the gates of his heavenly destination.

CRYSTAL WINDOWS

The glory of God brought out the best in John. If you could have peered into the depths of his soul, you would have observed glorious shades of love for Jesus. James Culross describes it vividly:

> We must look for those qualities and characteristics whereon the love of the Son of God rested…These qualities are nowhere catalogued in a formal way, and we are left to discover them from what we know of the Lord Himself. They must have been qualities in which He could take delight, such as the tender and delicate sensibility of the Apostle's nature, his profound and pure affectionateness, his childlike simplicity, as if you looked through crystal windows into his soul, the deep truthfulness of his spirit, his gentleness and holiness, his reverence, his capacity of meeting and returning the love of which he was the object with undivided heart.[1]

"GLORY IN THE BUD"

What heaven saw in the soul of John, Christ's grace and glory drew forth. What God's grace *appoints* for a man, his glory *anoints* in a man. Charles Spurgeon defined grace as "glory in the bud."

And what is it that makes up for our shortcomings? What fills the gaps? What gets us beyond ourselves and into the Promised Land?

One thing. The grace of God. His glory at work in our lives.

Jesus proves this in paramount fashion. God's grace appeared within his life at its greatest just before his darkest hour, the Cross.

THAT MOMENT

My mind reels with wonderment over just what John saw and experienced from the box seat Jesus gave him at his transfiguration:

Was this the launching pad location of a life given to God, sinless and heaven bound? Did this catapult Christ into a deeper phase of ministry? Did a booster rocket fall off here?

Was this the place where Jesus came to count the cost of the cross?

Was Jesus so close to being transported to heaven that Moses and Elijah had come as chaperones?…or did they come as coaches?

If the baptism of Jesus was his inauguration into ministry, was the Mount of Transfiguration his coronation into a greater glory?

Would Moses discover that day the real meaning of the word promise *in Promised Land when he for the first time felt much anticipated Promised Land soil between his toes?*

Did God want Moses' eyes, that had seen thousands of Passover lambs slaughtered for the sins of the people, to behold not just a lamb of God, but the Lamb of God?

Would Elijah offer the encouragement of another prophet, the original forerunner who knew how to face a whole nation of people who had turned against God with nothing but a fiery prayer and a pure heart?

And what did they talk about (Moses, Elijah, and Jesus) on that mountain while the disciples were sleeping?

JOURNEY TO GLORY

First and foremost, Christians are people who are on a journey toward the glory of Christ. Paul says that "we reflect the Lord's glory." This is because we "are being transformed into his likeness with ever-increasing glory, which comes from the Lord, who is the Spirit" (2 Corinthians 3:18). Paul describes our process of growing in God this way: "Those he predestined, he also called; those he called, he also justified; those he justified, he also glorified" (Romans 8:30). David said: "You are a shield around me, O LORD; you bestow glory on me and lift up my head" (Psalm 3:3, CEV).

John caught the mystery that Jesus is so generous that he longs to share his glory with his people. In the letter he penned to the "angel of the church in Laodicea" (Revelation 3:14) this incredible promise: "To him who overcomes, I will give the right to sit with me on my throne, just as I overcame and sat down with my Father on his throne" (Revelation 3:21).

A Master who not only demands worship, he also desires to share some of his glory with his people. Incredible to ponder. Most miss it. John caught it and caught it deeply.

Second, the glory comes to those who pray. Jesus climbed mountains for one reason and one alone: to pray, to renew his close walk with God, and to seek the face of God amid the challenges of life.

The account of the Transfiguration is introduced this way: "About eight days after Jesus said this, he took Peter, John and James with him and went up onto a mountain to pray" (Luke 9:28).

J. Oswald Sanders asks an important question:

> Could any of the twelve have been among that favored group? Were the three specially selected by the Lord? With him there is no caprice or favoritism. Their relationship with Him was the result of their own choice, conscious or unconscious. It is a sobering thought that we too are as close to Christ as we really choose to be. The deepening intimacy of the three with Jesus was the result of the depth of their response to His love and training.[2]

Third, the glory brings out the best in a man. We humans all have this in common: We have a soul. Even Adolf Hitler and Mother Teresa had this in common. The soul is the place within every person that God longs to fill and flow through. It is the part of us that hungers to taste of the glory and the presence of God himself.

> "As he [Jesus] was praying, the appearance of his face changed, and his clothes became as bright as a flash of lightning." (Luke 9:29)

The Scripture tells us that when Moses came down from Sinai, his face was so aglow with the glory of God that it had to be covered with a veil. Something so powerful happened when he was in the presence of God that it caused his face to glow, to radiate that glory, for some time after.

Stephen, the first martyr of the church, while presenting a solid defense of the faith, was stoned by his accusers. They threw harsh words at him and pelted his body with rocks. The Bible says that while they did that his face became like the face of an angel and he looked up into heaven and saw Jesus standing next to God. As his outer body perished, the inner man began to glow even more. The spirit was engaging, the flesh disengaging. He wasn't overly impressed with his enemies, his accusers, or even the stones they were throwing at him. Why? Because he was riveted on the glory of God in the face of Christ. He was awestruck with the wonder, the power, and the love of Jesus. The glory of God was once again bringing out the best in a man.

All of this is enveloped in the fact that we are on a journey toward the glory of Christ. John wrote, "The Word became flesh and made his dwelling among us. We have seen his glory, the glory of the One and Only, who came from the Father,…" (John 1:14).

Jesus doesn't want to keep his glory to himself. He wants to give it as the engagement ring—or the wedding ring—to his bride, the church. He wants her to wear his glory. He wants to endow you and me with his glory. Remember, Jesus promised that "to him who overcomes, I will give the right to sit with me on my throne" (Revelation 3:21). Not just at his feet, but "*with* me *on* my throne." You say, "That's overwhelming!" Certainly it is, but that's the grace of God. That's what he wants to give to you and me. This thing called Christianity is not just about making a decision or taking out a fire insurance policy. It is about getting to know the Lord and loving him with all your heart, mind, soul, and strength, and watching the power and presence of his glory emerge in you as a person. It is something spiritual and powerful.

Picture the moment with me: Peter, James, and John are on this mountain with the Lord and they're asleep. Little did they know all that was going on while they slept. They would have loved to listen in on that conversation, I'm sure. Moses, Elijah, and Jesus talking! And then "when they became fully awake," they saw that Jesus was changing physically. His glory was appearing.

Suddenly, Jesus is transfigured. The cocoon is momentarily removed, perhaps slightly, and the butterfly almost emerges. The veil is pulled back and the disciples look up and see the glory of Jesus. They see a Jesus they have never seen before. They have watched him feeding the hungry. They have watched him laying hands on people and them being healed. But that was only a tidbit. Now Jesus is covered with glory. The glory of God is all over him and within him and breaking forth around him and surrounding Moses and Elijah. The whole mountain is encompassed with the glory of God.

Wouldn't you love to have measured the size of their eyeballs in that moment?

Matthew uses the word *glory* four times in his Gospel. Mark uses it three times. Luke uses it nine times. But John uses it eighteen times. He was impressed with the glory of God because he was on that mountain. Of the four writers, he was the one who actually saw it. The body is designed to display the glory of God. That's what God made us for.

THE GRIME AND THE GLORY

The spirit of man and the Spirit of God act powerfully upon the body and show themselves through it. Positive and negative attitudes project themselves through the countenance of a person. Love gleams. Indignation flashes. Anger flares. Concern radiates. Scorn and hatred constrict. Hope shines. Disappointment pales. All the passions that are allowed to fuel the soul come forth and show themselves in the eyes, through the lips, and upon the countenance of a man or woman. Holiness is, in itself, a transfiguring influence.

Christ's glory in us shines. There is no getting away from it: Inward excellence is the source of true outward beauty. Clinique and Maybelline have yet to come up with a make-up that can hide sin on a person. Someone has said, "Beauty is only skin deep...but ugly goes to the bone!" I disagree. Ugly goes deeper. Ugly goes to the spirit! No tailoring, cosmetics, or perfume will make beautiful the face and form behind which beats an ugly heart. Selfishness and pride and bitterness will never look anything but unsightly and repulsive. On the contrary, the godly thoughts that breathe, the Christ-inspired feelings that glow, the Word-nourished spirit that animates, and the character that shines through—these are the things that beautify, adorn, make truly attractive, and win confidence and love. These are the most valuable things to care for, tend to, cultivate, and cherish.

To paraphrase Matthew 16:26, "What good shall it do for a man if he gains the whole world and loses the person he is inside? What shall it profit a man? Not a thing."

We watch the stars of the sky and we are intrigued with those that are the brightest and glow the most. What about heaven's inhabitants? What do they look at? I think they look for the souls that radiate the life of Christ the most. They view us as "children of God without fault in a crooked and depraved generation, in which [we] shine like stars in the universe" (Philippians 2:15). Spiritually, God is building a constellation right here on this planet, and he is calling men and women to let him fuel their souls with the life of his presence, changing them from the inside out.

THE SEVEN WONDERS OF JOHN'S WORLD

When John Ashcroft entered the governor's mansion of Missouri for the first afternoon he would spend as governor, there were a few surprises in store. Shortly before dinner, the resident butler inquired as to what kind of wine the new governor would like to have with his dinner.

"Oh, you have alcohol in the governor's mansion?" the new governor responded.

"Of course, Governor. Is there a problem?" the worker replied.

"Why, yes, now that you mention it. There is. You see, I'm a teetotaller. I would like you to get rid of all the alcohol in the mansion. We won't be needing it."

The next day the St. Louis newspaper front page read like this: "Miracle in Governor's Mansion: Ashcroft Changes Wine into Water!"

I love that story. It's a true one, by the way, and it leads us to the topic of miracles.

Of all the miracles that took place under Jesus' ministry on earth, John chose to record only seven of them. These seven, however, were quite significant in his mind. Each of them was placed in his Gospel account not so much to teach a lesson, I believe, but to make an impression. To John, each act of power was more than a miracle. Each miracle was, in fact, an unfolding of more of the glory of God in the person of Christ. They were much more than an act of power, they were a display of the overwhelming love of the God he served. While others were amazed, John was enchanted. While others saw a wonder performed, John saw a kingdom imparted. While some saw them as gifts from the *hand* of God, John saw among them glorious glimpses of the *face* of God.

Jesus was a worker of miracles and John the Beloved saw that. He had eyes to see the miracles and much more. Uniquely in his Gospel, when he lists the miracles, he describes them as *signs* (John 2:11a). But signs of what? John answers that question for us: "[Jesus] thus revealed his glory, and his disciples put their faith in him" (2:11b). There is much talk about miracles in our world today, much fascination and intrigue. Let us look more closely at each of them through John's eyes.

The first place Jesus chose to reveal his glory (work a miracle) was not in a synagogue service, not at a prayer meeting, not even during an evangelistic crusade. He worked his first miracle at a wedding (John 2:1–11). He seemed reluctant when Mary involved him in the need. But before the day was over, something more than just wine would be out of the bottle. This, the first of his miraculous signs, clearly accomplished much more in John's mind than the obvious. The obvious is, we know, that at what could have been an embarrassing moment when the families of the bride and groom ran out of wine, Jesus overcame the problem and turned it into a wonderful moment for teaching (2:11). This wonder *revealed Jesus Christ as Lord over material substance* as he changed the water physiologically into wine. The operative phrase for the faithful follower of Jesus here is "do whatever he tells you," as Mary wisely advised.

The second wonder Jesus performed and John recorded was the healing of the royal official's son (John 4:46–54). In this instance, John recalled that a certain royal official whose son was ill with great fever encountered Christ and his healing power without ever going near him. He not only asked Jesus for a miracle, he begged. Jesus' response was not one brimming with compassion, but seeming disgust. He rebuked the man and then provided the miracle. At this point, the word was out: Jesus was the miracle worker. And yet, clearly, Jesus rebuked the official because he "didn't want the kingdom to become a side-show attraction."[3] He wanted to do more than hand out quick answers to temporal problems; he had come to, first and foremost, save souls. This act of grace, this glory-demonstrating miracle, however, clearly *revealed Jesus as Master over distance and space*. Faith was released at a specific point: "The man took Jesus at his word and departed." His son was healed.

The third wonder John recorded was Jesus' healing of the paralytic at the pool (John 5:1–9). This pathetic man, an invalid for thirty-eight years, had placed all of his hope in what seemed to be a superstitious healing legend. His feeble hope required that a man enter the pool of Bethesda at the time the water stirred. It was believed that these stirrings were caused by angels and would supposedly bring a healing to the lucky one who entered. Ironically, of course, the paralytic did not have the ability to place himself in the pool. Ultimately, Jesus enabled this man to walk. In John's eyes this miracle *revealed Jesus as Lord over time and space*. The contact point was clear: "Get up...pick up your mat...and walk."

The fourth wonder John saw and recorded is better known: the feeding of the five thousand (John 6:1–14). After they had observed him performing various miracles and teaching, a large crowd had apparently followed Jesus a far distance and they were now hungry.

The disciples calculated that feeding them was financially impossible. Once again, their impossibilities became Christ's agenda. That day Jesus multiplied the sack lunch of a young boy and fed a virtual city. To John, this *revealed Jesus as the Master over quantity of need and as the multiplier of our small gifts.* The point of contact involved yielding to Jesus, giving him what you have.

The fifth wonder was perhaps the most astounding—walking on water (John 6:16–21). Certainly the memory of the storm was vivid to John. After all, he had been in the boat when it brewed up. He, like the other disciples, was afraid. What amazed him the most was not that Jesus walked on the water, nor that Peter did. Instead, he seemed to be in awe of how this act *revealed Jesus as the Lord even of the storm.* And the secret to walking through the storm? Looking to Jesus.

The sixth wonder was the healing of the man born blind (John 9:1–12, 41). This miracle *revealed Jesus as the one who opens eyes.* Jesus was always opening eyes, physically and spiritually. Wherever he went, he always left people with a transformed view. And the act of faith he required? "Go...and...wash."

The seventh wonder was the raising of Lazarus (John 11:1–46). Mary and Martha faced a mountain of their own prior to their miracle. Their mountain, at first, appeared to be Jesus' tardiness despite their blazing need. As Ken Gire has expressed it:

> But Mary and Martha can't see backstage in heaven. All they can see is an expansive, black curtain drawn across their lives. They sit at home, despondent, as in an empty theater, their tearful prayers returning to them like hollow echoes off indifferent walls.
>
> It has been four days since their brother has died, but a mountain of grief still looms before them. It is a steep climb for the two sisters, and they feel they will never get over it.[4]

While the world marveled that a dead man's body was dead no more, John saw something much more significant. This wonder had *revealed Jesus as the resurrection and the life himself*. The wonder is not simply a dead man walking, but the one whose presence can conjure such. And the Lord who causes corpses to rise and walk also weeps. Wonder of wonders. And the faith point of contact: simple belief in Jesus.

The mountain changed John's whole view. Without the mountain, his soul was too earthbound and his eyes much too landlocked. He was too close to earth and not near enough to heaven. It took a trip to a mountain to change his view.

Landlocked eyes saw a second glass of wine being poured from a water jug; Illumined ones saw the hand that poured it.

Landlocked eyes saw that the royal official's son was better; illumined ones considered the words that had authority over distance.

Landlocked eyes watched a paralytic take his first paces; illumined ones pondered the one who was unhindered by the dictates of time and space.

Landlocked eyes saw five thousand people eat from one boy's lunchbox; illumined ones were awestruck by how Jesus could do so much with so little.

Landlocked eyes were amazed that Jesus taught Peter to walk on water; illumined ones considered that eyes of faith make great flotation devices.

Landlocked eyes were stunned to watch a dead man walking; illumined ones were amazed to behold the one whose words could make it so.

Eyes that never rise above the gravity pull of life, that never climb a mountain and look about, miss much.

Sometimes the view from a mountain can be spectacular.

Chapter Twenty

THE JESUS
JOHN SAW

[H]is eyes looked like flames of fire.
REVELATION 1:14, CEV

*Bad religion answers the unanswerable;
good religion cherishes the mystery.*
MARTIN DALBY

*J*ohnny had been working on his drawing longer than all of the other students in Mrs. Sorenson's kindergarten class. Her assignment, given some twenty minutes earlier, was to draw a picture of something or someone important to them. As the interested teacher walked back to Johnny's desk for the third time, she put her arm around his shoulder and asked, "Johnny, what are you drawing?" Without looking up, he said, "God."

"But, Johnny," the teacher responded, "no one knows what God looks like."

"They will in just a minute," he said.

SNAPSHOTS OF JESUS

Jesus wore an earth suit as he walked the planet, and yet we have no instances within Scripture of anyone, anywhere, at anytime endeavoring to give us any descriptions of what he *looked* like.

Imagine. With the multitudes of words written to describe him, we have no basis to form any artistic composite of his looks. We don't know what color his hair or eyes were. We don't know his height or approximate weight. We have no descriptions of his facial features or posture.

The most descriptive guide we have is a prophetic one recorded hundreds of years before Jesus was born: "He wasn't some hand-some king. Nothing about the way he looked made him attractive to us. He was hated and rejected; his life was filled with sorrow and terrible suffering. No one wanted to look at him. We despised him and said, 'He is a nobody!'" (Isaiah 53:2b–3, CEV).

What reasons would the four Gospel recorders have for includ-ing not so much as a verbal snapshot of his image? I can imagine only five:

1. His extraordinary character overshadowed his physical appearance.
2. He was very ordinary looking.
3. They felt that his physical appearance was irrelevant.
4. They assumed that someone else would record that information.
5. A physical composite was not their purpose for writing.

The record is clear. God has in fact allowed us to see what he wanted us to see in the record of Jesus and his earthly ministry. As we read the Gospels, we don't see the color of his hair, but we do see the purity of his thoughts. We cannot tell the tone of his voice, but we can surely hear the sounds of his wisdom and counsel. We do not know how much he weighs, but we can discover how much he loves.

And yet at the very onset of John's record of the Revelation of Jesus Christ, he begins by giving us a specific physical description of Jesus Christ—the only one in the entire New Testament. It is as if Jesus has pulled back his earth suit and walked into John's life in all, or at least *more*, of his glory. The sight was unforgettable. It had to be remembered. It had to be recorded. It had to be told:

> I am John, a follower together with all of you. We suffer because Jesus is our king, but he gives us the strength to endure. I was sent to Patmos Island, because I had preached God's message and had told about Jesus. On the Lord's day the Spirit took control of me...
>
> When I turned to see who was speaking to me, I saw seven gold lampstands. There with the lampstands was someone who seemed to be the Son of Man. He was wearing a robe that reached down to his feet, and a gold cloth was wrapped around his chest. His head and his hair were white as wool or snow, and his eyes looked like flames of fire. His feet were glowing like bronze being heated in a furnace, and his voice sounded like the roar of a waterfall. He held seven stars in his right hand, and a sharp double-edged sword was coming from his mouth. His face was shining as bright as the sun at noon.
>
> When I saw him, I fell at his feet like a dead person. But he put his right hand on me and said:
>
> "Don't be afraid! I am the first, the last, and the living one. I died, but now I am alive forevermore, and I have the keys to death..." (Revelation 1:9–18, CEV)

JESUS IS THE REVELATION

I'm most surprised as I read the book of Revelation not by what John tells us about the *Anti*Christ, but over what he tells us about the Christ. Before we ever read about bowls of wrath, we read about candles of light. Before we observe the wrath of God, we hear the encouragement of Christ: "Don't be afraid!" Before we receive any robes of righteousness, we see him clothed in his own. Before our eyes are ever opened, we see his eyes absolutely ablaze. Before we have a chance to speak, we hear his voice like a rushing river. And before our feet approach God's throne, we see his feet tempered and bronzed. And that face of his shone like the sun in all its glory.

This was the revelation of Jesus Christ that John had so long awaited. It was what had to be recorded first. The revelation John saw was not just some timetable of future world events. It was much more to him than bowls of wrath and seals of judgment. To John the Beloved, Jesus himself *was* the revelation. Today in our reading of the book of Revelation we are much too quick to jump beyond the first chapters in our frantic search to figure out what is next in world events. Too often, we seek an inside track of information instead of an inward experience of transformation.

When we read this important book, we would do well to look for more than prophetic insights. We should look for Jesus. Whoever does so with a whole heart will find him throughout, all over every page and in between each line. We will see him revealing himself, his purpose, his power, and his coming kingdom.

THE REWARDS OF OBEDIENCE

When John received this astounding revelation, he was a prisoner on the island of Patmos, a small, eight-by-four-mile island just twenty-four miles off the coast of Turkey. The Roman government had rock quarries on Patmos and banished prisoners and other enemies of the state to life sentences upon it. Probably the somewhat cryptic and mysterious language used in this book was due to the realities of imprisonment and the need for caution in relaying information.

THE JESUS JOHN SAW   289

The antagonist John faced in this saga was none other than the Emperor Domitian. This caesar was perhaps the most vicious and bloodthirsty of them all. He insisted, for the first time in Roman history, that all of his subjects address him as "our Lord and god." He was the first emperor to mass produce images of himself, place them in all of the houses of worship, and insist that people worship him. When the early Christians refused to worship the emperor, they were executed by the thousands—some by burning at the stake, others by the lions of the Coliseum, and some even dipped in tar and lit as human torches for the royal garden.

Interestingly, John, who had served as the pastor of the capital city of the Roman province of Asia, was not executed but was exiled during this difficult time. Although banished, John seemed to have the freedom to move about the island.

The question emerges: Why among all of the disciples was John chosen to receive the revelation? Why was he most privileged among men to see what others could only imagine? Of all the souls God could have confided in and entrusted with highly privileged intelligence information, why the one who had once been called a "Son of Thunder"? I have pondered this question for quite some time.

It was not accidental that John was present at Patmos on that Lord's Day. It was a part of God's plan that he would be there. And yet, I believe that John had a God-allowed part to play in that choice. Certainly, it was sovereign, and yet it is also in keeping with a wonderful promise that poured from Jesus' lips and was solely recorded, and perhaps remembered as well, by "the disciple whom Jesus loved."

Whoever has my commands and obeys them, he is the one who loves me. He who loves me will be loved by my Father, and I too will love him and show myself to him. (John 14:21)

Among all of his disciples, John truly had Jesus' commands.
Above all of his disciples, John sought to obey Jesus' commands.
Amid all of his disciples, John loved Jesus deeply.

In keeping with the scriptural promise, who would better fit the bill to be the eyes and ears that would get to see and hear the revelation of Jesus Christ?

In the ecstatic opening moments of John's incredible vision and revelation of Jesus Christ three things were cemented in his soul:

- As Christians, we have a hope that will always endure.
- We have a vision of Jesus himself.
- We have a reason never to fear again.

WE HAVE A *HOPE* THAT WILL ALWAYS ENDURE

Why?

1.   *Because Jesus Is Not Coming Back for You or Me, He's Coming Back for Us*

"*I am a follower together with all of you*" (Revelation 1:9a, CEV)—The hope that filled John's soul was one that flowed out of the fellowship he shared with other dear believers. It was one that was never meant to be isolated, but rather shared.

The Word that gives life was from the beginning, and this is the one *our* message is about. *Our* ears have heard, *our* own eyes have seen, and *our* hands touched this word. The one who gives life appeared! *We* saw it happen, and *we* are witnesses to what *we* have seen. Now *we* are telling you about this eternal life that was with the Father and appeared to *us*. *We* are telling you what *we* have seen and heard, so that you may *share* in this life with *us*. And *we share* in it with the Father and with his son Jesus Christ. (1 John 1:1–3, CEV, emphasis mine)

John saw the vertical intimacy of knowing God as one directly connected to the horizontal. Loving God has everything to do with loving man. Loving man has everything to do with loving God.

My dear friends, we must love each other. Love comes from God, and when we love each other, it shows that we have been given new life...God is love, and anyone who doesn't love others has never known him....if we love each other, God lives in us, and his love is truly in our hearts...If we keep on loving others, we will stay one in our hearts with God, and he will stay one with us. (1 John 4:7, 8, 12, 16, CEV)

2. *Because There's a Reason for Our Suffering*

"*We suffer because Jesus is our king*" (Revelation 1:9b, CEV)—The Bible teaches that, as Christians, we face three primary enemies—the world, the flesh, and the devil. R. C. Sproul has identified those three archenemies respectively as the "fallen planet," "fallen man," and "fallen angels." Someone has said, "If that which is above us is not greater than that which is within us then we will fall prey to that which is around us."

Throughout this divine revelation John received from the Lord, he was not on vacation in some villa, nor was he itinerating at a distant church. John was in exile, being punished, on the rock heap of an island called Patmos. By this time, he was elderly. Some scholars believe he could have been ninety years old when he went to this concentration camp. At such an age, surely he must have suffered many aches and pains that go along with being older. And yet, he records little detail of his suffering and much of his revelation.

> I, John, your brother and companion in the suffering and kingdom and patient endurance that are ours in Jesus, was on the island of Patmos because of the word of God and the testimony of Jesus. (Revelation 1:9)

Many people would look at this account and complain, "How could God allow such a wonderful soul to be banished to such a terrible place as Patmos?"

John, however, would shout: "How could I have been so privileged to be the one chosen to receive such a glorious vision of my Lord himself?"

The pessimist sees Patmos as limiting; the optimist, or perhaps the realist, views it as absolutely liberating.

3. *Because God Gives Us Strength to Overcome*

"*But he gives us the strength to endure*" (Revelation 1:9c, CEV)—Perhaps John's most difficult season of trial and struggle came at this final period of his life. After all, isn't this when men and women begin to engage retirement or, at the very least, a second, less-demanding career? Not John. He was steady in his love and devotion to Jesus. They banished him to a stoneworks facility and, no doubt, gave him some taxing physical labor. Yet he clearly embraced this season of his life. Perhaps he, as Paul, saw himself not as a prisoner of the state but as a "prisoner of Christ Jesus" (Philemon 1:1). One of the ways the Lord fills us with his strength is that he becomes what we need in our struggles. For example: In our weakness, he is our strength; in our doubt, he is our hope; amid our fear, he is our confidence; when our doors close, he is an open one; and when we go through a desert, he is the river in the midst of it.

As Tozer has written:

The Christian soon learns that if he would be victorious as a son of heaven among men on earth he must not follow the common pattern of mankind, but rather the contrary. That he may be safe he puts himself in jeopardy; he loses his life to save it and is in danger of losing it if he attempts to preserve it. He goes down to get up. If he refuses to go down he is already down, but when he starts down he is on his way up.

He is strongest when he is weakest and weakest when he is strong. Though poor he has the power to make others rich, but when he becomes rich his ability to enrich others vanishes. He has most after he has given most away and has least when he possesses most.

He may be and often is highest when he feels lowest and most sinless when he is most conscious of sin. He is wisest when he knows that he knows not and knows least when he has acquired the greatest amount of knowledge. He sometimes does most by doing nothing and goes furthest when standing still...

He loves supremely One whom he has never seen, and though himself poor and lowly he talks familiarly with One who is King of all kings and Lord of all lords, and is aware of no incongruity in so doing.[1]

4.   *Because the Holy Spirit Wants to Give Us a Clearer Revelation of Jesus*

"On the Lord's Day the Spirit took control of me…" (Revelation 1:10a, CEV)—Don't you long to have a more vivid view of who Jesus is? I once read of a seminary professor who was very respected among his students for his strong spiritual commitment. On one occasion, a hungry-hearted student asked the professor if he would be willing to meet with him privately one hour a week to discuss the most effective ways to interpret Scripture. Much to his surprise, the usually-accomodating prof refused him. Instead, he said, "No. I won't give an hour a week to interpretation. But if you want to meet one hour every week to learn how to love God and follow Jesus more, I'm ready!"

The primary source of many of our spiritual ills today is not a lack of knowledge or insight. This has been one of the most teaching-enriched and insight-bombarded seasons in history. We have invested too many of our energies, however, in programs and not in relationships. Jeremiah told us that the only thing worth boasting about is the fact that we know the Lord (Jeremiah 9:24).

The revelation of Jesus that John received and passed on to the church was given to provide us a glimpse of our future, just enough perhaps to inject a solid dose of hope into our present. The word for *hope* used in the Bible communicates something much more substantial than what the word connotes today. "Hope" in the Scripture is a deep assurance based on a guarantee God has given us. You can count on hope. You can bank on it. You can stake your life on it. Biblical hope is more than a whim or positive notion; it is an anchor.

We have this hope as an anchor for the soul, firm and secure. (Hebrews 6:19)

This revelation of Jesus is given not just to intrigue us with future events, but to bolster us with a deep and abiding confidence.

The goal of the book of Revelation is not to simply create a group of people who are more eschatologically informed, but to equip an army of God's people who are spiritually and motivationally empowered to face today—and tomorrow—in Jesus' name. John made it clear in his first epistle what loving God involves and the blessings it leads to: "This is love for God: to obey his commands. And his commands are not burdensome, for everyone born of God overcomes the world. This is the victory that has overcome the world, even our faith" (1 John 5:3–4).

Special promises and incredible privileges are reserved for those who overcome. Growing up I heard that Jesus could save us *from* sin, but I never heard much about what he could save us *for*:

> "To him who *overcomes*, I will give the right to eat from the tree of life, which is in the paradise of God." (Revelation 2:7, emphasis mine)
>
> "He who *overcomes* will not be hurt at all by the second death." (2:11, emphasis mine)
>
> "To him who *overcomes*, I will give some of the hidden manna. I will also give him a white stone with a new name written on it, known only to him who receives it." (2:17, emphasis mine)
>
> "To him who *overcomes* and does my will to the end, I will give authority over the nations. I will also give him the morning star." (2:26, 28, emphasis mine)
>
> "He who *overcomes* will...be dressed in white. I will never blot out his name from the book of life, but will acknowledge his name before my Father and his angels." (3:5, emphasis mine)
>
> "Him who *overcomes* I will make a pillar in the temple of my God. Never again will he leave it. I will write on him

the name of my God and the name of the city of my God, the new Jerusalem,...and I will also write on him my new name." (3:12, emphasis mine)

"To him who *overcomes,* I will give the right to sit with me on my throne, just as I overcame and sat down with my Father on his throne." (3:21, emphasis mine)

"He who *overcomes* will inherit all this, and I will be his God and he will be my son." (21:7, emphasis mine)

Just imagine...

...Sitting with Jesus on his throne.

...Eating from the tree of life, in the paradise of God.

...Having Jesus tell the Father and all of heaven that you are his friend.

WE HAVE A *VISION*— OF JESUS HIMSELF

Since this is the primary physical description we have of how Jesus actually appeared to John at the onset of his revelationary and revolutionary experience, let's not rush through it. It deserves some careful pondering. After all, when John saw him, he "fell at his feet as though dead" (Revelation 1:17a). Consider the possible significance of what John saw when he laid eyes on Jesus. When Jesus walked the earth, John saw him for at least three years. Now, however, Jesus appeared in his post-Resurrection state. You get the definite sense that he had never looked quite this way before.

This day was "the Lord's day." It was probably Sunday, since this was the day Christians traditionally worshiped. It is interesting that John kept a count of what day it was while in such a banished state. And he was "in the Spirit." I believe this means that he was in a state of worship and prayer to God, not at all unlike Jesus' prediction of true worshipers who would arise to "worship in spirit and in truth" (John 4:24).

While in the Spirit, John heard a "loud voice like a trumpet." Notice he did not say he heard a trumpet, but a voice that reminded him of one. We are moving with him into a vision and experience so powerful that words to adequately describe it seemed to escape him. As Earl Palmer puts it, John is describing here "the flood of visions that are too immense for the limited possibilities of language."[2]

Palmer goes on to say:

> The vision is frightening, but not devastating. He [John] is struck down by its impact, and then quickly lifted up. He discovers both the sovereign, divine otherness of Jesus Christ, so vast that words fail to describe the wonder, and also the kindness and sensitivity of Jesus. Jesus is not a ghost, a vapor from the realm of death, and this is the first great fact John is told. "Fear not, I am...the living one" (Revelation 1:17–18, RSV).
>
> The result for John, as it was for Peter at Galilee, is not despair, but joy. The Lord who *found* John and the disciples on that first day of the week after Good Friday has again found His friend at the rock quarry of Patmos on the first day of the week. What a reunion![3]

1. *Jesus Is Our High Priest*
"*He was wearing a robe that reached down to his feet*" (Revelation 1:13b, CEV). The robe represents Jesus' role as priest. Time and time again, under the Levitical priesthood, Hebrews would enter the tabernacle with a sacrificial animal in tow and would come face to face with a priest. The priest would offer up their sacrifice to God and would proceed to represent them before God. Now we find John "in the

Spirit on the Lord's Day" proceeding to enter into a holy place of deep revelation, perhaps greater than any man has ever seen. And who does he encounter? A priest, but not just any priest—the Priest of all priests.

2.   Jesus Is Our King

"A gold cloth was wrapped around his chest" (v. 13c, CEV). The gold sash draped around the Lord's heart was a sign of royalty. It is interesting to notice the order in which John observed these physical characteristics of Jesus. We must remember that this particular passage of Scripture is not a record of words that Jesus spoke in reference to himself, but of observations John noted as he looked upon Jesus. He noticed the robe and then the sash. You could say he noticed first that Jesus was there to represent him and, second, to rule over him.

The gold around his heart is also a symbol of Jesus' deep love for his people, of his understanding and compassion, of his grace and forgiveness.

3.   Jesus Is Our Wisdom

"His head and his hair were white as wool or snow" (v. 14a, CEV). As John looked up at the face of Christ, his description was reminiscent of the name of the Lord, the Ancient of Days. Instead of the young and vibrant carpenter from Nazareth, this is a picture of an older Christ, full of wisdom. It was as if the words of Christ that earlier echoed in John's ear were unfolding tangibly: "If you have seen me, you have seen the Father."

4.   Jesus Sees Right through Us

"His eyes looked like flames of fire" (v. 14b, CEV). The gaze of Jesus into the face of John was one of power and penetration. As we read in Hebrews: "Nothing is hidden from God! He sees through everything, and we will have to tell him the truth" (Hebrews 4:13, CEV).

The Jesus John saw has eyes that burn through the veneer of our lives and deep into the substance of our souls. In this moment, perhaps the beloved disciple became transfixed not just over his view of the Master, but over the Master's view of him. This moment reminds us of the importance of not just seeking the hand of God, but of seeking his face; not just what he might provide, but what we might perceive of him, of his heart, his will, and his nature.

5. *Jesus Brings Us through the Flames*

"His feet were glowing like bronze being heated in a furnace" (v. 15a, CEV). There are two vivid pictures of Jesus' heart and ministry here: First, all of the instruments used in the outer court of the tabernacle were made out of brass or bronze: The altar (where fire burned), the laver (where the priests washed), the tongs, and all of the instruments. This image represents the judgment of God upon human sin.[4] And, second, Jesus' feet are possibly revealed to be "like bronze" because of all the times he walks, or carries, his followers through the flames of trial, struggle, and adversity.

> When you pass through the waters, I will be with you;
> and when you pass through the rivers, they will not sweep
> over you.
> When you walk through the fire, you will not be burned;
> the flames will not set you ablaze. (Isaiah 43:2)

Many are the times Jesus has walked me through the flames of fear, doubt, uncertainty, and conflict.

Anne Graham Lotz reminds us:

> These were the same feet that had walked the dusty roads
> of Palestine...

The same feet the disciples had neglected to wash because they were too busy arguing about which of them was greatest...

The same feet that walked up Calvary...

The same feet that were nailed to a Roman cross...

The same feet that were bruised by the serpent while crushing the serpent's head.

The same feet that walked out of the empty tomb...

The same feet that walked with the disciples on the Emmaus Road...

The same feet that ascended into heaven...

The same feet under which God has placed all things...[5]

6. *Jesus Speaks Clearly and Forcefully to Us*

"His voice sounded like a roar of a waterfall" (Revelation 1:15b, CEV). When Elijah waited for a sign from heaven after his tremendous victory on top of Mount Carmel, you will remember that a great wind and an earthquake came and God was not in either of them (1 Kings 19:11–13). However, as the storms and turbulence died down and the quiet set it, God spoke to Elijah in the form of a "gentle whisper." Now, following the death and resurrection of our Lord, that voice has become like the roar of a waterfall or "rushing river."

> The sound of the "roar of a waterfall" or of "many waters" refers to "many messages, many messengers, many prophets, although there is but one great, eternal word, one great voice. As a mighty river pouring over the falls is gathered from many streams and many sources, so His voice is as a sound of many, many waters..."[6]

In the past God spoke to our forefathers through the prophets at many times and in various ways, but in these last days he has spoken to us by his Son...(Hebrews 1:1–2a)

I have often stood within feet of the torrential cascades of Niagara Falls. When you get that close you get covered with the mist, and the noise is so great you cannot hear your voice or anyone else's. You are engulfed with the voice of the rushing water. That is how it is when God speaks to us.

7.   *Jesus Holds His Church in His Hands*

"He held seven stars in his right hand" (Revelation 1:16a, CEV). I no longer call the church I pastor "my church." For years I was in the habit of doing just that. I stopped calling it my church because of the way God got my attention through a series of circumstances and struggles. Within the first few years of arriving at the church I pastor, the Lord allowed me to go through some physical challenges that caused me to depend on him in ways I never thought I would. Those days were dark and difficult, and yet, somehow, filled with a fresh vision of Jesus. I needed him in ways I never had before. As I sought him, he did much more than comfort my soul...he confronted it. Through his deeply challenging and convicting promptings the Lord redirected my vision of him and of the ministry. No insight was more profound, however, than this one: "I will build *my* church, and the gates of Hades will not overcome it" (Matthew 16:18, emphasis mine).

Jesus loves his church, for it is exactly what he came to earth to build. He thought of it, he started it, he anointed it, he died for it, and one day he will regather it for a great feast in heaven. I can't wait! In this passage, he holds the church in his hands; it is the stars in his universe, the lights that he holds forth. Remember, it's not your church, it's not my church...it's his.

8.   *Jesus Is the True Judge*

"*A sharp double-edged sword was coming from his mouth*" (Revelation1:16b, CEV). John had always been impressed with the Word of God. In fact, he began his Gospel account referring to Jesus as the Word of God.

> In the beginning was the one who is called the Word.
> The Word was with God and was truly God.
> From the very beginning the Word was with God.
> And with this Word, God created all things.
> Nothing was made without the Word. (John 1:1–3a, CEV)

John had by now observed that Jesus' mightiest weapons as he walked the planet were not his miracles or healings, but his words. His words had captivated audiences, transformed souls, confounded scholars, opened blind eyes and deaf ears, forgiven prostitutes and tax collectors, turned fishermen into evangelists, and stilled storms. How privileged we are as Christians to have the Bible, the very Word of God, to read, treasure, ponder, and absorb.

And his words have two edges. Those words can at the same time convict and comfort, stir and support, rebuke and reconcile. The Jesus standing before John in that moment was a judge to be terribly feared and yet a friend to be deeply embraced.

9.   *Jesus Is Our Light*

"*His face was shining as bright as the sun at noon*" (Revelation 1:16c, CEV). Someone has said that our bodies were designed to "glow" when they are or have been in the presence of the Lord. I don't presume to know how that works. I do know that when Moses descended the mountain of the Lord his countenance was glorious, so much so that it had to be veiled. Additionally, we know that the holiest place of all in the ancient wilderness tabernacle, which housed the ark and presence of God, was shielded from the general public, even from the priests, by a thick material veil because of the bright power of God's glory. There is a definite brightness and joyous radiance about the person who walks closely with the Lord.

The light at the end of the long, dark tunnel of our lives is the face of Jesus.

10. *Jesus Redefines the Word* Awesome

"When I saw him, I fell at his feet like a dead person" (v. 17a, CEV). I have a pet peeve with our use of one particular word in the English language. The word is *awesome*. I don't know why it concerns me so much (neither do my kids, for that matter), but it does. Perhaps it is because I hear the same superlative used to describe the holiness of God and the taste of a hot dog. When we do that, I believe we dilute the power and significance of the word. I have a hard time referring to an A on a test, a slam dunk on the basketball court, or a new car on the lot as *awesome*. To me, none of those items is worthy of such high commendation.

Awesome must have been what John viewed when he turned around and saw Jesus standing before him in all his glory. The impression was so all-consuming that he "fell at his feet like a dead person." Like Isaiah, he was done in or "undone" by the presence of God. He fell apart under it. It was overwhelming, captivating, and overtaking. It was uniquely awesome.

W. A. Criswell recounts John's awestruck moment:

He could not see, his eyes were blinded by the glory of that light, the face of Jesus shining as the sun in his strength. He could not hear; he was stunned by that voice of many waters. His soul was overpowered and overwhelmed. His consciousness, his very life, seemed to ebb away. "...I fell at his feet as dead..." That response is most strange. It would seem that he would have looked upon the face of his Master with ecstatic bliss and joy beyond words to describe. I would suppose that John, this beloved disciple, knew the Lord all of his life. Their mothers were sisters, which would mean, according to the flesh, that John and Jesus were first cousins. He was a beloved disciple in that inner circle who lived next to the very heart and ministry of our Saviour. He laid his head on Jesus' bosom at the Last Supper. He stood at the cross. He saw that blood and the water flow out like a fountain from His heart. It was this beloved disciple John who, in obedience to the loving, tender, shepherdly word of the Saviour, took Mary, the Lord's mother, to his home and cared for her. Yet, when he sees the Master on the Isle of Patmos he falls at His feet as dead. I repeat, it would seem that he would have looked upon the Lord with joy unspeakable, with a bliss and a gladness that would be indescribable. Instead, great fear fell upon him, so much so that it caused the first words of the Lord spoken to him to be ones of comfort and encouragement, "Fear not."[7]

John was clearly now seeing Jesus as never before: unveiled and full of glory. He had shed his earth-suit. Just think, throughout this revelation his eyes looked upon great wonders: a jasper throne, an emerald rainbow, seven lamps, the crystal sea, and the hosts of heaven, and yet he stood. Just one look at Jesus, however, just one look at his resurrected and glorified body, and he fell at his feet as if dead. That, my friend, is awesome!

11. *Jesus Anoints and Authorizes Us*

"But he put his right hand on me and said: Don't be afraid!" (v. 17b,

CEV). How often had Jesus laid his hand on John before and done exactly this? We know that he did so at the Mount of Transfiguration. One of Jesus' most oft-used phrases to his disciples was "don't be afraid." Now that John had looked upon Christ and beheld "the King in his beauty" (Isaiah 33:17), the Lord proceeded to place his blessing on the disciple. Perhaps in this moment John felt an awe similar to what King David expressed in Psalm 139:

> You have laid your hand upon me. Such knowledge is too wonderful for me, too lofty for me to attain. (v. 5b–6)

WE HAVE *REASON* NEVER TO FEAR AGAIN

The First Reason: Jesus Was *Before* It All—
   "*Don't be afraid! I am the first...*" (Revelation 1:17c, CEV)
The Second Reason: Jesus Will Be *After* It All—
   "*I am...the last.*" (v. 17d, CEV)
The Third Reason: Jesus Is *in the Midst of It Right Now*—
   "*I am...the living one...now I am alive forevermore,...*" (v. 18a, CEV)
The Fourth Reason: Jesus Has Gone before Us Even into Death Itself—
   "*I have the keys to death and the world of the dead...*" (v. 18b, CEV)

Before Jesus spoke to John about coming apocalyptic events, before he dictated prophetic postcards to the seven churches of Asia, he revealed more of himself to John. Before John viewed what would have certainly traumatized and overwhelmed anyone else, Jesus fortified the beloved disciple's soul. This vision of Jesus reassured and even more deeply convinced John that Jesus was not just a powerful part of his past, but that he was in his present and would be in the rest of his life. Jesus not only knew the first and last and current chapters of the disciple's existence, he held them in his hands. They were under his absolute authority and jurisdiction. So John would never need to fear.

I remember eight years ago when God was stirring my soul to make a move from the Midwest to New England. We had heard all of the horror stories of this being the "land of ministerial suicide" and of it being "the burnt-over district." Reports came that this part of America, which had once known the depths of revival and had been stirred by the ministries of Whitefields, Wesleys, Finneys, Edwardses, and the like, had "seen it all" and was no longer interested. I felt a stirring that laid the Boston area heavily on my heart and I kept it in my prayers over a four-year period.

As God opened the door for us to take a faith journey to New England and look at this land I felt so called to, someone gave us a song. It was from an album by the group Truth, and the words captured my heart:

You're already there, you've gone before me.
You're already there, to you the future is now.
You're already there, waiting to show me around.

Hearing afresh that Jesus was not only in our past and present, but also in our future, was deeply reassuring. I could trust that he not only knew my future, he had it planned out and was completely comfortable with it. So much so that he was just waiting for me to get there so he could show me around. Well, after almost eight years of ministry in New England, he has proven to be quite an exceptional tour guide! He can walk you through your today and take you boldly into your tomorrows.

Because John sought to be closer to Jesus, he was given a vision of Jesus glorified. As I read the early chapters of this revelation I see

a pattern of deepening intimacy. Not at all unlike the stages of intimacy through which a man and woman journey through the
covenant of marriage, so our covenant relationship with God
unfolds. Consider these three levels of closeness that John experienced with Jesus:

- **Beholding** ("I saw...someone 'like a son of man'..." [Revela-
  tion1:12–13]). Once we behold Jesus working through
  another person ministering to us or simply at work in the
  events of our lives or guiding us through the wisdom of his
  words, we are never the same. The Holy Spirit causes something to happen deep within our spirits and, somehow, we
  begin to not just read the Bible, we hear the words of God; we
  no longer simply enjoy having good friends, we share in a
  deep fellowship with other believers; we cease to labor at
  praying the right way, and we begin to bask in his all-consuming presence. We behold Jesus.
- **Touching** ("Then he placed his right hand on me..." [1:17]). It
  is one thing to see the Lord at work in and around your life. It
  is altogether another thing to sense that he has placed his hand
  upon you. The hand of God upon a life represents his blessing
  upon it and his power to make it spiritually effective and purposeful. Whatever he touches is set apart for something glorious. Glorious in his eyes, mind you, not necessarily in our eyes
  or in the eyes of the world. David marveled, "You have laid
  your hand upon me. Such knowledge is too wonderful for
  me, too lofty for me to attain" (Psalm 139:5b–6a).
- **Disclosing** ("Come up here, and I will show you what must
  take place..." [Revelation 4:1b]). In the marriage covenant
  there is a nakedness and openness that is enjoyed by a husband and wife. A strong relationship is one in which love and

mutual support craft out an environment in which full disclosure is possible. A deep level of trust and knowledge can result. Our relationship with Jesus is similar in that there is opportunity for mutual disclosure. We bear our souls to him and he reveals his glory to us. Though with our human eyes we may not see God, the eyes of our spirits can behold more than we ever imagined possible.

Open my eyes, Lord.

Chapter twenty~one

KNOCK, KNOCK, KNOCKING!

GOD AT THE DOOR

Behold I stand at the door and knock...
JESUS
REVELATION 3:20A, NKJV

All happenings, great and small, are parables whereby God speaks.
The art of life is to get the message.
MALCOLM MUGGERIDGE

The era of the door-to-door salesman seems to have come and gone. I remember, however, when a knock came on our door one Saturday afternoon. I was about six and my parents and my baby brother were taking a nap. Instead of asking them first if I should open it, I went ahead and checked to see who it was.

When I opened the door, I quickly recognized the familiar face. It was the milkman. In those days—the mid-1960s—the milkman delivered your milk and eggs to your door every few days, saving you the trouble of purchasing them at the supermarket

"Hello, young man!" There was a sales pitch attached to the greeting. "We have ice cream today. Would your parents like a carton? What's their favorite flavor? Are they around today?"

"No. They're resting, but I'll go ask them," I responded hopefully.

Quickly running down the hall, I knocked on my parent's door. "Mom, Dad…the milkman wants to know if we want some ice cream today?"

"No, not today, Son," my mom softly answered, sounding quite sleepy.

Disappointed, my quick run turned into a slow walk down the hallway. I wished I could make the decision myself. Somehow I just knew that if Mom and Dad were completely awake, they would come to their senses. After all, it was Saturday afternoon, and who doesn't like ice cream?

"Well, what will it be, young man?" the milkman cheerfully asked.

"Uh…we'll have a carton of ice cream. Um, vanilla, please," I said confidently. Vanilla was my favorite.

Somehow, the opportunity seemed too good to resist. The potential taste of smooth and cool vanilla on my palate overshadowed any notions of a rod of discipline on my rear end. I think my response was so sudden that even *I* was surprised by it.

A few minutes later my mom walked in the kitchen and found me: Ice cream container opened (Exhibit A), spoon in mouth (Exhibit B), and a satisfied smile on my face (Exhibit C). I was caught red-handed and vanilla-moustached.

What I *did* know is that that ice cream was the best I'd ever had. What I did *not* know was what my parents were going to do about my transgression.

In the endlessly long moment that followed, my mom and dad were so surprised by my actions that they found them not defiant, not devious, not in the least bit dastardly, but somehow cute. Now they tell me that they put that act right alongside another memorable moment in my childhood when I ate one dozen Krispy Kreme donuts by myself and had started on the second dozen when they caught me. And that was at age three.

Thank God, and Art Linkletter, for cute moments.

What if a visitor knocked on your door? What would you do if Jesus came to the door? No, not just a door or any door, but to *your* door. What if you heard a knock on your door this very moment, even while you're reading this book, and you opened it only to find Jesus staring you in the face. What would you do? What would you say? More importantly, what would he have to say to you?

A handful of Laodiceans had that very experience one day. Take a close look at what happened:

> I am the one called Amen! I am the faithful and true witness and the source of God's creation. Listen to what I say.
>
> I know everything you have done, and you are not cold or hot. I wish you were either one or the other. But since you are lukewarm and neither cold nor hot, I will spit you out of my mouth. You claim to be rich and successful and to have everything you need. But you don't know how bad off you are. You are pitiful, poor, blind and naked.
>
> Buy your gold from me. It has been refined in a fire, and it will make you rich. Buy white clothes from me. Wear them and you can cover up your shameful nakedness. Buy medicine for your eyes, so that you will be able to see.
>
> I correct and punish everyone I love. So make up your minds to turn away from your sins. Listen! I am standing and knocking at your door. If you hear my voice and open the door, I will come in and we will eat together. Everyone who wins the victory will sit with me on my throne, just as

I won the victory and sat with my Father on his throne.
(Revelation 3:14b–21, CEV)

HE'S GOT YOUR NUMBER

When the Laodiceans met Christ at the door they were confronted by the same penetrating eyes that bore into John's soul.

"I know everything you've done," he said to them. Imagine the stunned state of the soul that hears Jesus say to it, "I know everything you've done." *Everything.* Every sin. Every good work. Every lie. Every shading of the truth. Every compromise. Every thought. Every question. Every doubt. Every tax return. Every entry in our checkbooks. Every television program viewed. Every video rented. Every word spoken. Everything.

The deduction is clear. It is utterly foolish to try to hide *anything* from someone who knows *everything* there is to know about you.

And Jesus not only knows what we've done, he knows the spirit in which we have done it. *He knows the temperature of our souls.*

"...you are lukewarm..."

His eyes see as no others do. For at the same moment he is viewing *what* we are doing, he is also perceiving *why* we are doing it. His eyes simultaneously see the methods, the means, and the motives of all our actions. Every single one of them. He gauges our passion by the moment and wants us to be on fire for him. The tone of his letter to the Laodiceans implies that they were not without works. It seems that they had many good works, but that their zeal and love for God had greatly diminished. This plainly turned Jesus' stomach. It caused deep concern and brought an open rebuke.

He also knows all of our lines. In a world conditioned to communicate in double-speak, Jesus would not fall for the stunts of the Laodiceans. His eyes stared them down with the truth. They soon found out that you don't play games with God, especially not when he shows up at your door, unexpected and unannounced.

"You claim to be rich and successful and to have everything you need. But you don't know how bad off you are. You are pitiful, poor, blind and naked."

Just look at the exposure and the confrontation.
"You claim to be…"
"But you don't know…"
"You are…"
What do you *claim* to be right now?…today?… this moment?
Is God trying to tell you something *you don't know?*
If he did, would you listen? Would you be willing to acknowledge that you are wrong? Even *completely* wrong?
Have you dared to invite him to give you an accurate assessment of your current spiritual state? Of your soul's temperature? If so, are you listening intently to his response?

One bright summer morning, a grandmother who had brought her two grandsons to DisneyWorld noticed that the thing she had feared had happened. One of the boys was missing. Worst of all, he was the youngest of the two. Tad was only five years old. Worried, she grabbed the hand of Eddie, her seven-year-old grandson and began to scour every corner of the Magic Kingdom. They went from Adventureland to Frontierland to Tommorrowland and still no sight of Tad.

After an hour of searching had passed, the grandmother, now in tears, went to the public service counter and had her grandson paged.

All over the park the message went out:

"Would Tad Swenson please report to the customer service desk right away please! Your grandmother is worried about you."

Two hours later, Tad's grandmother, now desperate but exhausted from all her walking, sat down on a park bench with Eddie and just sobbed. Wiping her eyes she could hear the sounds of the Main Street Parade making its routine journey down the main corridor. The parade came and went, and then she saw him. At the end of the parade right behind the band, there was Tad, marching and smiling and singing right along with the band.

She was overjoyed that she had found him.

Tad had in fact been lost, desperately lost. And, yet, he was so busy marching to the parade that he never recognized his condition. He was completely lost and did not know it.

That was the Laodicean church. That is often you and me, isn't it?

"You claim to be rich and successful and to have everything you need. But you don't know how bad off you are."

HE HAS THE RIGHT PRESCRIPTION

During the Western gold rush, countless thousands made their way to California to find their personal pot of gold. Stories are legend of the many who thought they had struck it rich and who were later disappointed to find that they had uncovered nothing more than pyrite, or fool's gold. The Laodiceans were like that. They were rich in all of the wrong things. They had attached value to things that were of little value to God.

When Jesus showed up at their door, he was determined to transform their value system. Much of our world today would like to use Christ like a seasoning shaker, to simply add a little of him to their already-set worldview or standards and values. The ambitious entrepreneur might desire to add enough of Christ to be socially respectable. The avid sports-aholic might want to check out church on Easter and Christmas, when no games are on. The self-made man might choose to acknowledge Jesus as merely a good teacher, all the while dismissing his call to repentance as too much to expect.

"Buy your gold from me. It has been refined in a fire, and it will make you rich." Clearly, Jesus wants more than the fool's gold of lip service, he wants heart surrender. He alone is the Judge of what is truly valuable.

Jesus repeatedly calls us to closeness in our relationship with him... to faith, to friendship. He not only wants to provide us with a cleansing and a covering for our sins, he wants to be our covering himself.

"Buy white clothes from me. Wear them and you can cover up your shameful nakedness."

The Laodiceans were known for their production of salves and creams used to medicate the eyes. Jesus chose this metaphor to speak to the Christians in Laodicea of their own spiritual blindness. Throughout his letters to the seven churches of Asia, Jesus packed his words with several eye-openers including:

The truth that the way you begin in Christ is important, but so is the way you finish.

The truth that our first love for Christ must be consistently renewed.

The truth that faithfulness will be rewarded.

HE'S KNOCKING AT YOUR DOOR

When I became a Christian, one of my first memory verses was Revelation 3:20. I was always taught that it was Christ speaking to people who had never heard the gospel. Since then, I've studied the passage and found a completely different message and context.

> Look! Here I stand at the door and knock. If you hear me calling and open the door, I will come in, and we will share a meal as friends. (Revelation 3:20, NLT)

This was actually an invitation to those who had already met him. This letter was not addressed to the lost, but to the found; not to the unchurched, but to the churched; not to the sinners, if you will, but to the saints. This was not an invitation to *come* to Christ. This was an invitation to come *closer* to Christ.

Note the way Jesus comes here to the Laodiceans. It reminds me of the way he has often come in my life. Somehow the knock sounds familiar:

- He comes *unannounced,* without a forewarning. The point when Jesus enters your life and mine usually lacks any notice. He comes suddenly into our lives, bringing his confrontation, his truth, and his encouragement.

- He comes *personally,* without a delegation. When the Lord comes to our door, he sends no representative. His call is up close and personal. As the saying goes, For God so loved the world that he did not send a committee.

- He comes *speaking,* with promise for those who hear. Our challenge is to hear his voice above and beyond all the other voices in our lives. The fact is that Jesus is speaking to many, even this very moment. Few, however, will get focused and interested enough to truly listen.

- He comes *calling* us away from our other doors. Jesus knocks at the door of our spirits. This is the part of us that comes to life at the new birth. The problem is that so many of us are tending to other doors instead. Often we tend to every door except the most important one. Some tend to the door of ambition, others to the door of wealth, and others to the door of some other relationship. Until we hear his knock and his voice at the door of our souls, we will miss the greatest gift of all.

- He comes *waiting* for those who will wait upon him. How many times does a person have to knock at your door to get you to open it? The picture here is one of patience and persistence. Interestingly enough, he who holds all power is depicted here standing, knocking, and waiting. Standing at the door of your life and mine. Knocking via the circumstances of our lives and the call of his Spirit. Waiting for the invitation to register and for the knob to turn and the door of our lives to open. He wants us to open fully to an ever-deepening and ever-developing relationship with him.

- He comes not to preach at us, but *to dine* with us. Isn't it interesting to consider the purpose for which the Son of God is standing at our door? He does not say that he is primarily standing there to be worshiped, or to lead us in a religious ceremony. He does not even imply that he comes to teach us something or to show us anything in particular. No, he says that he comes to dine with us. Just think of it! The Son of God wants to sit down with you, to share a meal, to talk, to laugh, to confide, to know, to share, to befriend, and to have us become one.

- He stands on the other side of our doors. No peep hole is provided. There is no sneak preview of what the experience might be like once we open the door of our hearts to Jesus. The only precursors to that experience are a knock and a voice. Once you take the step to open your door, you're committed. There he is and there you are. But it is exactly the kind of heart-opening faith to which the Lord calls us.

FOUR INTIMACY KILLERS

On January 1, 1861, Abraham Lincoln signed the Emancipation Proclamation in the Lincoln bedroom, officially ending slavery in

America. At that moment, legally, Lincoln said "It is finished" to slavery and slave trading. However, did every slave actually become free that day, or that month, or even that year?

The answer, of course, is *no*.

Imagine that. Every slave was set free—suddenly, legally, and officially—but thousands did not become free. The law said they were free; their lives said they were not. Why not?

There are at least four reasons many slaves remained in bondage:

> *They had not heard the word.*
> *They were afraid to go free.*
> *Their slavemasters became even more oppressive.*
> *They were too unfamiliar with freedom.*

Too often, we make better excuses than we do plans, don't we? When children miss school, they are usually required to turn in what is referred to as an excuse. I came across this list of actual excuses turned in by elementary students to their teachers. They are a bit telling, as you will soon discover:

"Please excuse Freddie for being out yesterday because he had the fuel."

"Please accuse Michael from being absent on January 30, 31, 32, and 33 because he was aleing."

"George was absent yesterday because of a sore trout."

"Please excuse Betsey for being absent. She was sick and I had her shot."

"Joseph has been absent becuz he had two teeth taken off his face."

"My son is under doctor's care and should not take fiscal ed. Please execute him."

"Please excuse Harriet for missing school yesterday. We forgot to get the Sunday paper off the porch, and when we found it Monday, we thought it was Sunday."

"Please excuse Ralph from school on Friday. He had very loose vowels."

We often use the same four excuses that kept legally freed slaves in practical bondage to avoid taking hold of the freedom that is ours in Jesus Christ. These are the four intimacy killers that keep us from realizing what John realized—the depths of knowing Jesus personally and powerfully in his life. Which one have you fallen prey to?

Word-Neglect—Some Christians stay in the shallow end of the experiential pool because they neglect to pick up and use the tools God has given them. When you give your heart to Jesus, your life becomes a garden. That garden needs tending. Perhaps early on, you receive assistance from a pastor, small group leader, or trusted friend. They invest in your spiritual growth. But now, you're a big girl or boy and it becomes time to pick up the garden tools and cultivate your friendship with Jesus. Paramount among these garden tools are Bible study and prayer. The Scripture is more than a book of wise sayings; it is the Declaration of Independence for your soul. Read it deeply and eagerly to discover the astounding invitations it contains from God's heart to yours.

Trust-Neglect—Some of us have lived in the throes of our hurts, pains, and disappointments so long that we fear that we would not know how to act if we were free. We feel like the player on the sidelines at the Super Bowl who, while keeping the bench warm, dreams of catching the winning pass. But, truth be known, he fears that if it were passed to him, he would cave in under the pressure. The biggest mistake we make when we fall prey to this is looking at ourselves and not at God. Margaret Jensen has said, "Faith is when you realize that that which is behind you is greater than that which is in front of you." Study the powerful works of Jesus in the Gospels. Rehearse his answers to prayer in your own life. Keep your eyes fixed on him...and step out.

Spiritual Harassment—These are believers who sincerely want more of God in their lives, but who find themselves under a barrage of spiritual attacks. They feel more like undertakers than overcomers. The worst part is not what these problems have done to the exterior of their lives, but to the interior, to the soul. If you feel that the enemy has designs on you, you're right. He does. But remember, even the struggles you face are tools in God's hand to bring the glory out in you. Instead of rehearsing the enemy's attacks on you, try on a new lens, or a new view. Consider often what the Lord may be doing through your difficulties to shape the image of Christ within you. For a Christian, a crisis calls for clinging to Christ, not publishing press releases for your enemy.

Fear of the Unknown—Probably the saddest stories after Lincoln's proclamation were the ones about the slaves who could go free, but who were so accustomed to living in bondage that they almost feared freedom. The story is told of a bear cub that was captured in the wild and placed in a ten-by-ten-foot cage. He grew up there and spent the first few years of his life pacing ten feet this way and ten feet that way. When he reached five years of age, the zoo ran out of funding and was closed down. As a result, all of the animals were returned to their native habitat and released in the wild. When the bear was let go in a vast wooded reserve, he exited the cage, and for weeks he paced ten feet this way and ten feet that way. They got the bear out of the cage, they just couldn't get the cage out of the bear.

Remember, Jesus is full of grace and glory and he is determined to set us free to know him in his fullness. Follow him one step at a time and you will find him bringing you to a place of great freedom. "He whom the Son sets free will be free indeed." Recognizing the deep liberty that was purchased on the cross for us is the beginning of a fuller walk with Christ.

Remember, He has reserved a seat just for you—Overcomers!

I believe the most astounding promise made to Christians in the whole New Testament is found in Revelation 3:21, CEV:

Everyone who wins the victory will sit with me on my throne, just as I won the victory and sat with my Father on his throne.

The friend of Jesus is promised the best seat in the house. Do you hear him knocking?

THE LAST TIME
HE EVER SAID
"FRIEND"

Friends, haven't you any fish?
JESUS
JOHN 21:5

A man with few friends is only half-developed;
there are whole sides of his nature which are locked up
and have never been expressed.
He cannot unlock them himself, he cannot even discover them;
a friend alone can stimulate him and open him.
RANDOLPHE BOURNE

The church bells were polished, but never rung.

Joe Scriven's wedding day proved to be the most difficult one of his life. Everything was set. The church was prepared, the bridal party was in place, and the minister was ready to do his part. No one thought that such a blessed day would become such a nightmare.

Nothing could have prepared Joseph Scriven for the news he would receive the night before his wedding. His fiancee was dead. It had been an accidental drowning.

It was not long before Joe felt compelled to leave town. His parents had been bothered by his spiritual zeal for some time. Even more so now. Joe found it very difficult to face the familiar sights of his hometown—Dublin, Ireland. Every one of them conjured up wonderful memories of his courtship. Everywhere he looked, he saw her face. Every familiar sound reminded him of her voice. And so he moved.

> *What a Friend we have in Jesus, all our sins and grief to bear!*
> *What a privilege to carry everything to God in prayer!*
> *O what peace we often forfeit, O what needless pain we bear,*
> *All because we do not carry everything to God in prayer.*

The hurting empty place in Scriven's soul eventually began to fill with an increased love for and devotion to Jesus. As he reread the Sermon on the Mount, Joe became convinced that it required much more than meditation, that it called for a radical lifestyle change. Before any religious people had a chance to put his fire out or to write off Jesus' counsel, Joe began to give liberally of his earthly possessions. On some occasions he would even remove an article of clothing he was wearing and give it to a person in need who crossed his path. Additionally, he devoted his handyman skills to helping financially strapped people with household projects.

On one occasion a man saw Joseph Scriven in the streets of Port Hope, Ontario, with his sawhorse and saw in tow. Inquiring of a friend, he asked, "Who is that man? I want him to work for me." The answer came back: "You cannot get that man; he saws wood only for poor widows and sick people who cannot pay." His benevolent practices caused some to respect him and others to call him eccentric.

> *Have we trials and temptations? Is there trouble anywhere?*
> *We should never be discouraged. Take it to the Lord in prayer.*

Can we find a friend so faithful Who will all our sorrows share?
Jesus knows our every weakness. Take it to the Lord in prayer.

A letter came telling Scriven that his mother was seriously ill. The great distance between them prevented Joseph from scurrying to her side, and yet he was determined at least to write. When he put pencil to paper, what followed was a simple poem, which he sent to her. He hoped that it would bring comfort and courage to her. Months later, when Joe himself was sick, a visiting friend noticed the scribbled poem on scratch paper near the bed. After reading it, the friend inquired as to whether Scriven had truly penned the verse. Joe, always the modest one, responded, "The Lord and I did it between us." In 1869 this and other poems penned by Scriven were published in a book.

In 1886, Joe Scriven took it to the Lord in prayer for the last time in this life. He too died of an accidental drowning. His most lasting legacy, touching millions, grew from a seed of thoughtfulness scribbled to merely encourage one mother's heart. Its message and appeal is so central to the Christian life that countless missionaries around the world have made this one of the first hymns they teach new converts, "What a Friend We Have in Jesus."[1]

Are we weak and heavy laden, cumbered with a load of care?
Precious Savior, still our refuge. Take it to the Lord in prayer.
Do thy friends despise, forsake thee? Take it to the Lord in prayer.
In His arms He'll take and shield thee. Thou wilt find a solace there.

Friend was one of John the Beloved's favorite titles.

It was much more precious to him apparently than that of *disciple* or *apostle* or *follower* or *student*. In addition to the astounding invitation passage we have considered earlier in John 15, I find only four other instances in the Gospel accounts in which Christ used the word *friend* when addressing someone.

The first time was when the paralytic was lowered down through the roof into the house where Jesus was staying. Determined friends of the suffering man chose this route because they couldn't get him through the large crowd surrounding the Lord. "When Jesus saw their faith, he said, '*Friend,* your sins are forgiven'" (Luke 5:20, emphasis mine).

The question begs to be asked: *Of all the names Jesus could have used to refer to this paralytic, why did he choose to use this one*—friend? *Why didn't he just say* man, *or* sir, *or* son, *for that matter?* After all, this is just a guy who dropped in on him unexpectedly, right? Why such an endearing name for such a sudden and abrupt acquaintance? One that literally just dropped from the sky? *Friends are there when we need them…and when they need us.*

I believe Jesus may have called him *friend* for many reasons. For instance, just look at the lengths to which this man went just to get close to Jesus. "You will seek me and find me when you seek me with all your heart" (Jeremiah 29:13). The next time you have difficulty just getting up to have your devotions when the alarm sounds, just think about this guy. You know, he's the one who was carried through crowds, had his buddies dig a hole in the roof of a house, and then was lowered through a roof just to get to Jesus. *Friends will go to great lengths to help you out.*

The second instance occurred when Jesus was warning his disciples to beware of the Pharisees: "Meanwhile, when a crowd of many thousands had gathered, so that they were trampling on one another, Jesus began to speak first to his disciples, saying: 'Be on your guard against the yeast of the Pharisees, which is hypocrisy…I tell you, my *friends,* do not be afraid of those who kill the body and after that can do no more. But I will show you whom you should fear: Fear him who, after the killing of the body, has power to throw you into hell. Yes, I tell you, fear him" (Luke 12:1, 4–5, emphasis mine).

Friends will give it to you straight. In these sentences Jesus speaks to his disciples in terms both of friendship and of the fear of the Lord. I can almost see him. While the Pharisees are lurching around the neighborhood stirring up strife and hoping they can catch Jesus having just a little too much fun doing God's will (you know the type!), I see him putting his arms around a couple of disciples' shoulders and saying, "Listen, friends. I have something to tell you and I don't want you to miss it."

As Jesus' disciples' ears perked up over what their Lord promised, he proceeded to give them soul-freeing advice:

Don't let hard-noses put pressure on you.

Don't fear a bunch of hot-heads.

But most of all, don't underestimate the influence of the Almighty.

The third occurrence is found at Jesus' arrest. It is an irony of ironies, and I would imagine that John certainly pondered the moment more than once and recorded it for us to remember and reflect upon. Not only had Jesus knelt and washed the feet of his soon-to-be betrayer, Judas, at the Last Supper, he even elected to call him by his most affectionate term at the brink of his betrayal. It was Judas who led the mob to a private site, making way for Jesus' arrest:

Now the betrayer had arranged a signal with them [the chief priests and the elders]: "The one I kiss is the man; arrest him." Going at once to Jesus, Judas said, "Greetings, Rabbi!" and kissed him.

Jesus replied, "Friend, do what you came for." (Matthew 26:48-50, emphasis mine).

Even in the face of one who has turned over his life to his ene-mies, Jesus refuses to abandon his friendship. To Jesus, a covenant is sacred and his grace holds out even in the face of bitter betrayal. His love is not only strong, it is tough and stubborn. So, whether he finds us down and out physically on a stretcher, down and out emo-tionally in the face of ridicule from the Pharisees, or down and out spiritually on the brink of betrayal, Jesus' brand of friendship is one that never, *I mean never,* fails.

When Jesus referred to his followers in a radically new way—no longer as servants, but as friends—he issued what constitutes his greatest gift to us. A. W. Tozer has written, "Unquestionably the highest privilege granted to man on earth is to be admitted into the circle of friends of God. Nothing is important enough to be allowed to stand in our relation to God…God is not satisfied until there exists between Him and His people a relaxed informality that requires no artificial stimulation. The true friend of God may sit in His presence for long periods of silence. Complete trust needs no words of assurance."[2]

Jesus differentiated between servants and friends, but what exactly is the difference? *Serving* is work oriented, while *befriending* is relationship oriented. *Serving* begins with doing something to gain approval; *befriending* begins with knowing someone who's freely giving it. *Serving* is a duty; *befriending,* a privilege. *Servants* don't dare pry into their master's business; *friends* are regularly given the inside track.

THE DIVINE APPOINTMENT

As a relationship characterized primarily by friendship, Jesus emphasized the fact that this compelling commitment begins with something more than volunteer entry or a randomly selected draft. No, there was more of an in-depth and deliberate process than that.

The fact is that before any of his disciples *chose* to follow him, they were first *chosen* to follow him. It is merely the fact that they were *chosen* that gave them the desire and ability to, in fact, *choose*.

Jesus put it this way:

"You did not choose me, but I chose you and appointed you
to go and bear fruit—fruit that will last" (John 15:16a).

There is no joy like that of being picked or being chosen. Whether on a sandlot baseball team or a place on an off-Broadway play cast, being selected is an invigorating proposition. According to the Bible, those who Christ chooses are not only invited to play on the team, they are fully adopted into a family and inducted into a kingdom.

THE RESULTANT PRIVILEGE

Not only had Jesus issued a new command to his followers ("Love each other as I have loved you") and painted the supreme example of a man who lays "down his life for his friends," he issued an astounding invitation of actual friendship with God. And the invitation came with the authority of a Father who has himself chosen us and who is eager to grant us our deepest desires: "Then the Father will give you whatever you ask in my name" (John 15:16b).

THE FINAL INVITATION

The toughest people to give gifts to are those who think they have it all. So often Peter came across as someone who had something Jesus must need. Perhaps he thought his loyalty would please Jesus. His devotion would outshine the others. His diligence would make the difference. He. Him. His. That was Peter. Ever the doer. Pushing. Striving. Reaching. Talking a lot, but saying little. Running hard and getting nowhere.

That's why Jesus in his post-Resurrection appearance at the Sea of Galilee had to pick up his personalized invitation to Peter, dust it off and extend it to him all over again (John 21:5,15–17). Peter needed reminding. And John needed some reassuring. Sometimes we do, too.

The final time Jesus used the word *friend*, it wasn't whispered in the ear of a nearby disciple sharing a meal and leaning against his back. Nor was it silently written in sand or kindly taught to the masses. No, on this climactic occasion, it was called out, shouted from the shore of a lake at the start of a day:

> Early in the morning, Jesus stood on the shore, but the disciples did not realize that it was Jesus.
>
> He called out to them, "*Friends*, haven't you any fish?"
>
> "No," they answered. (John 21:4–5, emphasis mine)

Of all the Gospel writers, only John thought this episode important enough to include in his account of Christ. This final time that Jesus used the word *friends* fills my mind with a number of questions:

How did John, singly among all the disciples, know it was Jesus on the shore that day?

Were the others too busy at their tasks to relate?

Were the others too caught up in serving their own interests and agendas of the moment to be reminded of their previous priority?

Were they all too busy doing to truly know?

Or was it the tone of Jesus' voice that John, above all of the others, recognized?

Was it the nature of his question that caused John to know it was Jesus?

Was it the authority with which he spoke?

Or, was it that name he used to describe them that gave him away— *"Friends"?*

He said, "Throw your net on the right side of the boat and you will find some." When they did, they were unable to haul the net in because of the large number of fish.

Then the disciple whom Jesus loved said to Peter, "It is the Lord!" As soon as Simon Peter heard him say, "It is the Lord," he wrapped his outer garment around him [for he had taken it off] and jumped into the water. The other disciples followed in the boat, towing the net full of fish, for they were not far from shore, about a hundred yards...Jesus said to them, "Bring some of the fish you have just caught...Come and have breakfast." (John 21:6–8, 10, 12a)

Doesn't that sound like the perfect friend? "Come and have breakfast."

Listen to the Lord, and your catch is increased.

It is interesting to me that nine of the eleven disciples stayed and held onto the net. They were glad to see Jesus, but perhaps not enough so to let go of their net and dive in.

How did John know it was Jesus on the shore? The same way you know that he is calling you. It was not because of his appearance, for that had somehow changed. It was not, I believe, simply the tone of his voice, for they were some distance away. It was not primarily because of the miraculous catch. The voice that John recognized and responded to that day was the same one that cried out to Joseph Scriven in his darkness and in his loss. What gave Jesus away that day on the shoreline of Tiberias is what still gives him away today. It was not the tone of his voice or the power of his provision. It was the word he carefully selected and used to address them on this most momentous occasion.

"Friends…"

STUDY GUIDE

Chapter One

THE ASTOUNDING INVITATION

IMPORTANT THOUGHT

Jesus has called you and me to do far more than serve him, he has extended an invitation for us to befriend him. His desire isn't just that we walk in his paths by obedience, but that we walk by his side in a meaningful relationship.

1. What is the difference between knowing *about* someone and truly knowing them *personally?*

2. What are the main stages of emotional intimacy a man and woman walk through from their first introduction until they have been married several years? What key changes usually occur along the way? How are these stages like spiritual growth?

3. How did you react to the story about John Newton and the painting he observed in his neighbor's home? Did you have any *paradigm shift* or change of view? Which of the two ways cited have you most tended to view God?

4. Do you think Jesus lived a truly *solitary* life? What brings you to this conclusion?

5. Do you consider yourself a *servant* of Christ or a *friend?* In what way?

6. Is the invitation Christ extended in John 15:14–15 truly astounding? Explain why.

Passages to consider: Genesis 16:13, John 12:1–8, 15:13–15.

Chapter Two

EDEN AGAIN

IMPORTANT THOUGHT

In the Garden prior to the fall of man, Adam feasted upon intimacies of all kinds. There was a fullness, a wholeness, and a balance to his life in the Garden that stands out like a bright star against the dark backdrop of the lives that have followed, all the way to yours and mine. In a real sense, Eden remains our model for relationship with God.

1. In what ways must the Garden of Eden have been like heaven on earth for Adam and Eve? What were some of the intimacies they enjoyed?

2. Pick up a hymnal and read the lyrics to "In the Garden." In what ways do these words describe what Adam and Eve must have experienced? Which of the phrases are the most appealing to you and why?

3. What were the results of the contaminant of sin entering the clean room of Eden? How has it impacted humanity to this day? What difference does the sin of Adam and Eve make in your life in the here and now?

4. Discuss the first promises God made to Adam and Eve in Genesis 1:26–2:17 and how they set the parameters of life as they knew it. What privileges were the first couple afforded? What were their primary responsibilities?

5. Which of the connections God invites us to enjoy do you most identify with? Which metaphor do you find the most compelling? Why?
- The Vine and the Branches
- The Shepherd and His Sheep
- The King and His Subjects

- The Captain and His Soldiers
- The Bridegroom and His Bride

Passages to consider: Genesis 1–3, Luke 22:29, John 10, 15, Ephesians 5:32, Hebrews 2:10.

Chapter three

NONE WALKED CLOSER

IMPORTANT THOUGHT

Of all the disciples, John was arguably the closest to Christ. He sat next to the Lord at the Last Supper. Among the disciples, he alone stood by Christ all the way to the cross. And on that eventful Resurrection morning, his passion caused him to outrun even Peter to the empty tomb.

1. If we were an investigative reporting team endeavoring to do a story on John the Beloved, what facts could we assemble about him and his life? What is his significance?

2. Why do some people seem to find God in a way others do not?

3. What are the most vital commandments? And what causes them to rise above the others?

4. If we gave the twelve disciples a personality test, how would Peter, John, and Thomas test out?

5. Which of Jesus' twelve disciples do you most identify with personally? Explain why.

6. What does it mean to have a passion for God? How is it acquired?

7. Was John truly the closest disciple to Christ? In what way?

Passages to consider: Exodus 20, Mark 3:17, 12:28–31, 23:24.

Chapter Four

A FAITH WITH A VIEW

IMPORTANT THOUGHT

The motivation to do God's will is somehow connected to the grace of being able to see more of who he is and more of what he has already done for us. The best way to strengthen our commitment to God is to improve our view of him.

1. What is the most impressive or massive structure you have ever seen? How did you feel as you came close to it? What impression did it make? What thoughts did you have?

2. In what way does our view of God impact our service to him?

3. How do most people view God today?

4. Do you agree that we live in an age of option tenders? Why are people so reluctant to make commitments today? Have you struggled with this? In what way?

5. Can having the right view (or vision of God) help us resist sin and temptation? How?

6. What comes to mind when you consider the *Life* magazine editor's description of heroes?

"[H]eroes are a rare breed. They have the uncanny ability of rising above their fears and doing what they really believe in. To a hero, what he cannot see is infinitely more real to him than what he can see."

Do you know any true heroes?

Passages to consider: Romans 11:33–36, 12:1, Hebrews 11:1, 6.

Chapter Five

WILL THE REAL JESUS
PLEASE STAND UP?

IMPORTANT THOUGHT

It is vital that we grow in our understanding of the Jesus of the Bible. Most of us have grown up with a culturally conditioned view of who Jesus is. Too often in the church today we are quick to make Jesus after our own image.

1. How could Paul Goebbels and so many others have fallen for such a false savior as Hitler? Could this happen again today in our world? Explain your reasoning.

2. In what ways have you experienced these varied culturally conditioned views of Jesus? What are their positive or negative impacts?

- The White, Anglo-Saxon Protestant Jesus
- The Republican-Conservative Jesus
- The Social Activist Jesus
- The Passive Jesus
- The Icon Jesus
- The Good Teacher Jesus

3. Would Jesus have been comfortable with any of these labels? If so, why? If not, why not?

4. What will it require for us to truly get to know the Jesus of the Bible?

5. How would you describe Jesus' personality? Does it defy description, or can it be observed in the stories and teachings of the Gospels? In what way?

6. What about Jesus intrigues you the most?

7. If Jesus came back and walked this planet as a man for one more week (this week), what would he do with those 148 hours? How would he spend them? Where? With whom?

Passages to consider: Matthew 7:21–23, Romans 8:29.

Chapter Six

FRIENDSHIP WITH JESUS

IMPORTANT THOUGHT

There is a basic need in all of us for friendships. God has designed us so that we do not function well without meaningful relationships with him and with other people. At the level of our souls we crave intimacy. Friendship is truly not an option. It is a basic human need.

1. In what ways have the price tags been switched in our culture? Do we *love* what we should merely *like*? How so?

2. Which of the four chosen tracks to God have you found yourself on?

- Debt Repayment
- Performance
- Religious Affiliation
- Friendship

3. What has led us to believe that we can come to God one of a number of ways, when he has prescribed just one? What did Jesus say about this in John 14:6 and 10:1, 7?

4. Can life be truly full without friendships? Are they just as important to an introvert as they are to an extrovert? How so?

5. Which of the four tracks (i.e. question 2) is the hardest to walk on? Why?

6. Should true friends focus more on peace-keeping or truth-telling? How come? Which of the seven characteristics of a true friend cited in this chapter matter the most to you?

7. Why were Abraham and Moses the only two men in the Old Testament referred to as the "friends of God"? What about their relationship made it uniquely a friendship?

8. Do you approach Jesus as a friend? What helps you most in cultivating that friendship?

Passages to consider: Proverbs 17:17, 18:24, 27:17, John 10:10, 15:5–13.

Chapter Seven

"I WILL SHOW MYSELF TO HIM"

IMPORTANT THOUGHT

All through Scripture we see obedience and faith as the magnets within man that draw God near. After all, among all the people on the planet whom God could have chosen to initially bless, why did he choose Abraham? The Scripture tells us it was his great faith in God. Bottom line, Abraham's faith got the attention of God and great blessings in his life and lineage resulted.

1. What is God's primary "love language?" What within us does he respond to?

2. In what ways were the great men and women of the Bible abandoned to God? How would you define the word *abandonment* in this context?

3. What about Mary caused the Lord to choose her womb to bear his only begotten Son? Why was she among all women so highly honored?

4. In what ways does our relationship with God operate like a good marriage? What part does prayer and obedience play in the flow of it?

5. What causes us to feel close to Christ? How important is this?

6. In what way is obedience the track God has given us to run on? What does it take to stay on track?

Passages to consider: Genesis 15:5, 22:1–2, Luke 1:26–38, John 14:21, Romans 1:17, James 2:17.

Chapter Eight

FRIENDSHIP HAS ITS PRIVILEGES

IMPORTANT THOUGHT

The fear of the Lord is where God awakens us; friendship with Jesus is where he embraces us. It must begin, however, with the fear of the Lord. "The fear of the LORD is the beginning of wisdom" (Proverbs 9:10a). Without that sense of awe and reverence, we will never come to marvel over the fact that a great and awesome God calls us into friendship.

1. What do you think about the deal the McDonald brothers made with Ray Kroc in 1961? Was it a deal or a steal? Was it the realization of a dream or the collapse of one?

2. In an age in which we are taught that fear is such a bad thing, why is the "fear of the Lord" a good thing? Why do we need it so?

3. What do the fear of the Lord and a friendship with Jesus have in common? Are they opposites or somehow interrelated?

4. Which is the best deterrent of sin—fear or friendship?

5. Do you most often see God's will as a set of rules to keep, or as a relationship to fulfill? In what way?

Passages to consider: Exodus 20:20, Proverbs 1:7, 9:10, Isaiah 33:5–6, 1 John 2:3–5, Revelation 3:21.

Chapter Nine

HARNESSING THUNDER

IMPORTANT THOUGHT

When Jesus found John, he called him "the Son of Thunder." He was impulsive, explosive, soiled up and sooty, his edges rough. This guy was raw and unrefined and yet ultimately he became the disciple who walked the closest to Christ. A closer look at John paints a picture of how God makes a man into a man of God.

1. In what ways is a soul like a diamond?

2. What do we know for certain about the raw material of John's life? What was he like when Jesus found him?

3. What misconceptions of John and his nature have been propagated throughout history?

4. Why did Jesus first refer to John and his brother James as the "Sons of Thunder?" How did they earn that title?

5. What was the purpose of James's and John's special request in Mark 10:35–38? What does it reveal about them? How do you think the other disciples felt about it? Was it ever answered by Jesus?

6. Was John the kind of person you would hire for a job? Why or why not?

7. In what way does Jesus have to look beyond the blue ground of your life to find the diamond?

Passages to consider: Isaiah 61:3, Luke 9:51–56, Philippians 2:15–16.

Chapter Ten

MIRROR TALK

IMPORTANT THOUGHT

John referred to himself as "the disciple whom Jesus loved." In other words, the best thing there was to know about John was that he was someone who was loved by God. From the moment he became consumed with an awareness of the love of Jesus, John seemed to take this love with him everywhere he went. To him, it was more than an established doctine; it was a consuming experience.

1. When you were seven years old, were you a masterpiece or a master?

2. How would you answer the question Bob Crosby was asked in his sociology class: "Who are you as a person?"

3. Do most people today have a strong or a weak sense of identity? How is it generally established in most of our lives?

4. What experiences in your life have enhanced your sense of identity? Who God has designed you to be?

5. What does John's self-descriptive title ("the disciple whom Jesus loved") say about him and his sense of identity?

6. Have you ever before thought of yourself as "the Beloved?" What impact does this thought have on you today?

Passages to consider: Jeremiah 31:3, John 13:24.

Chapter Eleven

LEANING ON JESUS

IMPORTANT THOUGHT

John was a leaner. In his mind leaning was synonymous with believing. The picture of John just casually leaning against Jesus' back is one of the most relaxed and at-ease images in the entire New Testament. John seemed so at home around Jesus, so disarmed and comfortable in his company.

1. Who did you sit next to at the dinner table when you were ten years old? What were those meals like?

2. What premium do we place on having the inside track in the business world today? Who possesses it? How is it obtained?

3. Knowing that the social and political tensions were heating up around Jesus at that time, what do you think the disciples were expecting Jesus to say at the Last Supper?

4. What power tool did Jesus use at the Last Supper? What kind of power did it represent? Did the disciples know how to use it?

5. Is it easy or difficult to let God love you? What contributes to this being so?

6. What is most significant about John's posture at the Last Supper? In what ways is it symbolic?

Passages to consider: Psalm 34:15, Matthew 7:7, John 13:18–30, 16:24, 1 John 3:1.

Chapter Twelve

HOW FAR?

IMPORTANT THOUGHT

We are on a journey of growing closer to Christ. The pathway is one of friendship characterized by obedience and love. The question remains: How far are you willing to follow Jesus? To the places of feeding and receiving? To the places of working and serving? To the places of leaving all? To the places of prayer? Or all the way to the places of the cross?

1. What is the scariest adventure you have ever been on? Would you do it again?

2. In what ways do we tend to look to God as a cosmic vending machine? What are the end results of such an attitude and approach?

3. Has your journey with Jesus taken you through some of the stages of following listed below and described in this chapter?

- Places of feeding and receiving
- Places of working and serving
- Places of leaving all
- Places of prayer
- Places of the cross

4. Pray a prayer of consecration and illustrate it by taking out and holding a few emblems as you pray:

- (car keys) Asking God to guide and direct the course of your life.
- (family picture) Blessings on your family.
- (business card) Wisdom at your workplace.
- (ATM card) Wisdom for your stewardship of God's provision.

5. What was it about John that caused him to be the only dis-

ciple who made it all the way to the cross with Jesus? Why were the others not there?

6. What is the next step you need to take to more fully follow Jesus? How can I pray for you?

Passages to consider: Psalm 27:8, Matthew 4:18–22, 25:35–40, Mark 8:34–36, John 1:43, 6:1–15.

Chapter Thirteen

OUTRUNNING PETER

IMPORTANT THOUGHT

Life is so full of dyings and new awakenings. Of chapters closing and new ones opening. Dark Fridays and bright Sundays. Shattered dreams and hopes fulfilled. And yet it is not the dark Fridays or the bright Sundays that require the greatest grace. The greatest grace is most needed during the eternally long Saturdays of life, those days that exist between our deaths and new births.

1. How good a runner were you at ten years of age?

2. In what ways was Peter always first among the Twelve?

3. What experiences do the following terms represent in this chapter?

- Dark Fridays
- Bright Sundays
- Difficult Saturdays

4. Can you describe a situation or experience you have had that included each of the three days? How did each of the three phases affect you and your spiritual life?

5. What thoughts must have gone through the disciples' minds and hearts on that long Saturday before Jesus' resurrection and after his crucifixion?

6. What impressed you the most about Maggie McKinney's experience in her marriage relationship?

7. Why was it so important to John to express four times within the space of just a few sentences the fact that he beat Peter to the empty tomb (John 20:4–8)?

8. What makes the principle of remembrance so important?

Passages to consider: Luke 9:23, John 20:4–9.

Chapter Fourteen

AN UNMISTAKEABLE CALL

IMPORTANT THOUGHT

Recognizing the voice of the Lord in your life is an important part of developing intimacy with Jesus. John the Beloved listened more closely to that voice than any of the other disciples. As a result, he recognized it at a most critical season when no one else could or would.

1. Have you ever endured a season in which you felt abandoned by God? Would you describe it briefly? How did it make you feel? How did you come out of it?

2. What emotions must John and Peter have experienced as they went back to their old fishing boat and nets after Jesus had left? How had their normal daily schedule of activities changed?

3. Why, among all the disciples on the boat that day (John 21:1–14), was John the first to recognize Jesus?

4. Are you fishing anywhere in life where the fish just don't seem to be biting? How are you dealing with it?

5. Do you sense the Lord's voice in your life today? How does Jesus speak to you?

6. What is the most difficult step of faith you have ever had to take?

7. Is there a step of faith God is calling you to take right now? Would you describe it? What will it require of you to take it?

Passages to consider: Psalm 139:7–12, John 21:1–14.

Chapter Fifteen

EAVESDROPPING!

IMPORTANT THOUGHT

Our lives are constantly filled with opportunities and challenges that call upon us to act with power or in love. Power seeks to control. Love seeks to influence. Moment by moment, every one of us must decide what will motivate our actions, reactions, and responses. Power or love. Jesus chose to love and to lead. He knew that wielding a weapon could pierce the flesh, but that washing feet would open up the soul.

1. How many remote controls do you have at home? Who uses the television remote control the most in your household?

2. In what ways does our use of a remote control typify the ways we wrongfully treat people? List an example or two.

3. In what ways was Peter the king of the remote control?

4. In what ways was this Peter's lowest moment (John 21:15–25)?

5. What tensions must have existed between Peter and John at this point in their relationship? What contributed to those tensions?

6. Why did Jesus ask Simon "do you love me" three times? What was the significance?

7. Have you ever had a major pity party? What was it concerning? How did you get over it?

8. Why did Peter ask Jesus "What about him" (referring to John)?

Passages to consider: Matthew 26:33, John 7:67–69, 18:10–11, 25–27, 20:3, 21:15–25.

Chapter Sixteen

FINDING CHRIST IN YOUR CONFLICT

IMPORTANT THOUGHT

When the disciples' storm blew over them, Jesus was not far off; he was right with them in the boat and in the midst of the storm. We tend to only want to associate God with the blessings that touch our lives, not the difficulties. He, however, has chosen to utilize both the mountains and the valleys in his process of molding us into the image of his Son.

1. Can you remember a major frustration that turned into a blessing? Describe it.

2. How do you generally feel when an unexpected storm hits your life?

3. In what ways can storms serve to "propel us forward in the direction of God's will?"

4. Oswald Chambers referred to God as "the Engineer of our Circumstances." What does this imply? How should it affect my view of the positive and negative experiences in my life?

5. How can our limitations be used by God? Consider the *swamp* and *river* contrast discussed in this chapter.

6. Have you ever experienced rejection as God's direction in your life? How so?

Passages to consider: Genesis 50:20, Psalm 139:16, Mark 4:35–41, 5:35–56, Romans 8:28–29.

Chapter Seventeen

PLAYING FAVORITES?

IMPORTANT THOUGHT

Jesus seemed to favor John. Somehow God playing favorites doesn't jibe with the theology I was raised on. The God I learned about in Sunday school is one who shows absolute equality in his expression of love toward men. He doesn't have favorites. Still…the Jesus I read about in the Bible did have a favorite disciple.

1. Have you ever had a teacher, coach, or leader who had a favorite among the bunch? How did that make you and the others feel?

2. If John were seeking to prove in a court of law that he was Christ's favorite disciple, what evidence would he have?

3. How do you account for this unique sense of favor with Jesus that John possessed? What was the reason for it? Is it available to us today?

4. This chapter describes three different types of relationships—requiring, reciprocating, and replenishing. Which people did Jesus encounter and which category would their respective relationships have fallen into in Jesus' eyes? Also, describe some of your current experiences with each of these three types of relationships.

5. Do you have any extra-grace-required people in your life now? How do you handle them? How would Jesus do so?

6. Why do you think Lazarus was such a special friend to Jesus?

7. How can you and I minister to Jesus?

8. What are you learning from John's relationship with the Lord about spiritual intimacy?

Passages to consider: Matthew 3:11, 16:22, Luke 7:28, 22:33, John 10:38–42, 11:1–44.

Chapter Eighteen

BREATHING LESSONS

IMPORTANT THOUGHT

The Holy Spirit is the breath of God to the body of Christ, to every believer. Without him we cannot breathe spiritually and without breath we cannot truly live. However, to live as overcomers and not merely survivors, in God's world God's way, we must learn to inhale the Spirit of God daily and to breathe deeply.

1. Do you think about breathing every day? Why or why not? How important is it?

2. Read and compare Genesis 2:7 and John 20:22. What do they have in common? What is their significance?

3. What did the Great Outpouring ceremony at the Feast of Tabernacles symbolize?

4. Have you ever experienced running on empty...in your car?...in your soul? What is it like?

5. How do you usually cope when your soul feels empty? What do you do?

6. In what ways has the Holy Spirit helped you to face the truth?

7. Have you received the Holy Spirit? Are you inhaling his presence daily?

Passages to consider: Genesis 2:7, John 7:25–44, 20:22.

Chapter Nineteen

ONCE YOU'VE SEEN THE GLORY

IMPORTANT THOUGHT

Mountain climbers and bench sitters. How can two people made by the same God and living on the same planet be so completely different? In a word, *passion*. The only difference is the nature of their inner compelling drive—a hunger in the heart of one that the other has never known and may never know or understand. To one, the mountain must be climbed; to the other, it is only considered. One is compelled to have the mountain under his feet; the other is content to have it in his view.

1. Have you ever been mountain climbing? What were the high and low points of your experience?

2. C. H. Spurgeon defined grace as "glory in the bud." How do you interpret this?

3. How have mountains played a special part in the Bible? Which men and mountains have made a difference?

4. In what way are we going from glory to glory as believers?

5. Consider the phrase "Christians are people who are on a journey toward the glory of God." What does this mean to you?

6. What do you think happened when Jesus was transfigured? What does the Bible say happened?

7. Why is it significant that John saw them as seven wonders and not just seven miracles?

Passages to consider: Exodus 34:29–35, Psalm 121:1, Matthew 17:1–13, Mark 9:2–13, Luke 9:18–36, 2 Corinthians 3:18.

Chapter Twenty

THE JESUS JOHN SAW

IMPORTANT THOUGHT

The revelation John saw was not just some timetable of future world events. It was much more to him than bowls of wrath and seals of judgment. To John the Beloved, Jesus was the revelation. Too often, we seek an inside track of information instead of an inward experience of transformation. When we read this important book, we would do well to look for more than prophetic insights. We should look for Jesus. Whoever does so with a whole heart will find him throughout, all over every page and in between each line. We will see him revealing himself, his purpose, his power, and his coming kingdom.

1. What is the most amazing sight you have ever seen?

2. Is Revelation more a book about the Antichrist or the Christ? How can you tell?

3. In what ways do our weaknesses work to reveal more of the glory of God in our lives?

4. What does it mean to be an overcomer? What does the Bible promise to this elite group?

5. Which of the descriptions of Jesus in Revelation 1:9–18 do you like the best?

Passages to consider: Isaiah 53:2b–3, John 14:21, 1 John 4:7–16, Revelation 1:9–18, 2:7.

Chapter twenty-one

KNOCK, KNOCK, KNOCKING!

IMPORTANT THOUGHT

I was always taught that Revelation 3:20 ("Behold I stand at the door and knock...") was Christ speaking to people who had never heard the Gospel. It is not. This was actually an invitation to those who had already met him. This letter was not addressed to the lost, but to the found. This was not an invitation to *come* to Christ. This was an invitation to come *closer* to Christ.

1. When was the last time you were visited by a door-to-door salesman? Was it a positive or negative experience? Why?

2. Does the lost grandson at DisneyWorld describe the state of lost souls today? In what way?

3. What surprised you the most about how Jesus came into your life?

4. How does the Emancipation Proclamation speak to those who are being tempted by Satan?

5. Which of the four intimacy killers do you struggle with the most in your Christian walk?

Selected Passage: Revelation 3:14b–21.

Chapter Twenty-two

THE LAST TIME HE EVER SAID "FRIEND"

IMPORTANT THOUGHT

When Jesus referred to his followers in a radically new way—no longer as servants, but as friends—he issued what constitutes his greatest gift to us.

1. Get out a hymnal and read the lyrics to "What a Friend We Have in Jesus." Then discuss them: Which of these phrases holds out the most hope to your soul and why?

2. Of all the names Jesus could have used to refer to the paralytic, why did he choose to use this one—friend?

3. What important warning did Jesus give to his "friends" in Luke 12:1, 4–5?

4. Why did Jesus call Judas "friend" as he came to betray him?

5. What is the difference between *serving* God and *befriending* him?

Passages to consider: Jeremiah 29:13, Luke 5:20, John 15:16a, 21:5, 15–17.

Notes

CHAPTER ONE

1. Lawrence Richards, *Expository Dictionary of New Testament Words* (Grand Rapids, Mich.: Zondervan Publishing House, 1985), 298.

2. Alexander Whyte, *Bible Characters* (Grand Rapids, Mich.: Zondervan Publishing House, 1967), 74–75.

CHAPTER THREE

1. A. W. Tozer, *The Pursuit of God* (Camp Hill, Penn.: Christian Publications, 1982), 66–67.

CHAPTER FOUR

1. Jerry White, *The Power of Commitment* (Colorado Springs, Colo.: NavPress, 1985), 9.

2. Ibid.

3. Tozer, *The Pursuit of God,* 89.

4. Ibid., 91.

CHAPTER FIVE

1. Oswald Chambers, *My Utmost For His Highest,* January 6, ed. by James Reimann, ©1992, by Oswald Chambers Publications Assn., Ltd. Original edition ©1935 by Dodd Mead & Co., renewed by the Oswalds Chambers Publications Assn., Ltd., and is used by permission of Discovery House Publishers, Box 3566, Grand Rapids, MI 49501. All rights reserved.

2. Philip Yancey, *The Jesus I Never Knew* (Grand Rapids, Mich.: Zondervan Publishing House, 1995), 88.

3. Charles R. Swindoll, *The Grace Awakening* (Nashville, Tenn.: Word Books, 1996), 275.

CHAPTER SIX

1. Lee Iococca, *Iacocca* (New York: Bantam Books, 1984), 36.

2. Whyte, *Bible Characters,* 74–75.

CHAPTER SEVEN

1. *Los Angeles Times* (21 February 1982).

2. Jeanne Guyon, *Experiencing the Depths of Jesus Christ* (Beaumont, Tex.: The Seed Sowers, 1975), 35.

3. A. T. Robertson, *Word Pictures in the New Testament,* Vol. 5 (Grand Rapids, Mich.: Baker Book House, 1930), 255.

CHAPTER EIGHT

1. John F. Love, *McDonald's: Behind the Arches* (New York: Bantam Books, 1986), 202.

2. Joy Dawson, *Intimate Friendship with God* (Grand Rapids, Mich.: Chosen Books, 1986), 20.

3. Howard W. Ferrin, *Twelve Portraits* (Providence, R.I.: self-published, 1949), 31.

4. James Culross, *John, Whom Jesus Loved* (London: Elliot Stock Publishers, 1872), 30–31.

5. John Bevere, *The Fear of the Lord* (Lake Mary, Fla.: Creation House, 1997), 172–73. Used by permission.

6. Nehemiah Adams, *Christ, A Friend,* 6th ed. (Boston: D. Lothrop and Company, 1875), 227–28.

7. John White, *Daring to Draw Near* (Downers Grove, Ill.: Inter-Varsity Press, 1977), 17.

8. Archie Parish and John Parish, *Best Friends* (Nashville, Tenn.: Thomas Nelson, 1984), 18.

CHAPTER NINE

1. Charles R. Brown, *These Twelve: A Study In Temperament* (New York: The Century Co., 1926), 48–49.

2. Ferrin, *Twelve Portraits,* 29–30.

3. Ibid., 23–24.

4. Dale Martin Stone, quoted in Paul E. Billheimer, *Adventure in Adversity* (Wheaton, Ill.: Tyndale House, 1984), 33–34.

CHAPTER TEN

1. Robert C. Crosby, adapted from *Now We're Talking—Kids!* (Colorado Springs, Colo.: Focus on the Family, 1996), xiii-xv. Used by permission.

2. Al Bryant, comp., *Day by Day with C. H. Spurgeon* (Waco, Tex.: Word Incorporated, 1985), 215.

3. *Metropolitan Tabernacle Pulpit,* Vol. 32, (Carlisle, Penn.: The Banner of Truth Trust, 1971), 322–323.

4. C. H. Spurgeon, *The Treasury of the Bible,* Vol. 7 (Grand Rapids, Mich.: Baker Book House, 1981), 732.

5. Brennan Manning, as quoted in *Abba's Child* (Colorado Springs, Colo.: NavPress, 1994), 49.

6. Whyte, *Bible Characters,* 43–44.

7. Manning, *Abba's Child,* 50.

CHAPTER ELEVEN

1. Oswald Chambers, *My Utmost For His Highest,* June 3.

2. Manning, *Abba's Child,* 124.

3. Max Lucado, *No Wonder They Call Him the Savior* (Portland, Ore.: Multnomah Press, 1986), 88.

4. J. I. Packer, *Knowing God,* as quoted in Charles R. Swindoll, *The Tale of the Tardy Oxcart* (Nashville, Tenn.: Word Books, 1998), 236.

CHAPTER TWELVE

1. *Pulpit Commentary, Gospel of John*, vol. 17 (Peabody, Mass.: Hendrickson Publishers), 452–53.

2. A. W. Tozer, *The Divine Conquest* (Camp Hill, Penn.: Christian Publications, 1950), 62.

3. A. W. Tozer, *The Root of Righteousness* (Camp Hill, Penn.: Christian Publications, 1950), 63.

4. Ferrin, *Twelve Portraits,* 30.

CHAPTER THIRTEEN

1. Maggie McKinney, "Return to the Future," My Turn Column, *Newsweek* (6 March 1995).

2. Whyte, *Bible Characters,* Part 2, 43-44.

3. Manning, *Abba's Child,* 130–31.

4. McKinney, "Return to the Future."

CHAPTER FOURTEEN

1. Culross, *John, Whom Jesus Loved,* 34.

2. Ferrin, *Twelve Portraits,* 30–31.

3. James Stalker, *The Two St. Johns* (London: Isbister and Company Limited, 1895), 8–9.

CHAPTER FIFTEEN

1. Orin Crain, quoted in Charles R. Swindoll, *Three Steps Forward, Two Steps Back* (Nashville, Tenn.: Nelson, 1980), 42–43.

2. Culross, *John, Whom Jesus Loved,* 32–33.

3. Robert C. Crosby, adapted from *Living Life from the Soul* (Minneapolis, Minn.: Bethany House Publishers, 1997), 96–97. Used by permission.

CHAPTER SEVENTEEN

1. Ferrin, *Twelve Portraits,* 29.

2. Culross, *John, Whom Jesus Loved,* 30.

3. Dinah Craile, quoted in Stu Weber, *Tender Warrior* (Sisters, Ore.: Multnomah Publishers, 1993), 112.

4. Culross, *John, Whom Jesus Loved,* 23–24.

CHAPTER EIGHTEEN

1. Crosby, *Living Life from the Soul*, 56.
2. A. W. Tozer, *The Divine Conquest*, 74.

CHAPTER NINETEEN

1. Culross, *John, Whom Jesus Loved*, 23-24.
2. J. Oswald Sanders, *Enjoying Intimacy with God* (Chicago: Moody Press, 1980), 19–20.
3. Ken Gire, *Incredible Moments with the Savior* (Grand Rapids, Mich.: Zondervan Publishing House, 1990), 14.
4. Ibid., 94–95.

CHAPTER TWENTY

1. A. W. Tozer, *That Incredible Christian* (Camp Hill, Penn.: Christian Publications, 1964), 12.
2. Earl F. Palmer, *The Communicator's Commentary: Revelation*, ed. Lloyd Ogilvie (Waco, Tex.: Word Books, 1982), 121.
3. Ibid., 122–23.
4. W. A. Criswell, *Expository Sermons on Revelation* (Dallas, Tex.: Criswell Publishing, 1995), 147.
5. Anne Graham Lotz, *The Vision of His Glory* (Dallas, Tex.: Word Publishing, 1996), 36.
6. Criswell, *Expository Sermons on Revelation*, 148.
7. Ibid., 152–53.

CHAPTER TWENTY-TWO

1. Kenneth W. Osbeck, *101 Hymn Stories* (Grand Rapids, Mich.: Kregel Publications, 1982), 275–77.
2. Tozer, *That Incredible Christian*, 121.

Printed in the United States
by Baker & Taylor Publisher Services